P9-CKX-634

ROCKNE

ACKNOWLEDGMENTS

No one in the history of American sports left a more stirring legacy of memories among those who knew him, than did Knute Kenneth Rockne. Fortunately, a great number of those who played for him, or were among his intimates, are still around, and were glad to distill their remembrances of some of the richer moments that come back to them.

To countless Notre Dame players and alumni; to many eager and helpful archivists; to a myriad body of literature, and press and periodical coverage, I owe a monumental debt of gratitude.

More specifically, to Notre Dame athletic director Edward (Moose) Krause, Notre Dame sports information director Roger Valdiserri, Jimmy Crowley, Judge Don C. Miller, Judge Norman Barry, Rip Miller, Bert Metzger, Frank Carideo, George Vergara, Mary Jean Rockne Kochendorfer, George Strickler, Kenneth L. (Tug) Wilson and countless others.

Also, to Ethel Robinson and the Cleveland Public Library; Anton Masin, director of Special Collections, and Herb Juliano, curator of the International Sports and Games Collection, the University of Notre Dame Memorial Library; to the South Bend *Tribune* and the former South Bend *News-Times;* and to two individuals whose memories and works were so particularly key to my research: Francis Wallace, the peripatetic and talented Notre Dame alumnus-novelist-sportswriter-author-scenarist, who knew Rock so well and who illuminated their relationship in so many ways, and Chet Grant, a remarkably enthusiastic octogenarian, former Notre Dame quarterback, assistant coach and brilliant writer, whose life and times with Rockne go back further than that of anyone extant.

Without the cooperation of all these people, and their guidance to so many other sources, this book would not have been possible.

J.B.
Roslyn Hts., N.Y.
May 1976

FOR ONE OF MY ALL-TIME,
FAVORITE TEAMS—ELLEN AND NEIL J

CONTENTS

Prologue / 3

1. THE FLIGHT OF NC-999 / 7

2. TIME OF A GIANT / 20

3. IMMIGRANT FAMILY / 33

4. NEW BOY IN TOWN / 43

5. DORAIS-TO-ROCKNE / 57

6. THE ASSISTANT / 70

7. GIPP / 82

8. AMBUSH—AND A WEIRD AFFAIR / 98

9. THE SHIFT / 113

10. THE FOUR HORSEMEN / 121

11. PICKING THE ROSES / 135

12. MAKING IT MESH / 145

13. A VERY PERSONAL DAY / 163

14. BUILDING THE PROGRAM / 178

15. THE EMBARRASSMENTS / 192

16. THE PIED PIPER / 201

17. THE GHOST OF GIPP / 217

18. THE CRIPPLE / 226

19. RETURN TO THE TOP / 241

20. AFTERMATH / 260

ROCKNE

PROLOGUE

The Telegram

"... *Then Rock took out the telegrams he'd received before the game. He always read them to us. Stuff from the mayor of South Bend, or the president of the alumni association, people like that. Always the same go-get-'em-good-luck business. He read these; then, almost as an afterthought, and kind of tenderly, he pulled one more out of his pocket . . .*"

—Jimmy Crowley,
one of the Four Horsemen

It was going to be a key game for Notre Dame. And Knute Rockne, though guardedly confident, was concerned. It was evident in many little ways during practice that week. A bit of impatience here, a heavier tinge of sarcasm there. A subtle sense of urgency in his routine.

It was mid-October 1922, and the Irish were getting ready to play Georgia Tech. At Atlanta. Therein lay the difference. Road games normally held no terror for Knute Rockne. He once said: "We use the same boys and the same plays on the road as we do at home. Our execution is expected to be the same. At home we're the hosts, and I never liked the idea of being embarrassed in front of so many of our friends. On the road we're somebody else's guests —and we play in a way that they're not going to forget we visited them."

Being the guests for that approaching Saturday in Atlanta presented a somewhat more clouded set of circumstances. For the most part, the Irish had done most of their performing in the Midwest, with an occasional trip to the East.

They had never ventured into the Deep South, but Knute Rockne was embarked on his program to gain truly national recognition for his team and his school. Cannily, he began to schedule maneuvers which would take him to different parts of the country. The South would be first; the West Coast would follow.

But the Deep South presented some sticky psychological problems. Notre Dame, of course, was a Catholic school—quickly becoming the most notable such school in the land, with a considerable part of the credit due to its burgeoning football fame. Rockne was concerned with the anti-Catholicism still surfacing in the Deep South. The Ku Klux Klan was in its renaissance, with huge membership drives and widespread political influence. The Klan didn't like Catholics and, by extension, had little affection for Catholic football teams. Especially a team as powerful as this one coming in from South Bend.

Atlanta happened to be the Klan's national headquarters.

Rockne had known all this when he'd scheduled Georgia Tech. He was willing to take his chances, but he hoped the antagonism would be held to a minimum. Still, it was a nettlesome thing in Rockne's mind. This was the only kind of adversity his kids had never had to cope with, and who knew what mischief an ugly taunt or even a strategically placed fiery cross might do.

There were other worries, too. The trip was to be the longest a Notre Dame football team had ever taken—two days by train— and this could be translated into stiff muscles and loss of timing. There were already some nagging injuries afflicting the squad.

There was one other thing. Georgia Tech had a helluva football team. So never mind the collateral fears. The Engineers were a threat just on sheer talent. -

Rockne had the makings of his greatest club so far. He'd worked six or seven sophomores into his starting line-up, more than any Notre Dame team had ever fielded. And remember, this was single-platoon football, with no freshmen eligible. But, though more than half his club were neophytes, they had tremendous potential. (Later that season, the four backs destined to become the most famous backfield in football would appear together for the first time. Two years later, they would receive their name: "the Four Horsemen.")

This young team had won four in a row prior to the invasion of Atlanta, and if they were nursing hopes for an unbeaten season, they seemed to have the ability to make it happen. Rockne felt they were the cockiest bunch he'd ever suited up, but he was afraid a mid-season loss could deflate them disastrously. So Georgia Tech, on the road in Atlanta, could be a watershed weekend for the Irish.

Don Miller and Jimmy Crowley, the two surviving members of the Four Horsemen, recalled that Saturday with cherished pleasure.

"All things being equal," Crowley began, "we may not have been quite on a par physically with that Tech team. They were the biggest and toughest guys we'd faced yet, and Bill Alexander was a tremendous coach. They'd had visions of an undefeated season, but just the week before they'd been upset by Navy, 13–0, and they were going to salvage their season by knocking our heads off. The best thing we had going for us in that situation was Rockne . . ."

Don Miller picked up the thread: "By now, Rock was becoming known for his pre-game pep talks. We knew we were going to get the full treatment in that locker room in Atlanta. But Rock was somewhat subdued—for him. He called off the names of the guys who were starting, then warmed over the things we'd been working on all week, and that was about it. Somehow it just wasn't Rockne. It was as though he had something else more important on his mind . . ."

"Then," Crowley continued, "as he often did, Rock took out a few telegrams he'd received before the game. He usually read them to us. Stuff from the mayor of South Bend, or the president of the Alumni Association . . . people like that. Always the same go-get-'em-good-luck business. He read them to us. Then, almost as an afterthought, and kind of tenderly, he pulled one more out of his pocket. We were all staring at it . . ."

"I'll never forget the way he unfolded that one," Miller said. "Sort of hesitantly, and I'd have sworn his hands trembled a bit."

"It seemed he couldn't make up his mind whether he really

wanted to read this one," Crowley said. "But he did. 'It's from my son, Billy,' Rock announced. Then he paused just a bit. 'Billy is ill and has been taken to the hospital,' he told us. Then Rock read the telegram: PLEASE WIN THIS GAME FOR MY DADDY. IT'S VERY IMPORTANT TO HIM."

"We all knew Billy, of course," Miller went on. "He was Rock's little four-year-old, a tow-headed kid who often came to watch us at practice—a great favorite of the players. Well, I tell you, it really got us. Rock didn't say another word, just put the telegram back in his pocket and walked out. We burst out after him, onto the field, yelling and cussing our heads off. We tore that Georgia Tech team apart and beat 'em, 13–3. They never had a chance."

"That's not the end of the story," Jimmy Crowley added. "We got back to South Bend on Monday and were met at Union Station by the usual crowd of fans. And who do you think was the first one to come rushing up, whooping and hollering? Little Billy Rockne. You never saw a healthier kid in all your life. He hadn't been in a hospital since the week he was born.

"But the guys on the team never considered they'd been taken in by Rock. There wasn't even anything to forgive. We were used to Rock's drama—the real and the theatrical—and we'd find out over the next couple of years that Rock would use any ploy he could think of to get the most out of us, whether it was at practice or in a game."

"Nobody ever said anything to Rock about the telegram," Miller said. "And he didn't bring it up on his own. It just wasn't necessary, at either end. You either knew Rock or you didn't. Those of us who played for him knew him."

There were a few hundred who played for him and knew him. Unfortunately, not as many as there should or could have been . . . Fate took care of that . . .

1

The Flight of NC-999

*Wichita came on the radio to tell them something,
but static was garbling everything. But Wichita
heard Mathias say, anxiously, "I can't talk, now.
I'm too busy." There was another snatch of interrupted message, prompting Wichita to ask NC-
999: "What are you going to do?"*

A worried reply came back: "I don't know."

The deep-red and silver F-10 Fokker monoplane sat damply on the
runway at Kansas City, Missouri, rivulets of water running over
its striated metal fuselage as a cold drizzle enveloped it. Its three
motors growled evenly, its propellers cutting a glistening circle in
the drizzle. Tuesday, March 31, 1931, was a miserable day, and at
9 A.M. the pilot was giving the engines a pre-takeoff warm-up.

The Department of Commerce registration number, NC-999,
stood out starkly on the tail assembly, identifying the red Fokker
as a Transcontinental Western passenger and mail plane. The Fokker could accommodate ten passengers, five on each side, with a
narrow aisle between.

Its destination was Los Angeles. Takeoff time was 9:15, with the
first stop at Wichita at 10:25. There would be two mail stops
between Wichita and L.A., but no other passengers were scheduled
to board NC-999 at any stop.

For this trip the manifest registered six passengers and sixty-five pounds of mail, plus the pilot and co-pilot. There was no steward-ess. Commercial aviation was still in its infancy, and the emerging airlines were yet to discover the merchandising ploy of dazzling, shapely sex symbols aloft. You got aboard, found your own seat and, if you wanted to ward off hunger pangs between stops, you brown-bagged it or stuffed a couple of candy bars in your pocket. So much for creature comforts of airline travel in 1931.

The pilot was thirty-two-year-old Robert Fry; his co-pilot, Jess Mathias, thirty-one. No third officer or flight engineer, types like that. There was, however, a moderately reliable radio system be-tween plane and ground points. The Fokker was pretty much up to date in Kansas City.

Fry was not only experienced; he had made headlines a few years earlier. In 1928, stationed in China, as a sergeant-pilot in the U.S. Marines, he had become lost over unfamiliar territory and run smack into a raging sand-and-wind storm. It took a cool hand at the controls and a minor miracle to keep from crashing. When he finally made an incredible forced landing, he found himself in territory occupied by insurgent Chinese troops who were warring with the Nationalists—and had no love for American forces. They thought he was a spy, and only his fancy footwork and fast talking convinced them that he shouldn't be shot—or worse—and that he was only a lost aviator who'd like nothing more than to get the hell out of there and they could all still be friends. The incident put him on every front page of America.

The six passengers who were to board the Fokker were all men. H. J. Christen, of Chicago, a wealthy designer of department store fixtures, was on his way to the Coast for a reconciliation with his estranged wife; he was also a good friend of chewing gum magnate Phillip K. Wrigley. J. H. Happer, also of Chicago, an executive of Wilson Western Sporting Goods, was on his way to open a branch in Los Angeles. C. A. Robrecht, a produce merchant from Wheel-ing, West Virginia, was bound for Texas; this was his first plane trip. W. B. Miller, of Los Angeles, was an executive of the Aetna Insurance Co., going home after an Eastern sales meeting. Spencer Goldthwaite, a young New York advertising man, was on his way to visit his parents in Pasadena.

Goldthwaite, for some reason, had felt impelled to send an innocuous telegram back to his office, probably as an excuse to add an awe-struck afterthought. The wire said: PLANE TAKE-OFF DELAYED BECAUSE OF WEATHER. And then: KNUTE ROCKNE ABOARD.

Knute Kenneth Rockne, the sixth passenger, was the coach of the by-then fabled Notre Dame football team, the most famous football coach in the land, and one of the greatest names in all sports history.

Rockne was going to Los Angeles on—as usual—several missions. He always had to fragment his time wherever he went. Now he was going to Hollywood to sign a film contract; to speak at and be inducted into the illustrious Los Angeles Breakfast Club; to help J. H. Happer open his new sporting goods division; to speak at a gathering of Studebaker Motor Car regional executives and sales personnel.

His West Coast expedition was to last only two hectic days. Then he was to return to Notre Dame, where he was in the midst of spring football drills. He had given the squad a few days off for Easter Week and was anxious to get back to work. From the look of the team, the fall would bring him his third straight undefeated, national championship season.

In fact, just the night before, Rockne had visited the offices of the Chicago *Tribune,* where he'd chatted with sports editor Arch Ward. "We've lost several of our stars," he told Ward, "but I think we can do it again. Frankly, though, I'm a bit worried about Southern California . . ."

He had gone to dinner that night in Chicago with two good friends, playwright Albert C. Fuller and Christy Walsh, Rockne's personal business manager. Walsh was a sports entrepreneur who booked speaking engagements for Rockne and a few other leading sports figures and syndicated their articles to newspapers throughout the country. Walsh clucked over Rockne like a mother hen, getting him squared away for his varied meetings in L.A.

After dinner, Fuller drove Rockne to Union Station, where Rockne was to take the 8 P.M. Pullman sleeper to Kansas City. It would arrive in plenty of time for his morning plane connection. As Rockne got out of the car and handed his suitcase to a redcap, Fuller waved and shouted: "Happy landings, Rock!"

Rockne waved back and grinned. "Thanks, Al, but I'd prefer just an ordinary *soft* landing."

Knute Rockne was an enthusiastic air traveler. His Notre Dame teams, like all teams of that era, used trains for road games. Even Notre Dame's famed junkets to the West Coast to play Southern California were by train—a special train that always stopped en route, in Tucson, for a team workout, with a corps of accompanying sportswriters chronicling virtually every mile and every moment of the five-day journey. But by 1929 Rockne had discovered the early commercial airplane and was a frequent flier.

Just a few weeks earlier, he had taken a flight with L. W. (Chip) Robert, athletic director at Georgia Tech. It was Robert's first flight, and he was obviously nervous. Rockne had joked and reassured him: "Don't give it a thought," he said. "Each of us has a time to go, and when that time comes, no matter where we are, it strikes. So I figure it might as well be in a plane as anywhere."

Christy Walsh's wife didn't share Rockne's fatalistic philosophy. Walsh was to have accompanied Rockne on this trip and had phoned his wife in Los Angeles the day before to tell her his plans. She pleaded with him not to go by plane and made him promise he'd take the train instead. Walsh promised, and canceled his plane reservation.

It was the second such cancellation. Dick Hanley, the Northwestern University football coach, and a Rockne pal, was planning to make the trip with him, but that morning his wife had become ill and he cancelled his reservation.

The nation hadn't yet accustomed itself to routine commercial aviation. And multiple deaths in civilian air crashes were the new and dramatic form of disaster news. Still, in the decade of the 1920's there had been only twelve crashes, with eighty-four fatalities throughout the world. In 1930 there had been only two crashes: on January 19, 1930, sixteen people had been killed in a crash at

Oceanside, California; on October 6, eight people had perished at Dresden, Germany.

No famous person had yet lost his life in a plane crash. That kind of news had not yet been made, but there was no dearth of dramatic or titillating news stories on the nation's front pages of March 31, 1931.

Back home in South Bend, page one of the *News-Times* led off with the story of a devastating earthquake that had leveled Managua, Nicaragua, in less than twenty seconds, killing 1,100 people, including several Americans.

Another headline read:

HITLER FIGHTS
DICTATOR PLAN
FOR GERMANY

It seemed a rising young leader of German Fascists was unhappily protesting a decree by President Paul Hindenburg curtailing radical speech and assembly. Herr Hitler screamed that it was dictatorial and a violation of civil rights, and threatened to bring suit against it in Constitutional Court . . .

Another:

WITNESS SAYS
HE SAW MURDER
OF TRIBUNE MAN

This one dealt with one of Chicago's current sensational crime trials, in which a local mobster was accused of gunning down Jake Lingle, a *Tribune* reporter, because he knew too much.

And:

DOPE PEDDLER
KIDNAPS TOT
TO FLEE JAIL

And:

HUNT BANDITS WHO
ROBBED 3 PRIESTS

Another story described the armed guard thrown around the St. Joseph, Michigan, county jail, where one of Chicago gangland's master killers sat in an escape-proof cell while awaiting trial for cop-killing. ("It looks bad for me," he said.)

Perhaps the most provocative front-page piece was headlined:

WIDOW OF WAR FLIER
WEDS HUSBAND'S FOE

It was a real-life romance surpassing fiction. The widow of a World War I RAF officer had met a handsome German on vacation in Europe. Ultimately, she discovered the remarkable coincidence. It was the German who had shot down her husband over France. But she married him anyway.

This was the entire make-up of page one in South Bend. Before the day was over, however, the *News-Times* would have one more big story—in a special edition.

On the sports pages, it was noted that the sixteen major league baseball teams (remember those days?) were breaking spring camp and heading north. The big talk was that the Washington Senators (the Washington Senators . . . ?) were favored to dethrone the Philadelphia Athletics as American League champions.

It was announced that Cleveland had sewn up the heavyweight title bout between champion Max Schmeling of Germany and W. L. (Young) Stribling of Georgia, scheduled for Cleveland's giant new lakefront stadium in July.

Paul Berlenbach, only a shadow of the great champion he'd been, had begun a comeback to regain his light-heavyweight crown, and launched it with a third-round kayo of Six-Finger Eddie Clark of Harlem.

In other news from New York, it was reported that Babe Ruth's venture into the haberdashery business on Broadway had gone sour. An auctioneer conducted a sale that returned the Babe seven cents on the dollar.

It was not surprising—and it really wasn't the Babe's fault. Because, in the news columns and on many of the editorial pages, a new phrase was rapidly becoming commonplace: Economic Depression.

Wall Street, seventeen months earlier, had suffered its historic and horrendous crash. Now the repercussions were being felt around the world. Factories had begun to go on short shifts, and a creeping concern was showing up among bankers and politicians alike. As yet there were no street-corner apple sellers or soup lines, but they were just around the corner, along with hideous unemployment throughout the land.

It was in that economic climate that Knute Rockne was headed west to help sell Studebaker cars and make his first talking movie.

Following his Pullman trip from Chicago, Rockne's train pulled into Kansas City at 7 A.M., on time, Tuesday, March 31. Hurrying to the center of the station, he took up a post near the information booth. His two older sons, Billy, fourteen, and Knute Jr., twelve, had previously left Miami, where they had spent Easter vacation with their mother, and were on their way back to Pembroke School in Kansas City. They were due into Kansas City station at virtually the same time as Rockne, and he was looking forward to a brief reunion before rushing off to the airport. He hadn't seen his sons in several weeks.

Impatiently, he looked at his watch. It turned out their train was delayed and Rockne wouldn't be able to wait. He hailed a taxi and started for the airport. The boys' train came in fifteen minutes later.

When he got to the airport, Rockne found his plane's takeoff was being held up by incoming mail and the 8:30 departure was rescheduled for 9:15.

Heavy clouds massed darkly over the airport and the drizzle had not let up as the six passengers waited impatiently to board. Airport officials and airline representatives discussed the advisability of taking off at all. The weather ahead was even worse than here at the airport. Winter was giving way to spring only grudgingly.

But after a few minutes' discussion, the pilot, Fry, made his decision. They'd go.

Just before boarding, Rockne turned to another passenger, J. H. Happer, whom he knew quite well, and said: "I suggest you buy some reading material. These plane engines make an awful racket and just about shuts off most conversation."

At virtually the same time, Pop Warner, the famed Stanford coach, and Navy Bill Ingram, coach at neighboring University of California, were preparing to leave their homes for Alameda, across San Francisco Bay, where they were to board still another Transcontinental Western plane bound for Los Angeles.

The day before, Warner had phoned Ingram. Both were close friends of Rockne. "Hey, Bill," Warner said, "Rock is flying into Los Angeles tomorrow for some speeches and stuff. Let's go down there and needle him a bit."

Ingram chuckled and thought it a fine idea. Three hours after Rockne's plane was scheduled to take off from Kansas City, they flew out of Alameda. They planned to be at Rockne's hotel when he arrived, armed with some elaborately planned waggery . . .

The red and silver F-10 Fokker taxied into the wind, then began to roll down the Kansas City runway as Fry applied the power, water streaming along its sides and from the tail assembly. Six hundred yards down the runway, it began to lift off and start its climb. Within one minute, it was above the sullen clouds and obscured from view below.

Almost immediately Fry and his co-pilot, Jess Mathias, began a sputtering radio communication with airport weather observers along their westward route. Reception was poor.

Within forty minutes, the Fokker was over the Flint Hills cattle and corn country of southeast Kansas, its propellers ripping through the gusty, wet skies. Wichita was about twenty-five minutes away.

At that point, the Wichita tower came on the radio to tell them something, but static was garbling everything. Then Wichita heard Mathias say: "I can't talk now. I'm too busy."

There was another snatch of message, not quite decipherable, prompting the Wichita operator to ask NC-999: "What are you going to do?"

A worried reply came back: "I don't know."

As the Fokker neared Bazaar, Kansas, ranchers and farmers were working in the fields below, feeding their cattle, despite the weather. One of them, Robert Blackburn, looked up. He had often seen and heard the mail planes flying this route, and had given them only cursory glances. This one he could hear but couldn't see because of the low-scudding clouds.

Bazaar was a remote village with small ranches and houses dotting the adjacent, gently sloping valleys. Not far away were the long-abandoned ruts carved out by stage coaches on the rude road headed indifferently for Fort Sill, Oklahoma, in the 1850's and 1860's. History had passed this way and left its mark. Here, too, was where thousands upon thousands of Texas cattle had come up from the old Chisholm Trail, for fattening on Kansas' grassy plains.

The area was particularly treacherous for fliers. The surrounding hills contributed more than their share of wayward and bumpy air currents. From Kansas City to Wichita, mail pilots at night followed a route marked all the way by flashing signal lights on the ground.

Robert Blackburn, who understood tractors, combines and other mechanized farm equipment, knew about motors, and something about the sound of this plane's engines caught his attention and held it. He looked up sharply, lifting a hand in front of his face against the wet mist.

A mile away, Seward Baker, working on his 3,000-acre ranch with his son, Edward, also looked up. So did Clarence McCracken and Charles Carpenter, other farmers nearby. All of them, peering up intently now, saw the same thing.

Suddenly, a single-wing red and silver monoplane flashed through the cloud bank, angling sharply but not dangerously so, toward earth. It was as if the pilot were looking for a landing spot. Then, as though the pilot changed his mind, the motors, which had seemed to be missing slightly, roared solidly and the plane started to pull back up. Then its motors definitely seemed to miss again. A slight plume of smoke fluttered behind but nothing too serious. Planes often trailed smoke.

For an instant, the Fokker seemed to level off and steady itself as it skimmed along at an altitude of about 1,500 feet. Then the farmers heard a loud noise above the motors. Not an explosion, really. Just a loud bang. A second or two later, they were stunned to see the right side of the monoplane's wing snap off with a sharp report. The plane faltered, like a bird winged by a hunter, then nosed over in a slowly twisting dive, gathering speed as it plummeted toward the ground.

Halfway in the plane's descent, the farmers saw five bodies fall free from it, twisting and tumbling in the air like so many rag dolls. The five bodies smashed into the earth not far from each other, at about the same instant the plane ploughed into the ground with a shattering crash. Then there was silence. No further explosion. No flames. The farmers started racing toward the point of impact. All except one. Young Edward Baker started running, instead, two miles to the nearest telephone.

The torn wing, fluttering down more slowly, like a willow leaf caught in an updraft, clattered to the ground after everything else had hit.

It took more than an hour for ambulances and doctors to make their way over muddy roads to the scene of the crash. The last quarter-mile across the Baker farm had to be slogged by foot. As it turned out, the ambulances weren't needed. Baker, his son and two or three neighboring ranchers were standing mute and helpless as the medical party puffed in.

Three bodies were jammed together in the forward section of the plane—or rather what was left of it. They were the pilot, co-pilot and a passenger. Five other bodies lay where they had fallen.

A watch on the wrist of one of the victims had stopped at 10:45. The doctors quickly realized that positive identification of the victims was going to be difficult. All were mutilated horribly. One doctor shook his head sadly as he noted that one of the men had a rosary clutched in his hand.

The eight bodies were taken to the coroner's office at Cottonwood Falls thirty miles away, where a preliminary investigation would be conducted by the Chase County coroner, Dr. Jacob Hinden. He and an assistant started going through papers on the bodies. "My God!" said the assistant as he stared at some papers held in his trembling fingers. "It looks like this man is Knute Rockne!"

The victim was the one who'd been found with the rosary in his hand.

Positive identification was made within a few hours by two men hastily called to Cottonwood Falls. One was William L. White, a friend of Rockne's, and the author son of William Allen White, famed editor of the Emporia, Kansas, *Gazette*. The other, ironically, was Jess Harper, whose ranch was not far from the crash site. Jess Harper had been Rockne's coach at Notre Dame, the man whom Rockne eventually succeeded.

By now the word of a plane crash with eight people aboard had been phoned in to Kansas City and flashed over all three wire services—AP, UP and INS. The news broke upon the nation early in the afternoon of March 31. Every radio program was interrupted with the bulletin, and many newspaper editors scrambled to get out extras.

In Cottonwood Falls three girls at the switchboard of the local telephone office tugged wearily at their plugs as newsmen in New York, Boston, Los Angeles and elsewhere beseeched them for the latest news. Was it *really* Knute Rockne?

When a report reached Cottonwood Falls that one of the passengers, Christen, had been carrying a half-million dollars on his person, authorities hastily sent two deputies to guard the wreckage. The deputies found a chaotic, weird scene out of Dante or Daumier. Six or seven planes had flown in from Wichita, circled the area cautiously and then swooped down to bumpy landings, drawn by the magnet of airmen's curiosity about how and why one of their own had come to grief.

Hundreds of people from the towns of Bazaar, Matfield Green, Cottonwood Falls and Strong City were already swarming over the crazily twisted wreckage on the small hilltop, tearing off pieces of fuselage metal for souvenirs. Over everything lay the pervasive stench of gasoline, oil, gouged earth, split wood and torn fabric.

Four or five cowboys sat on their horses quietly, observing the grotesquerie without comment, even as more of the curious trudged toward them over the muddy turf from autos and trucks parked two miles away on the back road. Among them were ranchers, their wives, schoolboys and even small children.

Nobody ever found the alleged fortune in securities at the wreckage. There was none.

At Glendale, California, a Transcontinental Western passenger plane landed, and Pop Warner and Bill Ingram stepped off jauntily, intent on hailing a cab to take them to Knute Rockne's hotel in L.A.

They were met at the terminal doorway by an airline representative, who took them aside. Warner murmured, "Oh, my God!" and faltered. Ingram reached out to steady him. They looked at each other helplessly and decided they'd go right back to San Francisco, by train.

In the Oval Office at the White House, an aide hurried in to President Herbert Hoover, who, despite his high starched collars, was an avid football fan and had been student manager of the football team at Stanford. Told of Rockne's death, Hoover pursed his lips and then said quietly, "What dreadful, dreadful news."

Back at Notre Dame, Frank Carideo, the All-America quarterback on Rockne's 1930 national championship team, was shaving when he heard someone screaming across the hall in his dormitory. He stepped outside to see what it was. A student told him about the radio report. Carideo just stood there, the razor in his hand, unable to move, unable to speak. Downstairs in the same dorm, Marchmont Schwartz, the All-America halfback, was sobbing uncontrollably: "Nobody can make me believe it! It can't be true!"

At East Lansing, Michigan, a reporter called Jimmy Crowley from a newspaper office with the news. Crowley, who had been one of the Four Horsemen, was then coach of the Michigan State football team. He said nothing to his secretary, got up, put on his hat and walked to his car in the parking lot below. He started driving along the river road, aimlessly, uncomprehending, knowing only that he had to stay away from a telephone that would be ringing constantly, with people seeking his comment on the tragedy. And the one thing he knew for sure was that right now he wanted to keep his feelings to himself.

Down in Annapolis, Maryland, Rip Miller, a star tackle on that same team with the Four Horsemen, was coaching the Naval Academy. It was 3:30 P.M., and he was holding a spring practice session when a Naval officer hurried over. Miller was surrounded by his team as he held up a play chart. "Rip, it's bad news," the officer said, and tersely explained what had happened on the Kansas prairie.

There was a moment of suspended animation, as though Miller and the Navy football squad were frozen into some gold and blue tableau. Then, without a word from Miller, without a word from any member of the team, the players abruptly broke from their soundless transformation and, as if on cue, began running to the locker room, knowing instinctively there was no further practice that day.

In Chicago, Tug Wilson, athletic director at Northwestern (later Big Ten Commissioner) and a dear friend of Rockne's, was walking down Michigan Avenue. A man came out of a shop scanning the front page of a newspaper. Wilson glimpsed the black headline and snatched the paper out of the astonished man's hands. "Give me that!" he cried.

"You're nuts!" the man bellowed and tried to grab his paper away.

"You don't understand." Wilson's voice trembled. "You don't understand . . ."

The word had swept the city of South Bend, Indiana, long before the newspaper extras had hit the streets. And a strange thing happened. Stores began to close downtown in midafternoon as if by common assent. People left their offices. Total strangers, passing each other on residential streets, would nod, and inevitably one or the other would say: "Have you heard . . . ?"

In his office, the mayor called in his secretary and said: "We'll have to get ready. This funeral is going to be the kind of thing no one could ever imagine."

2

Time of a Giant

*When Notre Dame came to New York each year
to play Army, the New York press, wisely mindful
of its Irish and Catholic constituency, leaned on
the thing not so much as a sporting event but as a
visit by spiritual brothers. Any rooting for the Cadets was an aberration against God, nature and
Knute Rockne.*

For better or worse, the 1920's were Knute Rockne's decade.

Never was there a period in American history in which people
were so attuned to the spectacular, the outrageous, the maudlin—
the varied rites of passage of a nation come of age.

Come of age? Translation, please?

Well, yes. Here was a country which at the end of World War
I was the only big nation on earth not exhausted and enervated by
the war of 1914–18. As the 1920's dawned, we began to be aware
of this condition, and then, suddenly, with gathering momentum,
there was a tilt from a strait-laced, conservative, mostly rural
society to an urbanized one, with all sorts of attendant excesses.

The process rates a reprise, here. The prohibition scene . . .
gangsters . . . mob warfare . . . Tea Pot Dome and other political
shenanigans by the job lot . . . flappers . . . flagpole sitters. Also
a new music called jazz, the gestation of something called radio,
and a sensation-seeking press which set out to luridly chronicle the

era with only one thing in mind: circulation.

Hollywood, the new Babylon, cranked out miles of celluloid, flung up its tinseled back-lot façades and invented sheiks and sirens and synthetic heroes of the silent screen: Rudolph Valentino, Gloria Swanson, Douglas Fairbanks, Tom Mix, Clara Bow, and a wide-eyed waif named Jackie Coogan.

The nation was hooked. It was hooked, too, by Clarence Darrow's defense of reprehensible murderers like Leopold and Loeb; by the titillating Scopes "Monkey Trial" in Tennessee; by the tragic saga of young Floyd Collins, trapped eighteen days in a Kentucky cave; by silvery dirigibles crashing all over the countryside; by the Prince of Wales tumbling off every other horse in America; by Albert Coue, an itinerant French philosopher coming to our shores and urging Americans to parrot: "Day by day in every way I'm getting better and better" (or happier and happier, or slimmer and slimmer, or whatever); by shoeshine boys and candy store owners making mini-killings in Wall Street's insane financial gymnastics.

And hooked, too, by a new and overwhelming passion for sports. Concrete and steel-girdered stadiums and ball parks were rising everywhere as old wooden grandstands came crashing down, signaling the end of the dowdy and inadequate. A new opulence was being demanded to go with the "Golden Age of Sport." It was the emerging era of the "fan," a fitting short term for "fanatic," and from this new reaching out by the common people came the sports hero. And oh, did the 1920's ever manufacture them! With more gilt and worship, it might be added, than one American ever should have lavished upon another.

Instead of military heroes and other assorted leaders on horseback or perched on granite pedestals, the new breed of hero was being created for display in heavy black headlines of the press. Babe Ruth powering those prodigious home runs. Jack Dempsey parlaying a beetling-black scowl and two thunderous fists into boxing's first million-dollar gates. Bobby Jones, exquisite and elegant, taming golf courses as they'd never been mastered before, and making converts of ordinary people to what was recently a game for the wealthy and elite. Big Bill Tilden, supremely arrogant, and Poker Face Helen Wills making converts for tennis. Red Grange, the fabled No. 77 on his back, racing to football immortality. Gutsy Gertrude Ederle, the first woman swimmer to conquer the English Channel. Earle Sande, a jockey known to millions who didn't know a furlong from a fetlock but who knew the sports page poesy: "Gimme a handy guy like Sande!" Johnny Weissmuller, before he swung from trees in Tarzan's ersatz jungle, splashing to lasting swimming fame.

It seemed that the nation, finding itself in short supply of national leaders to look up to, briskly and enthusiastically created giants—athletic giants—with whom they were more willing to identify.

It was into this milieu of screwed-up passions and exalted public imagery that Knute Kenneth Rockne was projected.

There was a special magic in the man, and a kindred magic in his name. Inevitably, certain questions are posed. Did he become a living legend because of the checkered trappings of the fabled 1920's? Was Knute Rockne a product of his times or did he help make the times? Perhaps a little of both?

The questions are legitimate but not easily answered. The consensus would be that Knute Rockne was not just a synthetic hero manufactured in the process which gave America dozens of notorious, star-crossed celebrities. Knute Rockne was self-made, self-starting and self-propelled. He needed no publicity build-up, no false coloration, no trumpeting of nonexistent values.

No matter. He was unique. He was, after all, merely a coach. But such was his force of personality, his record of accomplishment, that despite the fact that he was a *non-performer* in a culture getting its biggest sports kicks from the stars, he was as luminous as any and outshone most.

And the state of his accomplishments? Begin, first, with the record—the numbers that forever persevere and tell you what winning and losing is all about over the long haul.

Knute Rockne in thirteen years as head coach at Notre Dame (1918–30) sent his team out 122 times, won 105, lost 12 and tied 5. Percentage-wise, that's .897. Impact-wise, it's awesome. No coach past or present has ever matched that record in major competition. Sing your praises of the Bear Bryants, the Woody Hayes, but no one is likely to do as well as he did.

Rockne had five undefeated seasons (1919–20, 1924, 1929–30), three national championships (1920, 1929–30) and a reasonable claim to a fourth (1924). Six teams (1921–23, 1926–27) lost only one game each year. Rockne did have one year of sheer disaster, by his standards. In 1928 he was five and four.

In those thirteen years of single-platoon football, Rockne developed fifteen All-America players, the second best percentage ever, just behind the twelve in nine years produced by Yale's Tad Jones in an era when it was still *de rigeur*—if not downright mandatory —for the Eastern All-America Establishment to name half its selections from the Eastern Seaboard.

And winning, after all, was what people in the 1920's were interested in—whether it was beating the stock market, the elements, an opponent, or even rising above one's origins and the prejudices of others. Knute Rockne became the archetype of the winner, a monumental hero for an age that was obsessed with heroes.

Rockne was a zealot, a fierce perfectionist at his trade who analyzed every phase of it in a way no man previously had ever attempted or was equipped to do. He was a psychologist with the instincts—if not the training—of a Freud or Jung. He was a supreme actor whose dormant talents were first brought out in student vaudeville and theatrical productions, and then exquisitely honed and polished as a football coach.

Wrapped up in the man was a hint of true genius, an uncommon charm, quick and biting humor, and, above all, great intellectual gifts—traits he could put to use instantly, for any occasion or circumstance, as needed.

He was described as a benevolent despot who was an intense, sure-minded driver, but with nothing harsh in his methods, and never abusive—an insistent master but an understanding one.

In sum, he dominated everything and everyone, whether on the football field, in the classroom (where he was an inspiring chemistry instructor even while coaching football), at a coaches convention, a social function, a business meeting. If one element of his personality was preeminent, it was his flair for leadership. Close behind in number two position was his quick perception in sizing up a person (rival coach, football player, *potential* player, student), a business affair, or, of course, a situation in a ball game.

There were many sobersided people, not given to extravagance, who claimed Knute Rockne would have been a shining success at anything he might have gone into. "He could have been a superb lawyer," insists Moose Krause, Notre Dame athletic director, who was a freshman when he first met Rock. "He could have been a terrific business executive, a scientist or a great politician—in the finer sense of the word—an outstanding congressman, senator, you name it. If it's true that certain men are created or born to leadership, Rock surely was one such."

Rockne also became a writer. And such was his personal integrity that when he agreed to write newspaper pieces for the Christy Walsh sports syndicate, Rockne imposed one, iron-clad rule. There would be no ghostwriting and nobody could lay a pencil on his copy. Not a phrase, not a comma could be changed. "If they're reading Rockne," he growled, "they're going to get Rockne—at his best or worst."

The 1920's were an era of emotional excess, but Rockne had the ability to arouse a strong, positive emotional response from all sorts of people: players, students, coaches, politicians, newsmen, schoolboys, business executives and the social commentators of his time. He was at least three decades ahead of one of today's fad words: charisma. The word, in fact, could have been invented for him. Look it up. Knute Rockne had it long before it got to be tossed about promiscuously as a label for too many show biz types, pols, and womanizing pro quarterbacks.

Even the U.S. Armed Forces recognized his appeal. In a trophy display in the Notre Dame Convocation Center is the ship's bell and wheel from the S.S. *Knute Rockne,* the only Liberty ship in World War II to bear the name of a sports personality.

Knute Rockne of Notre Dame was, yes, loved and lionized. Nobody ever hated or even disliked him. There were many among his coaching colleagues who envied him, and more than a few were jealous of him. But even the jealousy was laced through with an esteem and respect that would subsequently take a rare and dramatic form . . .

With the 20–20 wisdom of hindsight, we can see that Rockne did more for football than any coach who had yet come along. Harvard's Percy Haughton, Princeton's Bill Roper, Cornell's Gil Dobie and Pitt's Pop Warner had been bona fide giants of football in the East where, nobody can deny, the game had been invented. Nor can it be denied that its early heroes—the Hefflefingers, Brickleys, Thorpes, Mahans, Coys and others—were the headliners who provided the sport with its first glamour.

Chicago's Stagg, Minnesota's Henry Williams, Michigan's Fielding Yost and Illinois' Bob Zuppke were the Midwest's leaders and developed most of early football's emerging tactical weapons: the tailback formation, the screen pass, the six-man defensive line, the roving center, the statue-of-liberty, the spin-buck and other wrinkles that opened up the game and added spice for the spectator. These Midwestern giants brought their area's football up to par with the East and even surpassed it.

With Rockne's arrival as a head coach, college football was mushrooming into the nation's greatest sporting attraction (pro football was then only a poor country cousin). It would have reached its zooming heights with or without a Knute Rockne, but what he did with his Notre Dame teams and his sheer force of personality sure gave football one helluva leg up.

By the middle of the decade, a number of schools had already established themselves, episodically, as national football powers: the Ivies in their time; Chicago, Michigan, Army, Alabama, a few others. But, in truth, not one could be said to have a clear national focus—a magnetism, an *esprit* that could catch on in every section of the country.

The farm kid in Kansas wasn't captivated by what was happening in Michigan. The factory worker in Philadelphia didn't give a hoot about the rising Red Tide in Alabama. But Rockne set off something in South Bend, Indiana, that was national in its significance. Notre Dame was not only a winning football team but it was directed by a personality so dynamic, so highly visible, even in the limited media of the day, that the coach's image was inseparable from the ball club. For Notre Dame read Knute Rockne; for Knute Rockne read Notre Dame. It was sport's greatest and most successful marriage, and football fandom gave the Union a spontaneous and rousing blessing, claiming it as Family.

A new descriptive phrase would be needed to describe this national following and it was quickly supplied by the press: Curbstone Alumni. It was largely Catholic and visibly Irish, although Poles, Italians, Czechs and Germans were quick to claim admittance to the lodge, including thousands who had never advanced beyond grammar school. In Knute Rockne's Notre Dame team they had a champion who could lick anybody, and which was going around the country doing just that. Notre Dame was their very own, by adoption, and who the hell cared where South Bend, Iowa, was. (Illinois? Oh, it's in Indiana . . . ?) Wherever, it surely was as sanctified as Galway or Donegal.

In essence, Knute Rockne probably did as much for all Catholics in this country as he did for Notre Dame and football. America in the first quarter of the twentieth century liked to chant its annual Fourth of July litanies about democracy. But the truth of the matter was that there existed a strain of bigotry which, if not universal, was still etched deeply in our social fabric. And Catholics, the native-born as well as the continuing immigrant stream, suffered their socioeconomic lumps to a marked degree.

For decades, the notion of a Catholic president of the U.S. was just a millimeter short of preposterous. In 150 years of American nationhood, there were fewer than a dozen Catholic governors and about the same number of U.S. Senators. In the first two decades of the twentieth century, a Catholic chairman of the board or president of a big corporation was a rarity, and few Catholics gained admittance to country clubs. The stereotype of the Irish hod-carrier or tavern drunk was still a lingering theme in the jokebooks and on the vaudeville stage. The days of want ads ending with the phrase "Irish need not apply" were not far behind.

Aside from Al Smith, Governor of New York, and an occasional athlete, there were few Catholic public heroes in whom to take pride. In short, there was no central rallying point for Catholics aside from their religion. Knute Kenneth Rockne was instrumental in changing all that.

When Notre Dame came to New York each year to play Army, the New York press, wisely mindful of its Irish and Catholic constituency, leaned on the thing not so much as a sporting event but as a visit by spiritual brothers. Any local rooting for the Cadets was an aberration against God, nature and Knute Rockne. Wherever the Irish team went, NOTRE DAME TEAM ARRIVES was the top news of the day, and would sell more papers than your average flood or the peccadilloes of a wayward politician.

Curbstone Alumni . . . the phrase simply couldn't be improved upon. Whoever coined it deserves a niche in journalism's hall of fame.

An immigrant himself, Knute Rockne was well aware of what the melting pot had already produced in America. He knew that he was part of the immigrant dream that a man with brains, some muscle, and a lot of drive and energy could do great things, could compete with the best. He sensed the opportunity as a boy on Chicago's tough-fibered Northwest Side, and his way up from his American beginnings was so typical it was almost a parody.

His background encouraged him to remember that the players he was working with were, in many cases, the sons of immigrants like himself: Irish, Poles, Slovaks, Germans, the whole European Exodus thing of the late nineteenth and early twentieth centuries. He'd say to a player: "Dubrak . . . Polish or Slovenian, right? What town, exactly, did your father come from?" Or: "Petrillo . . . those blue eyes of yours . . . your folks were from northern Italy, right?"

He was at home with his players. They were comfortable with him, even when he was laying on a cutting edge of sarcasm for a missed block, or blasting a back for hitting the wrong hole. At moments like those he was Thor hurling a thunderbolt—except that the bolt was wrapped in velvet.

Bert Metzger, an All-America guard in 1930, says: "You not only took what Rock dished out to you but you sort of looked forward to getting blasted by him. If Rock gave you his undivided attention like that in front of everybody, you were *somebody*. You'd been *noticed*. We thrived on it. Maybe that sounds strange, but that's the way we felt about him."

All football coaches hate to lose. Knute Rockne, who did so little of it, found it all wormwood and gall. He put it succinctly to his players: "We count on winning. And if we lose, don't beef. And the best way to prevent beefing is—don't lose." Another way he put it was: "I don't want anybody going out there to die for dear old Notre Dame. Hell, I want you fighting *to stay alive!*"

"Staying alive"—and winning—really was what Rockne was all about. And although there was no formal Notre Dame "system," it was presumed around the country that anyone who played under Knute Rockne was his disciple and could duplicate his success anywhere in the coaching business. It was not so, but colleges all over the land were willing to find out for themselves. At the time of his death, twenty-three of Rock's boys were head coaches at colleges and universities. Dozens of others were assistant coaches and at least 150 were coaching in high school. Many tried (with varying degrees of success) to drill sixteen and seventeen-year-old kids in the choreography of the famed Notre Dame shift. It was a backfield maneuver so brilliant and devastating that Rockne's coaching foes found only one manageable way to cope with it: they got the rules committee to outlaw it.

But football had gotten Rockne by default, and the fact was forever in the back of his mind, like some small private room that held a haunting secret only he was privy to. Knute Rockne had wanted to be a doctor. (Significantly, he would be virtually his own team trainer for many years.) When dreams of a medical career dissolved among the hard facts of financial realities, he became a chemistry instructor after graduation from Notre Dame, so talented that his department head all but got down on his hands and knees, pleading with the young Rockne to pass up a coaching career and remain in the classroom.

Meanwhile, the physical man was a perfect adjunct to the psychic and professional man. Fate must have made a calculated decision in that respect. He was a man who, once seen or heard, was not easily forgotten.

Rockne was not Irish. He was Norwegian—and he proved that not all Vikings are tall, blond and lithe, with the sculptured musculature and handsome faces of Thor, Baldur, Hermod or Sigmund. This Viking from South Bend was only five feet eight inches tall and weighed 160 dumpy, irregular pounds, assembled, according to one observer, "as though the Master Chef had just flung together spoonsful of mashed potatoes and hoped they'd land with some semblance of order." His round, pumpkin-shaped head was balding on top, deeply furrowed above the eyes, and there were lines in his face with which a basset hound could have taken best-in-show. His nose, broken at least three times, was the wayward feature of the failed preliminary boy who never made a main event.

But then there was the famous Rockne smile—a broad, rippling, lopsided smile, soaked in instant warmth and charm, the blue eyes signaling the absolute truth in it. Someone once said Knute Rockne wouldn't know how to smile for accommodation or any effect less than truth. And for counterpoint there was his raspy, throaty chuckle, just as spontaneous and often more effective.

Westbrook Pegler, one of the widest-read columnists of the period, once described Knute Rockne as having a face that "looked like a battered oil can." The fact that he added ". . . which spouted champagne when he talked" didn't help much. Although Pegler was a great admirer of Rockne and his work, Rockne never forgave him for that one line. It was the first and only time his intimates ever knew he was sensitive about his looks.

Then there was the voice. It was said there were three incomparably recognizable public voices on the American scene in the late 1920's: those of Will Rogers, Knute Rockne and crooner Rudy Vallee. And Vallee had to be singing. There was as yet no distinctive voice from Hollywood. Politicians? Maybe Al Smith.

But there was no voice like Rockne's, and nobody used the human voice with more startling and unforgettable emphasis.

To describe Rockne's voice as flat, nasal, metallic, is to make a bare beginning. Each word emerged as though coated with brass, and pretested for hardness. And that was merely Rockne's normal speech. When he was truly animated, when he was all revved up with anger, impatience or sarcasm for a pre-game or half-time pep talk, Knute Rockne was a one-man vocal symphony.

In a single sentence he could start out slowly, calmly—then shift to a higher speed—slow down a bit for subtlety—push it two notches forward—hit a key word for explosive accent—and race pell-mell into a word or phrase repeated over and over. It could go something like this: "Now I want you to go in there and drive . . . to *drive* in there . . . to keep DRIVING alla*time* in there . . . DRIVE IN THERE . . . ALLATIME *DRIVING IN THERE* . . . until you've got that man OUTTA therRRRE . . . !" He had the trick of lengthening or holding a final sound on an upward, sliding note, in a manner that registered on the listener with remarkable effect. The whole thing in a clackety-bang mélange of consonants, vowels and shaded diphthongs which no speech teacher would have tolerated in a classroom but which would have mesmerized the teacher anyway.

Francis Wallace, who probably knew Rockne better than any sportswriter who covered him, once said that Rock could use his voice as a weapon or a sedative. It could also coax, cajole, frighten, charm, mollify and motivate.

When Pat O'Brien prepared to play Rockne in the 1940 film, he listened to virtually every foot of early sound newsreel film made on the Notre Dame coach. He scrounged for the few radio transcriptions that had recorded Rockne's voice. He buttonholed players, faculty and officials who had heard Rockne under varying conditions and mined their memories for the shadings and idiosyncrasies Rock exhibited. "Without a decent re-creation of that singular voice," said O'Brien, "no characterization would have been acceptable to people who knew him."

It was partly the voice but mostly the man and his distinctive vitality which the Studebaker Corporation, of South Bend, put to work for several years. They hired him to attend every national and regional sales conference and make inspirational speeches before the company's salesmen and executives. Rock never gave them a pitch on how to sell cars. He would get up there and talk about automobiles and people and how people thought and how they reacted to messages. For an hour or so, there was 110 percent attention riveted on the chunky, bald-headed man up front who held them in thrall. It was said that the month following every Rockne speech before Studebaker people, the sales of Studebaker cars would rise dramatically. "If Rock could have visited every

Studebaker showroom in America once a month," said one executive dryly, "we could have outsold General Motors and Ford combined."

In the spring of 1931, Rock was to have signed on as national promotion director for Studebaker, in complete charge of sales promotion and dealer relationships—a job that would have taken the full time of anyone else. But with his genius for organization Rock was going to handle it, if not between punts, then certainly between seasons. And according to Studebaker's schedule, the company's newest car—the Rockne Six—would be introduced in the fall. (It did come out, but disappeared soon after, a victim of the deepening Depression.)

If other men could achieve the unlikely or the spectacular with a few sentences, Rockne could accomplish the improbable with—well, just two words.

Once Notre Dame was trailing badly at half-time, and as the team trotted dejectedly to the dressing room, everyone expected Rockne to pour out a Niagara of acid comment on their play.

But Rockne didn't show up. For thirteen minutes the squad huddled on the bare wooden benches in enveloping silence. The assistant coaches fidgeted nervously, but just as silently, in front of a blackboard void of the usual X's and O's. An official stuck his head inside the door and yelled: "Team on the field in two minutes!"

Still no Rockne.

With thirty seconds to go, there was the sound of the dressing room door opening violently. Every head swung around. There stood Knute Rockne, hands on hips, glaring as only he could glare, the steam all but visible around his ears. He spoke only two words. Rather, he *spat* two words, nurtured in disgust and soaked in contemptuous disbelief:

"*Fighting Irish . . . !*"

Then, quickly, he spun around and left. He might have been blown out by the bellowing roar behind him. The Irish won by two touchdowns. He had taken no chances with this ploy. He simply knew his men.

Knute Rockne was a man who had scaled a monumental height,

as a personality and as a master of his craft. To reach that summit he had taken a route marked by the familiar milestones (and some not so familiar) of the immigrant accomplishment. It had begun among the snowy mountains and the deep, icy fjords of Norway. When the entire route is examined, his success, if not his field and his fame, was assured from the beginning.

3

Immigrant Family

The 10-year-old was fascinated with pole-vaulting. He scrounged a stout clothes pole or a tough, bamboo stick from the core of a new rug and vaulted six-foot backyard fences. He and a pal found a broken flat iron and taped a weight onto it. Presto, they had a shot-put. No back-alley cat was safe.

The immigrant family stood nervously but excitedly at the rail as the ship steamed slowly to pierside in New York Harbor. It was a raw spring day in 1893, and the young, blond mother encircled her two small daughters with protective arms. Her husband had preceded them to America by a year and a half, and had set up a home in Chicago. Now the eleven-day voyage in humble third-class passage from Bergen, Norway, to New York was drawing to its end. For Martha Rockne it was also a beginning, as it was for all immigrant mothers whose first sight of America certainly had to be one of the most thrilling moments of their lives.

Suddenly she looked around, a flash of alarm on her face. "Where's Knute? He was just here a minute ago." Quickly she shepherded the two girls—Anna, the older, and Martha, the younger, in front of her, as she frantically searched the deck. Knute may have been with them a moment ago, but a moment was all that was needed for a disaster. Time was a fragile and fleeting restriction on her son's movements. Any disappearance was cause for alarm. Then Martha Rockne saw someone pointing upward.

There, seventy-five feet up in the crow's-nest of the steamer, was a small boy, leaning precariously against the thin quard rail, staring out toward the upper harbor. She suppressed a scream, not wanting to startle him, and hurriedly found a crewman.

The crewman scampered aloft and carefully escorted five-year-old Knute Kenneth Rockne to the safety of the deck.

"I wanted to be the first to see the city," he explained. Martha Rockne nodded knowingly. He'd also wanted to be the first to board the ship at Bergen, and in his haste tumbled off the gangplank into the water. A sailor had to fish him out with a grappling hook.

A few months earlier, the boy had received a pair of gum rubber boots from his father in Chicago, and what better way to try them out than to go fishing on an ice shelf, frozen to the shore of the lake near him home in Voss, Norway. Age five was young for a boy to fish on the frigid lake, but adventuresome juices flowed early in this kid. The ice shelf broke off and floated out into the lake, which was almost ten miles wide. Luckily, someone spotted the dark speck far out on the water, just before dusk, and a platoon of villagers hastily manned a boat and rescued him.

The special gifts that make up the Viking psyche may or may not have been noted by Martha Rockne in her only son (two more daughters would be born to her in America), but if the Norse had their own version of Kismet, then it surely was written that this boy was already measured for greatness.

Martha Rockne could only hope that in the place called Chicago (it, too, was on a lake—a gigantic one) young Knute Rockne might, just might, rise to that measure.

It was easy to recall what friends and neighbors had said to her when he was born: *"Natte det ga ham godt."*

Visualize a picture post card, vintage 1880's. A Scandinavian village of about 4,000. Beyond, the greenish-blue mountains crested with fir and hemlock. The glittering lake that washes close to the main street almost shimmers with salmon and bass. Less than an hour away is one of the North Sea's hundreds of jagged, narrow, fingerlike fjords that scratch their ice-blueness inward from the coast.

The most imposing building in the village is the brown-board Lutheran church—the only church in town. About 800 years earlier it had begun as Roman Catholic, but Martin Luther's Reformation had changed that. Down the street is a bustling *lanhandleri*, the country store where one buys virtually everything needed in the home—from two pounds of *senafenalar* to a piece of *gjeitost* to a lovely pink and white *toerkle* to top off a lady's blouse.

The people who come into the *landhandleri* are close to being a demographic cliché. For the most part, blond, blue-eyed, fairfaced. Exploding with obvious good health and a sense of prideful satisfaction with things as they are. Why not? Take a deep whiff of that air. A tonic in the summer. Even more bracing in the winter.

Winter. Everything white-mantled and feathery. The snow and ice immune from alien soot and grime. Kids' voices crackling musically on the air as they skate and romp with sleds and toboggans.

Older men go skiing on honest, hand-fashioned wooden runners without fancy clothes because the word "après" hasn't yet been invented in its latter-day context.

The place, in fact, is so invigorating, so colorful, that it has been known for a half-century as a health spa, and the wealthy from Oslo, Bergen and even Berlin have discreetly discovered it.

Your picture postcard is Voss, Norway, and it was here, on March 4, 1888, that Knute Kenneth Rockne was born.

(A few years later, in America, his first name would be corrupted in pronunciation to *Nute*. In Norway, the name is pronounced as though there is a vowel between the "k" and "n." Thus, *Kanute*. And the surname was spelled "Rokne." The c would be added in America.)

The Rocknes traced their family back to the fourteenth century. Knute's great-grandfather, Knute Lars Rockne, started out as a farmer but was so adept at repairing things that he turned to full-time blacksmithing and became chief mechanic to most of the people in his village. Knute's grandfather, Knute Knutson Rockne, continued the blacksmith and repair shop, and in 1852 moved from his small village to the larger town of Voss, where he opened a hardware shop and was soon renowned as the Master Fixer of Southwest Norway. In 1882 Knute's father, Lars, took over the machining works, and soon became famous as a manufacturer of such two-wheeled vehicles as the *stolkjerre* and the *kariol* (carry-all), the most popular means of conveyance aside from a regular buggy—and even more so, perhaps, because they were cheaper and easier to maintain.

By the late 1880's Lars Rockne's *kariols* were so popular that wealthy patrons at the Voss health spa got interested in them. They became an absolute vogue when Kaiser Wilhelm of Germany spied one on a visit and ordered a stableful for his estates. With that kind of patronage, Knute Rockne's father was on his way. There had to be other worlds out there eager to snap up his beautiful woodworking wares and his buggies. America? Why not?

Voss was a prolific producer of immigrant talent for the New World. The Nelsons would provide a governor and senator from Minnesota. The Nestos, a governor of North Dakota. The Vinges, a member of the Wisconsin supreme court. The Lawsons, a founder of one of America's great newspapers, the Chicago *Daily News.* What, then, might the Rocknes provide?

One day, Lars Rockne scanned a Bergen newspaper. There it was. In the city of Chicago, in 1891, there was to be a great World's Fair. He had already won a prize for a carriage at the Great Liverpool Fair in England, but this festival at Chicago was to be the biggest fair the world had ever seen. It would attract artisans and exhibits from every civilized nation in the world. With Norse confidence, with Viking reach, he'd build the most beautiful and most practical carriage anyone had ever seen, and if he didn't win he'd spit in their eye and come home.

Lars Rockne never came home. In October, 1891, his carriage won the grand prize. He decided Chicago was a vital, bustling place. Here was where Louis Sullivan would build the world's first steel-girdered skyscrapers. Here, a lake port, though inland, rivaled anything in Norway. Here, too, were the world's greatest stockyards, and nearby were steel mills as roaringly productive as anything in Pittsburgh, or Birmingham, England.

Lars got a job. He wrote to Martha telling her he was enrolling in night school and that in another year she should start planning to bring the three children to America. A year or so, and he'd be ready for them.

Martha Gjermo Rockne was no less a Viking adventurer than her husband. The Gjermos also had contributed to the American Midwest melting pot: doctors, clergymen, educators and mayors in a dozen towns and cities. But Chicago? A city of (then) a million people must have been intimidating. Knute would have to leave his skating, romping in the fields, swimming in cold, clear waters. She needn't have worried, at least for Knute. Life for him wasn't going to be easy, but it would provide as much romp as the Rockne family could tolerate.

The Logan Square district of Chicago was representative of the immigrant neighborhoods in big American cities. There were plenty of Scandinavians to provide the comfort of common background and help ease the Rocknes into new ways. And there were enough Italians, Poles and Slovaks to remind them that the sensitive process of assimilation was not a lonesome one, and that everyone could learn from everyone else.

Young Knute had already had almost two years of schooling in Voss, but entered elementary school in Chicago knowing only the few words of English his father had already taught him. His teachers immediately discovered, however, that the moon-faced, towheaded kid with the constantly quizzical expression had a prodigious memory and tremendous desire. He was a human sponge, soaking up everything around him. Within two years he was considered, age for age, the most brilliant student in school. Math was a breeze. History was his hand-maiden. And his vocabulary, even with his rapidly disappearing Scandinavian accent, constantly charmed and amazed everyone.

But if he had a thirst for learning, he also exhibited a love of physical activity that was almost insatiable. The American thing to do was to get into sports. Or find an after-school job. Knute did both. Somehow he came into possession of a thin, battered baseball glove, and he was off. It took him only a few weeks to become a slashing line-drive hitter and to have his nose broken by a bad-hop grounder.

He washed school windows for a penny a window at four different schools. He picked beets and corn for ten cents an hour on farms north of Chicago and also held a part-time job on a Lake Michigan ferry. After school he earned three dollars a week running deliveries for a department store—and was already American enough to discover the pleasures of switching cows and horses in neighbors' barns on Halloween. All this before he was twelve.

But sports were his real passion, and he soon discovered his greatest love: track and field. He could outrun any kid his age—and many older—in races around the block. He became fascinated with pole-vaulting, scrounged a stout clothes pole or a tough bamboo stick from the core of a rug and was vaulting backyard fences. He and a pal found a broken flatiron and taped a metal weight on it. Presto, they had a shot put. No neighborhood cat was safe.

On a rainy Saturday morning, Knute and his friends would duck into somebody's basement where there might be a poster of Jim Jeffries, Bob Fitzsimmons, Joe Gans, or any of the current world boxing champions, and they'd go into a frenzy of shadowboxing, feinting, and exercises in nimble footwork. The only heroes to kids around Logan Square were sports heroes, and the average lower-middle-class kid wanted to be a Cap Anson, a Jim Jeffries, a Walter Eckersall, long before he ever came to grips with the thought of making a living. That part of life was almost preordained in Logan Square. A kid was going to be a hod-carrier, a mill hand—or a clerk if he didn't have the hands and muscles for anything else. If he was lucky, he might become a cop.

Soon Knute was living only for sports. His parents were at least mildly troubled. Lars and one of Knute's older sisters had begun thinking he was smart enough to go to college (few young men did then, and even fewer women). They even harbored some small hope that Knute could enter the newly minted University of Chicago.

Knute assured his parents he was interested in school, but they began to wonder when he came home one day and said he'd joined

—at age twelve—a special sports training club sponsored by Company F of the 132nd Infantry Regiment.

Like many immigrant fathers, Lars Rockne didn't know quite what to make of his son's athletic ambitions. Besides, at age thirteen, Knute was the smallest boy in his class. He was all of five feet tall and weighed ninety pounds, and nobody was predicting he'd ever be a Cap Anson or a Jim Jeffries.

Still, he played corner-lot football, a ragtag running and tackling game without much finesse. The Scandinavians (always called "Swedes" whether from Norway, Sweden, Finland or Denmark) often faced off against the Irish in these neighborhood blood-and-mud baths, without pads, helmets or even the flimsiest uniforms. Any kid's best protection was his mental toughness and an unflagging desire to bust somebody who always seemed bigger than he was. Referees were a luxury and were seldom there. At least five cops were *always* there because a free football game was the only football most of the neighborhood people could afford to see. And with a saloon on just about every corner, there was a lot of instant partisanship generated on the way to and during the games. The cops never had any trouble with the players. They were there, mostly, as Rockne wrote years later in his autobiography, "to make sure there were only 22 players on the field at a time, instead of a couple hundred who were only too willing to get out there and start swinging."

A player who had a lot of trouble on the field was the now-100-pound Rockne. He played in thin moleskin pants and a raveling sweater. The only obeisance he made to head protection was taping his ears to the side of his head so they wouldn't get torn off. A reedy, spindly-legged back who ran like a scared rabbit, young Knute was noted for breaking long gainers, but he took a terrible pounding. Once, playing against the Swedes' arch-rival, the Hamburg Athletic Club, he ripped free on a long run but, with a touchdown ahead, was nailed by a couple dozen Hamburg rooters who not only swamped him but stole the football.

The tough little Norse kid wondered whether legitimate, refined football would be more fun. When he entered North West Division High School, near Humboldt Park, his father reluctantly gave him permission to go out for the team. Lars Rockne could not have done less, recognizing as he did the boy's fierce desire.

By now, the boy had a shining idol: Walter Eckersall, the Mighty Mite of college football, the All-America quarterback of the University of Chicago. Knute had seen Eckersall in action as the star of the Hyde Park high school team. Hyde Park had invited Brooklyn Tech, the best prep team in the East, to come to Chicago for what was billed as "the high school national championship." Rockne sneaked into the ball park to see the 125-pound Eckersall lead his team to an awesome 105–0 victory over the Easterners. A cocky, assertive, signal-barking quarterback, a field general in every sense of the word, was what football was all about as far as Knute Rockne was concerned.

But at North West Division, the 120-pound Rockne never got much further than the scrub team, although he occasionally got into a varsity game in his junior year.

What he did do with moderate success at North West Division was track and field. He was a fair sprinter but not of championship caliber, so he worked up to the middle distances and managed to win a few points in the half-mile. Actually, he was more attracted to the pole vault, the fun thing of his earlier boyhood. But merely flirting with 10 feet got him no headlines.

Meanwhile, his preoccupation with sports was costing him points in the classroom, and his father quickly sensed it. One night, Lars Rockne told his not-quite-sixteen-year-old son that he ought to forget about college. He'd never get in and probably couldn't handle the work if he could. In fact, the father hinted that even a high school diploma was unnecessary and suggested that Knute find a full-time job.

The boy brooded for a few days. On the record, his father seemed to have summed up things quite perfectly. And despite his love affair with sports Knute realized he'd never make a living that way. So, a pragmatist, he opted for security. He took the civil service postal exam, passed it, and dropped out of high school at the end of his junior year to take a job at Chicago's main post office. In many respects, it was the wisest thing he could have done. It represented a chance to make good at something, on his own. He was appointed clerk, and on March 1, 1907, he reported for work.

His salary was $600 a year. Assignment: stamper, mailing division. Six months later, he was made a dispatcher and advanced to $800 a year. The work was gruelingly tough and constant. There was no letup in the flow of bulk mail in giant canvas sacks, often weighing seventy-five pounds or more, which he had to heave around. Nor was it very inspiring to be working the midnight to 8:30 A.M. shift.

The six-day work week was normal, and most weeks he worked seven days because of the huge volume. Chicago was the busiest rail center in the land, and the postal demands on the Chicago post office reflected this. Anyone wanting to advance up through the dispatching system would have to take an exam, proving he had mastered the network of postal arrivals and departures on the network of railroads serving the city. A dispatcher had to have a razor-sharp mind to keep an orderly flow moving.

Postal employees counted on six months to memorize everything before taking the promotion exam. Young Rockne's friends at work kept hammering at him to start studying the huge schedule books. Rockne kept putting it off. Although there was an occasional hour or so when there was a lull in the mail flow, he preferred to spend it with a book he brought from home, or the library, rather than pore over railroad timetables and mail routes.

One day, he looked at a calendar and panicked when he saw the exam was just two weeks away. He went into a cram session and even came back to the post office during his off-hours to study the postal books. He took the exam and scored in the high 90's.

Rockne spent most of his three and a half years' postal service on the night shifts because he wanted to use the days for his track training. He hooked on with the Irving Park A.C., and then was invited to join the prestigious Illinois Athletic Club, for whom he became a respectable half-miler and pole-vaulter.

It was his infatuation with sports which regenerated a desire: the possibility of going on to college, even though he'd never finished high school. He figured if he could ever put aside $1,000 he would talk the University of Illinois into giving him a special qualifying examination. Notre Dame, the small Catholic school over in South

Bend, Indiana wasn't even in the back of his mind. In and around Chicago, it was Illinois, the state university down in Champaign-Urbana, that got all the publicity.

But Rockne had a couple of close friends, Johnny Devine and Johnny Plant, runners on the Chicago track scene. They were headed for Notre Dame and talked Rockne into considering going with them. In the first place, they were sure that Notre Dame would allow Rockne to take some sort of high school equivalency exam to qualify him. More importantly, perhaps, Plant seemed sure that Notre Dame, in its zeal to enroll students, would find Rockne a part-time job.

Rockne wrote to Notre Dame. Yes, they would give him an admissions exam, even though he hadn't graduated from high school. And, maybe they'd dig up some sort of job for him.

Rockne broke the news to his parents and older sisters. His parents were startled. They were devout Lutherans, and their chief concern was whether Knute would have any problems adjusting to the Catholic environment. So, at twenty-two, an age when most people were graduating from college, Knute prepared to enter as a freshman. With slightly less than $1,000 as his four-year stake, and with a single suitcase containing all his clothes and personal effects, he took a New York Central train to South Bend. It was September 1910.

Outside of Devine and Plant, he didn't know a soul there. And he wouldn't have been able to name a Notre Dame football player —present or past—if his life depended on it.

4

New Boy in Town

At the end of Rock's junior year, the head of the chemistry department offered him an assistantship to teach an undergraduate course in his senior year. It was the first time in Notre Dame history that an undergraduate had been so engaged.

The sycamore trees, with huge leaves often twelve inches across, had not yet started to turn color when Knute Rockne arrived at the Notre Dame campus the second week in September, 1910. He walked around slowly, tentatively, soaking up the idyllic rural atmosphere, perspiring in his heavy wool suit, the only one he owned.

He talked to no one, tentatively returning a nod here and there as he passed a few students coming from the main building crested with the famous Golden Dome. It was as unlike Logan Square as Chicago had been unlike Voss, and he was facing another big adjustment. Except this one might be a bit more difficult.

At twenty-two, his hair was already beginning to thin, a portent of the famed balding head of so many later photos. Other freshmen were only seventeen or eighteen. He had known this when he decided to come here, but in Chicago it had been a somewhat remote fact. Here, as he noticed the peach-fuzz faces, his difference from the others gave him a small jolt. There was also the possibility that they might be better prepared for college than he was. He'd find out momentarily, when he reported for the special examination the admissions office had agreed to give him . . .

The college Knute Rockne hoped to attend was at least unique for the incredible circumstances of its founding and survival. Frontier Indiana had had a rich French heritage, a residue of early French missionary-explorers and fur trappers. By the late 1830's the French-born Bishop of Vincennes was alarmed. Hundreds of Catholic families far from Vincennes, and living amongst many "Godless adventurers, ne'er do-wells and malcontent frontier settlers," had no priests or religious training for their children.

The Bishop appealed to the Society of the Holy Cross in Le Mans, France, and the Society sent out young Father Edward Sorin and six teenage Brothers. It was a sixty-three-day journey of utter travail. Unbelievably foul steerage passage by sail to New York. Sluggish Hudson River steamboat to Albany. Horse-drawn barge canal to Buffalo. Savage, storm-tossed Lake Erie passage to Toledo. By canoe or rivers south and west to Indiana. Horse and wagon through rutted forest trails toward Vincennes. Frigid stream crossings and holdups at pistol point by highwaymen.

When he finally arrived at Vincennes, Father Sorin learned he was not to launch a school as he had hoped. Instead, the Bishop sent him into the boondocks to bring the faith to deprived Catholic families.

But Sorin had a dream and he persisted. Months later the Bishop capitulated, handed him $300 in cash and a deed to some Church-owned land in northern Indiana, and gave his permission to start a school—if he could.

The land, on lovely Lake St. Mary's in a settlement called South Bend, was all Sorin needed. Here, on November 26, 1842, he founded Notre Dame on the site of a log cabin chapel where an earlier French priest had hoped to build an orphanage—but didn't.

Sorin started with two students who paid their way in chores. Within a couple of years there were a couple of buildings of yellow handmade brick fashioned from lakeside mud. Sorin advertised the school in Indiana papers, promising strict discipline, a fourteen-hour school day of study, recitation, meditation, recreation and constant supervision. "Your sons will be well-trained and well-attended," he promised parents. There would be no smoking, drinking, swearing or disrespect for elders or faculty. Students from elementary school through college age would be admitted. Cost, including bed and board, would be $100 per year. For a few chickens or a pig thrown in, a boy would be given an extra course of study.

Twice the school burned down. Stubbornly, Sorin each time rebuilt even bigger. A devastating cholera epidemic hit South Bend and twenty-two members of the Notre Dame community died. Sorin kept some of the deaths a secret for fear parents of students would panic and withdraw their sons from school. Burial ceremonies for faculty were held at night so nobody would know.

But the school held on and prospered. Sorin had convinced everyone that Notre Dame was not just for Catholics and that boys of other faiths would be enthusiastically welcomed. By the end of the Civil War, it was on solid footing. Tuition, room and board were now $245 a semester. In the 1880's a survey of earlier graduates showed that 27 percent were lawyers; 18 percent, priests; 10 percent, businessmen; 7 percent, educators. A few reported insouciantly that they were "doing nothing."

Notwithstanding its French beginnings, Notre Dame already reflected the American melting pot with a tilt toward the Irish. Another survey of student nationality before 1890 brought this response:

Irish	183
American	155
German	75
French	21
Spanish	3
Scots	2
English	1
Italian	1

Thus, as Knute Kenneth Rockne contemplated his special admissions examination, it was perhaps symbolic that a college founded on hardship and faith would take a chance on a latter-day immigrant youth who, like Notre Dame, never had anything handed to him.

Anyone fortunate enough to go to college in 1910 almost by definition was headed for a profession of some sort. Knute Rockne's hopes were similar to those of the rest of the students. If Notre Dame admitted him, he planned to enroll in its pharmacy school and someday open a drugstore.

He reported to the admissions office and immediately sat down to a two-hour examination covering history, English and some mathematics. When he finished, the proctor told him to come back in two hours. They'd grade his papers and let him know right then and there.

During the three and a half years Rockne had worked evenings in the Chicago post office, his biggest interest had been amateur track. Luckily he'd also spent a lot of his idle daytime hours reading books he'd lugged home from the library. If his modest track feats were still to be an iffy item in his future, the books now paid instant dividends. He returned at the appointed hour and an official simply said, "You passed, Rockne. You have been assigned to a room in Sorin Hall." He was told one more thing. He would have the part-time job promised him: janitor in the chemistry lab.

The room at Sorin Hall was a dingy, basement-level cubicle with two small windows barely above the ground. On any scale of elegance it was just a cut above a dungeon. Rockne walked in and found a black-haired, angular-faced freshman surveying the room dourly, hands on hips. The kid turned and stuck out his hand.

"My name's Dorais. Charles Dorais. I'm from Chippewa Falls, Wisconsin."

"Mine's Rockne—from Chicago."

"I guess we're roommates."

"Yeah, I guess so," said Rockne, looking around. "Where you going to put your trunk? There's not much space here."

"I haven't any trunk."

Rockne grinned. "Neither have I. We'd better shake on that because we're starting even."

It didn't take long for Rockne to learn that the eighteen-year-old

Dorais, better known as Gus, had been a high school football star and had a passion to play at Notre Dame.

"How about you?" Dorais asked, casually noting the Chicagoan's 5′8″, 145-pound frame. "Hall football, maybe?"

"Hall football?" Rockne echoed.

"Everybody who has the time at least tries to play on his hall team."

"Oh," said Rockne, and let it go at that.

Years later Dorais recalled: "I sort of sensed that the old geezer —that's what he looked like to me—was sort of ruffled by my suggestion. I hadn't meant anything by it, but there was a funny glint in his eye that I hadn't noticed before."

The four- or five-year age difference between Rockne and his younger classmates didn't prevent him from exercising some of the spirit of fun that was part of his personality—and which was to show up in varied form after he got into coaching. Dorais offered testimony on that.

"There was a lot of the little boy in Rock," Dorais once said. "Breaking a rule was never a sign of rebellion or a mark of disrespect for the established order. Rock just acted on impulse, especially if there were some fun involved.

"Yes, as poor as he was he did have his fun. He came down here with possibly the smallest wardrobe of any freshman. He had that one suit, a couple pair of pants and a few shirts. Three neckties, I believe. One blue, one brown and one black. When he got his first letterman's sweater, he wore it all the time. In the winter, on a rare visit into town, he'd borrow a friend's overcoat. One of his pals was about 6′2″ and weighed 230 or so. You should have seen Rock in that coat. Incidentally, any time he'd go into town he'd walk the two miles to save the nickel trolley fare.

"Picking up a few extra bucks was always a major preoccupation with Rock. When he found out that the guys in the band or orchestra received small stipends, he sent home for his flute and auditioned. He was good enough to be taken on. I think they got a buck for every concert. That damned flute of his almost drove me wild, though. He practiced quite a bit because he didn't want to lose his place in the band, and he could fill that room of ours with some hideous music. There were times I'd take that damned flute apart when he was out, and hide the pieces all over. He'd find them every time and just grin and start tootling."

When pressed, Dorais admitted to other fund-raising gambits which were natural for their hustling spirits. Since nobody was allowed to leave the dormitory at night without permission, their ground-level windows in Sorin Hall were very handy for students who wanted to evade the rule—"skiving" in the Notre Dame argot. Gus and Rock would charge a quarter for skiving rights to their windows and could pick up a couple dollars a week that way.

Their biggest paydays, however, took a little more effort. At least on Rock's part. "Once in a while," said Dorais, "we'd disappear off campus and take part in club smokers in and around South Bend or Elkhart. Rock was the fighter—at 145 pounds—and I'd serve as his second. The guys he fought—often 160-pounders—for the most part were using these club dates as a step up the ladder to the Chicago big time. There were quite a few guys who lost their way when they ran into Rock. God, he was tough. And twenty bucks was a big purse for us."

The social Rockne, as recalled by Dorais and others of his era, was a young man, older than his peers, who was thought to be very shy. He was bashful, unsophisticated and not conversationally glib. He wasn't very successful at dating because he was so self-conscious and unsure of himself. According to Dorais, he rarely dated the same girl twice while in college. In fact, it was reported on a couple of occasions that he was so depressed and unhappy with himself that he might even quit school. Apparently, only his brilliant talent with his chemistry studies and, later, his football success, kept him going.

There was one other area that grabbed and held his interest: drama. He saw his first dramatic production as a freshman and was hooked. By the time he was a junior, there wasn't a campus dramatic production in which he didn't have a leading role—often a feminine part. He played an Indian squaw with long-braided wig and heavy make-up in *Girl of the Golden West,* and the role of Mrs. Smith in *David Garrick,* and drew rave notices in the South Bend papers.

There seemed to be no end to his versatility. In his junior year he got to the finals of the Notre Dame marbles tournament. "I lost to a farmer boy," he said later, "who had the toughest thumb in the county."

But the bedrock of his college success was in his role as a student. Father John Cavanaugh, president of Notre Dame during that period, was to write: "He had a tremendous reputation as an unusual student. He was never unprepared in any class, but to some of our professors' dismay, he would often—and innocently —sit in the back of a lecture hall with two or three of his buddies discussing politics or football—yet have the uncanny knack of following the lecture accurately and come up with a pertinent or challenging comment if called upon. Or sometimes when he wasn't called upon. No one knew how he could do that. It was as though he had a divided brain that could handle two functions at once.

"According to his friends his favorite way to study at night was to read a book at his desk for a few minutes, then get up and pace up and down, rolling a pencil between his palms while fixing the material in his mind.

"If someone came into his room one of two things would happen. Either Rock would ignore him completely or swing around and invite the newcomer to discuss something Rock had been studying."

Father Julius Nieuwland, Notre Dame's famed professor of chemistry, called Rockne the most remarkable student he ever knew. When in 1912, Nieuwland was doing research that would lead to his discovery of synthetic rubber, he took his prize pupil off his laboratory janitorial duties and made him an assistant in the research.

Rock, in fact, had taken honors in his freshman pharmacy course and was considering becoming a chemistry professor. At the end of his junior year the department head offered him an assistantship to teach an undergraduate course during his senior year. It was the first time in Notre Dame history that an undergraduate had been so engaged.

"Knute often audited classes in courses not in his program," said Cavanaugh. "His was a case of brain hunger. Especially in cultural things, the humanities and general literature."

Under other circumstances, Knute Rockne's academic honors and drive might clearly have shaped his future life, but sports were also a part of his destiny. There were only 400 undergraduates in the Notre Dame college division when he arrived as a freshman, and everyone was required to take part in some sort of physical education program. As many as possible worked out the obligation by playing on one of the hall football teams.

So in 1910 Rock went out for the Brownson Hall team, coached by Joe Collins, one of the varsity players, and within a week Collins suggested to the varsity coach that he take a look at a smallish but very tough freshman. Shorty Longman, a one-time Michigan star, was the Irish headman, and it took him only three days to decide that Rockne was a flop. Longman stuck him at fullback with the scrubs, where his longest gain from scrimmage was two yards. As a safety man he fumbled his first punt. When he tried to get off a punt of his own, he bobbled the snap and was smeared.

Rockne was upset. He was already feeling a bit strange at being what he thought was the only Protestant in a stronghold of Catholicism (actually there were several others), and he wondered whether that had anything to do with Longman's disenchantment. He decided he'd go out for track in the winter and spring.

Although he'd failed in football, he was an immediate success in track. He made the varsity as a freshman pole-vaulter and was awarded a varsity letter. Despite his rather small stature, he had excellent speed coming down the runway, and he got good lift from his muscular shoulders. (As a junior he would clear more than 12 feet and set the American indoor record in the event.)

Returning in the fall for his sophomore year, Rock was determined to prove that Shorty Longman's evaluation of him as a football player had been faulty. But he would have to prove it to a new coach, John L. Marks, a former Dartmouth man, latest in a long line of hopefuls who thought they could enjoy continuing success at the school on the Indiana prairie.

The football program that Knute Rockne was determined to be a part of had not been a long and glorious recital of success. In 1887 the University of Michigan had sent a team to South Bend to play in Notre Dame's first interscholastic game. It was one of the few times the schools would ever meet, and Michigan took the inexperienced Notre Dame team apart. After two more dismally unproductive seasons, in 1890–91 the school fielded no team at all. When play was resumed in 1892, there was a note in the Notre Dame *Scholastic,* the student publication, that put the local effort into proper perspective: "Our players are strong and willing but we need full-time coaches to teach individuals how to unite mind, body and spirit in the common cause: how to play with and for each other to the best interest of the team."

Nobody before or since has ever stated it more succinctly. What the student body was asking for was not just a volunteer who was here in September and gone in November, and not interested in returning. Finally, in 1896, there arrived in South Bend a crisp, serious-looking young man of about twenty-five who had played for Stagg at Chicago and had then gone East to do some coaching at Bucknell. His name was Francis E. Hering and nobody was ever going to say he was a laggard. He came to Notre Dame to coach, act as captain, play quarterback, teach English and study law on the side. He may have been paid as much as $100 in cash but also received sides of beef from the Notre Dame farm operated by the Brothers of the Holy Cross. Even if Hering had not qualified for a footnote in football history, he would have something else going for him: he was the founder of the national "Mother's Day," in memory of his own mother.

Frank Hering stayed only three years but he left his impact on the place. He convinced the administration that the sport would never survive successfully without financial support for decent uniforms, an extra football or two, and a field free of rocks and ruts. He also ran a program with some integrity. If you played for Hering at Notre Dame, you had to be a student. No more tough townies or tramp athletes would share their lumps anonymously with bona fide students who got whatever glory was up for grabs when the team won a game.

Hering produced three winning seasons and had begun to upgrade the Irish schedules. Such foes as the Illinois Cycling Club, the Indianapolis Artillery, and Chicago Physicians and Surgeons would for the most part soon disappear, and Notre Dame would go from a four-game program to eight and nine games.

But Notre Dame was troubled. When the Western Conference (later to be called the Big Ten) was organized in 1896, Notre Dame applied for membership. The Irish were turned down curtly and there was no disguising the fact that the new loop thought Notre Dame wasn't big-time enough. Naïvely eager, with an eye on future consideration, Notre Dame would soon adopt many of the Big Ten's eligibility and code-of-conduct regulations, hoping for later admittance. There would be more rebuffs.

Notre Dame under Hering also began to develop a reputation for its robust, devil-may-care execution of the flying wedge on kickoffs in what was a portent of the later Irish zeal.

Early Irish coaches surely believed in the physical part of the game. In 1899, Joseph J. McWeeney, a part-time wrestler who later would become South Bend's police chief, had a succinct bit of advice for his backs: "Go into the line," he told them, "with your fist doubled. You won't have to use it. They'll get the message." (And, presumably, to hell with the fumble potential when you only had one hand on the ball.) McWeeney lasted one year.

By the turn of the century, Notre Dame football, if not looming large in administrative hopes, was beginning to be a matter of fierce pride among the students. They'd had a taste of a full-time head coach under Hering and would accept no other system. Although subsequently there would be a succession of almost one-night stands (names destined for deepest anonymity like James F. Faragher, Henry J. McGlew and Victor M. Place), the administration was beginning to realize that football must succeed at Notre Dame because students demanded it.

In 1901, for instance, it was reported in the South Bend *Tribune* that, for the Indiana game, rooter preparations were being made on such a fierce scale that "every student will be there whether he likes it or not." No reference was made as to how the threat would be carried out. A prize was even offered for the best yell composed by a student. The winner was a native Irishman who whipped up his contribution in Gaelic:

Aurd-skuel aur Mahur
Na laochra town gon go
Feer laoch na mille trown
Skappig eud mor cho
Buallig agus Kawnig eud
Gus kurrig eud fay chra
Aurd-skuel aur Mahur
Go bragh, go bragh.

To be sung to the tune of "Marching Through Georgia," it was used at the Indiana game but never again. Mostly, according to the reports, because everyone free-lanced it into a wild, banshee howl.

In 1903 Notre Dame attracted national attention for the first time when Louis (Red) Salmon, a slashing 170-pound halfback, made Walter Camp's third team All-America, and with an undefeated nine-game season the Irish demanded to share Western championship honors with Fielding Yost's point-a-minute Michigan teams. Nobody listened to Notre Dame.

It wasn't until 1909 that anyone really took Notre Dame seriously as a pretender to national power. Frank (Shorty) Longman had taken over and had molded a collection of individual stars into a smooth-working machine. The most notable player became the first Irish superstar, Harry (Red) Miller, at halfback. Miller, who had appeared as a frosh in 1906, was the first of the Defiance, Ohio family that would send more members to Notre Dame than any other family in Notre Dame history. Something like thirty Millers would show up under the Golden Dome.

In 1908 Notre Dame had put a scare into Michigan before losing, 12–6. Longman asked Fielding Yost if they could come back in 1909. Yost demurred and questioned the eligibility of two Notre Dame linemen, Ralph Dimmick of Oregon and George Philbrook of Washington. Had they or had they not gone to an Oregon college? Finally, Yost agreed to the 1909 game, grumbling that it would be good practice for his Wolverines. Notre Dame was in a vengeful mood. Michigan had dropped out of the Western Conference in 1907 in a pique over league scheduling difficulties and Notre Dame once again applied for membership—and once again was snubbed. Somebody had to be *shown*.

The week before the Michigan game, the Irish, who had won three straight, went East to play one of Pop Warner's great Pitt teams. The campus almost went berserk when local headlines blared the news that Walter Camp, no less, was going to witness the game. The Irish had not yet come close to having a first team All-America player, and with the panjandrum of All-America selectors there in the flesh, maybe—just maybe—he'd name a Notre Damer.

The Irish whipped the heavily favored Panthers, 6–0. Camp called Notre Dame's Pete Vaughan the greatest fullback in the West—but subsequently did not name Vaughan or any Irish player to All-America. (It was Vaughan who, the year before, correctly or not, was given credit for launching the nickname "Fighting Irish." Once when the team was far behind and playing listlessly, Vaughan, so the story goes, shook both fists in the air at his teammates and screamed: "What the hell's the matter with you guys? You're mostly Irish and you're not even fighting!")

Then, on November 6, the Irish—again the underdogs, only more so—went to Ann Arbor for the long-anticipated meeting with Yost's Michigan powerhouse. The Wolverines were rated at least a two-touchdown favorite. Nobody could see the Irish running against a big Michigan line that had two All-Americas.

Yost again referred to his upcoming joust with the Irish as "a practice game," not only because he expected it to be that but because it had been scheduled grudgingly. Some practice game. The vengeful Irish ripped the Wolverines to pieces, beating them 11–3 and never allowing Michigan within the Notre Dame 20-yard line. After the game Yost sourly and publicly dismissed the defeat as "unofficial," and brought up the old "practice" wheeze.

Nobody else bought it that way, including the press. It was the lone defeat of the year for Michigan. For the Irish it was their first upset victory of epic proportions. They went on to an undefeated season and a bona fide claim as Champions of the West. (In their season finale they whipped neighboring Wabash, 38–6. The Wabash team was coached by a man named Jesse C. Harper, who would loom large in the Irish football picture in just a few years.)

The season was notable for another reason. The Notre Dame band, the first marching band in college history, played for the first time a tune that is easily the most stirring of all college pep songs: the Notre Dame "Victory March."

The sophomore Knute Rockne who reported to new coach John Marks in September 1911 had grown slightly. He was now five-eight and 160 pounds, with a good torso but slim legs. He was stronger than his weight would indicate, and it took Marks just two weeks to decide that despite his size the candidate kindled too many sparks to be left off the starting line-up. Knute Rockne, from opening game on, was the regular left end. His roommate, Dorais, started at quarterback.

Against Ohio Northern in the opener, Rock made an embarrassing debut. It was a cold day, and the first time Dorais tossed him a pass his fingers were chilled and the ball bounced away. "It was the first time I suspected that loose hands and relaxed fingers would be the key to pass-catching," he said.

Rockne also realized that day what an economic handicap Notre Dame struggled under to keep its football program going. "One of our linemen was injured," he recalled with wry humor. "Our coach had to use our entire roll of tape on him. A few minutes later when his substitute got hurt, they had to take some of the tape off the first casualty to fix the second. I never forgot that in later years. As coach and athletic director I determined that Notre Dame football players would have the best we could afford."

Again Notre Dame traveled to Pittsburgh to meet a tough Panther team, and this time there was an even bigger crowd than for the 1909 game. Notre Dame was beginning to be an attraction. It was also beginning to lure boys from all over. At least twelve states were represented on that Irish team. The press coverage was the heaviest in Pittsburgh history, editors having heard about the nimble, crafty Gus Dorais at quarterback.

No one scored in the first half. Opening the second half, the Irish tried a daring onside kick. Rockne zipped in, recovered the ball and raced for a touchdown. But the Irish had been offside and the play was called back. The game ended scoreless.

In Rockne's sophomore year the Irish went undefeated, winning six games and tying two. Then they won seven straight in 1912. At the end of the season, Rockne was elected captain of the team for his senior year. Most fans thought the captaincy would go to Gus Dorais, but insiders and those on the squad knew Rock's flaming leadership qualities.

Rockne also found himself mentioned as an All-America candidate for the following year, or at least All-Western. But shortly after the 1912 season was over his father died, and he seriously considered leaving college to help out his family. Only the dogged insistence of his older sister kept him on the campus. It was a fateful decision.

5

Dorais-to-Rockne

Eastern coaches mostly detested the pass. They were the purists, the traditionalists who had invented and developed the game, and had accepted the pass in the rules only because President Teddy Roosevelt had rammed it down their throats.

It was a typical gab session with Knute Rockne after the season was over, late in the 1920's. Rockne was relaxing in his New York hotel room with three or four sports writers. Joe Williams of the *World-Telegram* swished some illegal Scotch around in his glass. Perhaps the motion would add something to the suspect product that had found its way into Manhattan.

"Question, Rock," he began. "This story we keep hearing about that first Notre Dame–Army game in 1913—that West Point thought you guys were a bunch of untalented plow jockeys who'd provide them with a breather. Is that a myth or not?"

"Okay, let me set it straight, then," Rock snapped. "It's about time—and 'myth' is the right word. What a lot of surprised Eastern sportswriters didn't realize was that the Notre Dame success story had already been launched before 1913, but the word had some difficulty getting over the Appalachian Range." He stabbed a finger at Williams. "And another thing—Army was confident they'd beat us but they knew we were no plow jockeys."

Rock smiled thinly. "It was a helluva day."

It had all started with a short piece in New York newspapers on April 18, 1913, with a West Point dateline, announcing Army's schedule for the coming fall. With a line that was almost a throw-away, it observed that one of the interesting home games would be with Notre Dame.

Sports fans paid little attention. Football was a long way off. The New York Yankees, the New York Giants and the Brooklyn Dodgers had just returned to town a week earlier from their spring drills in Florida. That's where the news was—and besides, who and where was Notre Dame?

Quite obviously, Eastern observers had overlooked the fact that just a few years earlier, in 1909, the Irish had defeated one of Yost's best Michigan teams, and had put together undefeated seasons in 1911–12. Possibly, they were unaware, too, that some Midwestern critics had considered the Irish on a par with Wisconsin's Western Conference champions—a Badger team that had placed, amazingly, nine players on the eleven-man All-Conference team, as picked by Walter Eckersall of the Chicago *Tribune*.

The Irish were no mystery in the Midwest. In fact, Notre Dame was having difficulty booking games with Western Conference teams. So the new coach, Jesse Harper, looked East—not only to fill out his schedule but because he felt it was time Notre Dame made an impact on Eastern consciousness to lure a recruit or two to the Indiana prairie.

The Irish already had a November 8 date for a road game with Penn State, but November 1 was still open. And looked as though it would remain that way unless there was a minor miracle. Teams didn't make schedules seven, eight years in advance as they do today. But Notre Dame was operating virtually on a year-to-year basis. And any open date meant there would be no trip to the bank the following Monday. One of the things the still-young Notre Dame football program needed was money.

The miracle had started to evolve in 1912. Army and Yale had mutually decided to end their annual contest because—get this—coaches and administrators at both places decided the game was demanding too much from the players in terms of effort and emotion.

Suddenly Army had an open date for 1913 and sent out a blizzard of letters to Eastern colleges. Nobody could accommodate the Cadets. In some small measure of panic, the Army Athletic Association banged out a few more to Midwest schools, but by late March they still had no opponent for November 1. One day a handwritten letter came from a man who was still the head coach at Wabash College in Crawfordsville, Indiana. His name was Jesse Harper, and at the end of the school year he was to report to Notre Dame as the new head coach of the Irish. Notre Dame officials had received a letter from West Point with an offer of a game. Harper was replying on Notre Dame's behalf but wanted to know how much Notre Dame would be guaranteed for the game.

The brass at West Point were puzzled. Money? Schools like Yale, Penn and others always paid their own way to West Point. But they thought they could come up with $600. Harper replied that Notre Dame needed $1,000—and that he would hold his squad down to eighteen players. Army figured time was running out, and it had better make the guarantee or there wouldn't be a game at all. "Get 'em," said Charles Daly, the former Harvard and Army All-American who was the new Cadet coach. "They're not a bad team and it's a fair enough price for a good win."

So Notre Dame agreed to come to the Plains above the Hudson. They would travel light. Only eighteen players, each man carrying his own equipment in a modest satchel. According to one story, only fourteen of those satchels contained a pair of real football cleats.

Jesse Harper made sure he reported in at Notre Dame before his squad dispersed for the summer. The first person he collared was his captain, Knute Rockne.

"We've got a game with Army," he said tentatively. "How do you feel about that?"

His balding captain grinned lopsidely. It was the first time Harper was to see that famous, lopsided grin on his captain's face.

"Do you have to ask?" Rock said and dashed off to spread the word for a squad meeting.

What it turned out to be was the first step in a Crusade, a Holy War of epic proportions. The team wasn't going to be selfish about it, either. Not only were they going to strike a blow for Notre Dame —they'd also strike a blow for all of Midwest football. Nobody in the East thought much about the Midwest game and sniffed diffidently when cornfed chauvinists mentioned Stagg and Yost. Outdated muscle mechanics, no finesse, said the East. The game simply hadn't developed when Chicago and Michigan were rolling up all those victories in the early 1900's.

After the meeting, Rock and his roommate, quarterback Gus Dorais, came to Harper privately.

"We've got summer jobs at Cedar Point, Ohio, on the lake," said Rock. "And we're going to do some special practicing. Can we take a couple of footballs with us?"

Harper raised an eyebrow. "Well, yes," he said, "but what's so special?"

What was so special was an idea Rockne and Dorais had about some new rules governing forward passing, put into effect the previous year but not yet fully taken advantage of.

The weapon which Dorais and Rockne decided to refine on the shores of Lake Erie was not completely unknown, although a solid body of mythology has been built up suggesting that the two young Notre Damers invented it. The forward pass had gone through a rather quixotic and overmanaged evolution. Dorais and Rockne were not even the first famous pass combination.

President Teddy Roosevelt forced the rule makers into opening up the game by threatening to outlaw it because of the brutality of mass play. The forward pass, first allowed in 1906, was the handiest device the rule makers could think of. Except that they almost strangled it in its infancy.

A pass had to cross the line of scrimmage not more than five yards to the left or right of the center, and couldn't be tossed more than twenty yards. To help the referee's judgment, the field was chalked off into five-yard squares (hence the new nickname "gridiron"). An incomplete pass could be recovered by either side if the ball had been touched. A pass caught behind the goal line wasn't a touchdown, but a touchback, and the defending team took over the ball. With restrictions like that, it was no wonder that 95 percent of the college coaches considered the pass a handmaiden to the plague. When you ran the ball, you at least didn't need a road map of the field. The shape of the ball didn't help, either. In the hands of most throwers, it was more balloon than oblate. Many quarterbacks didn't pass it; they flung it awkwardly, and it looked more like a ruptured duck in a high wind.

Very few passers could spiral the ball, and virtually all receivers caught it as they would a medicine ball—in the pit of the stomach or cradled against their chest. And most pass routes called for a receiver to dash to a designated spot and wait for the ball. (Worse, the defenders were allowed to commit mayhem on receivers waiting to catch the ball.)

Although all the backs and both ends were eligible receivers, one man was normally designated to catch passes from the quarterback. And the most effective way to get the ball to the receiver was to toss up a high lob which the receiver waited for, or (if he were agile and daring) leaped high for. No one had yet thought of trying to fire the ball sharply to a receiver on the run.

So much for skill, technique and deception in an aerial game.

Amos Alonzo Stagg of Chicago and Eddie Cochems of St. Louis University, however, apparently had come up with a more mobile maneuver in 1907 or 1908, with the ball tossed to a man running out. In fact, to St. Louis goes the distinction of producing the first effective passing combination. Brad Robinson, the St. Louis quarterback, found the handle in learning to throw an overhand spiral, even with the fat ball of the period, and end Jack Schneider cleverly snagged it into his chest or stomach.

It still wasn't a very popular gimmick. Eastern coaches, particularly, detested it. They were the purists, the traditionalists who had invented and developed the game and had accepted the pass in the rules only because Teddy Roosevelt had rammed it down their throats. Okay, it was in the rules, but the rules didn't say they had to use it. Ground would be gained by a man lugging the ball overland, with somebody up front clearing the way for him. Let the fancy Dans and the Johnny-come-latelies throw it around—and lose it. Until proven otherwise, the forward pass was pure japery and nonsense.

But in 1912 the rule makers did away with the five and 20-yard restrainers and prohibited deliberate interference by the defense. Knute Rockne and Gus Dorais, prior to the 1913 season, figured it was time to take advantage of the new rules. They explained their plans to Harper. He gave them two footballs and his blessings. Later he was to say he had nothing to lose; Knute and Gus would have a way of keeping in shape, and they were both adaptable athletes. Who knows? They might even come up with something.

It is an oft-told story, of course, that Rock and Dorais went off to Cedar Point for a summer of clerking, janitoring and waiting on table, for which they got their room, meals and about $12 a week in wages. The story is wrong, however, when it tells about the duo practicing on the beach for hours at a time. They did do a lot of running in the sand because it was good for the leg muscles, and, yes, they did toss the ball around a bit on the beach. But mostly the duo worked out on a turf field near their hotel. They had to in order to perfect what they had in mind and get their timing down pat. Dorais, who could whip a perfect spiral, even with the more bulbous ball of the period, was going to throw short, medium and long. He would take an imaginary snap to fade back, or fake a handoff and scamper right or left before throwing.

"Rock kept repeating a phrase like a litany," Dorais was to say. " 'Mobility. Mobility and change of pace. That's what we need. They're not going to know where we're going or when we get there.' "

What Rock meant was that there'd be no camping out under a pass, waiting for it to arrive. He'd grab it on the run, in full stride, if possible, and with open, relaxed hands. No more breadbasket or medicine ball stuff. (He even experimented by catching it with one hand, but when they got back for fall practice Harper said nothing doing.) Rock freely admitted, later, that he was quite possibly the first receiver to use his hands that way.

They worked tirelessly, establishing pass routes and timing the patterns so that Dorais could lead Rock, or hit him over the shoulder, or put it right into him on a cut or curl back. It is safe to say that nobody ever thought of the possibilities those two did at Cedar Point.

One other significant thing happened to Rockne that summer at

Cedar Point. One day he met a lovely, slim girl from nearby Sandusky, Ohio. Her name was Bonnie Skiles . . .

When practice opened at Notre Dame early in September, Dorais and Rockne put on a demonstration, for Harper, of what they'd worked on at Cedar Point.

"Harper was pleased," Rockne later recalled, "but we decided we weren't going to show too much in our early games."

There was no need to, as the Irish demolished their first three foes—87–0 over Ohio Northern, 20–7 over North Dakota and 62–0 over Alma, of Michigan—for an explosive total of 167 points to 7. Although there was quite a bit of scoring on passes, Harper held his aerial game just enough in check so that the press wouldn't start gushing about a new Notre Dame offense.

"What we had fixed firmly in our minds," said Rock, "was that November 1 date at West Point."

It was probably the best team that Notre Dame had yet fielded. Paired at end, with Rock, was tough Fred Gushurst; Deak Jones and Ralph Lathrop were the tackles; Freeman Fitzgerald and Emmett Keefe were the guards; Al Feeney was the center; Dorais, of course, was the quarterback; Joe Pliska and Sam Finegan were the halfbacks; Ray Eichenlaub, a bullish runner, was the fullback. As good as the unit was, they had no idea they were going to carve out a little bit of immortality for themselves. They only knew that Army probably had the best team in the east.

The Cadets featured a fearsome backfield: master strategist and slick runner All-America Vern Prichard at quarterback and the three "H" boys, halfbacks Ben Hoge and Leland Hobbs and fullback Paul Hodgson. The line was headed by All-America Lou Merillat, an end, and future All-America center Johnny McEwan.

"The entire student body was caught up with the team's spirit," Rockne recalled. "The morning we left—Thursday, two days before the game—everyone in the dorms got out of bed long before breakfast and marched downtown to accompany the team to the depot. It was the first time I'd ever seen anything like mass hysteria generated on the campus—and it wouldn't be the last."

With its limited travel budget, the Irish entourage of about

twenty-three, including the eighteen players, took along sandwiches and fruit, packed by the kitchen ladies in the refectory, to
save money for dinner aboard the train. It took a full day to get
to Buffalo, where, at about 11 P.M. they gawked at the luxury that
awaited them—a transfer to a sleeping car, with Pullman berths.
Lowers for regulars and uppers for the seven substitutes. "It struck
me," Rock once said, "as a rather reasonable discrimination. It
remained so fixed in my mind that I used it for later Notre Dame
trips when I became head coach."

It was also the first time anyone in the party had ever slept on
a train, and the players were so awed that few of them got the kind
of sleep Harper always prescribed for the week of a game. He
worried about it when they tumbled off at West Point at 8 o'clock
next morning. He needn't have; Irish adrenaline was going to flow
at riptide velocity.

The Notre Dame team was cordially received, was given the
freedom of the Officers Club and was housed overnight at Cullum
Hall. They entered, however, for some reason not entirely clear,
through the kitchen. It was to lay the groundwork for an Irish
superstition. Every year after that, the Notre Dame teams insisted
on coming into Cullum through the kitchen.

On Saturday afternoon there was only a moderate crowd in the
stands at West Point, although one day three times that many
would claim they were there.

Jess Harper knew, of course, that he and his team hadn't arrived
at West Point as total strangers. Charley Daly, the Cadet coach,
had dispatched an assistant to Cartier Field to check on the Irish
against Alma. Although Alma had been obviously outclassed, the
scout came back to West Point and reported that Notre Dame had
a slashing offense. Dorais, he said, was a magician at handing off
to Eichenlaub or the halfbacks, and they all hit with a lot of drive.
Harper had allowed only three passes against Alma, just to keep
the franchise warm, so the Army scout didn't have much to warn
Daly about. Daly wouldn't have been impressed, anyway. Although he incorporated some modest passing in his own game—
and had, in fact, beaten Colgate earlier in the year only because of
three complete aerials in the second half—Daly actually had an

indifference bordering on contempt for the pass.

He prepared his team to stop Notre Dame's quick-hitting ground game, then to destroy the Irish with his own bulldozing offense behind a line that outweighed the Irish forwards by almost fifteen pounds per man. His battle plan was to maintain some respect for the visitors but to use them as just another stepping stone in Army's surge for the Eastern championship and maybe a claim as the best in the nation.

The New York papers must have figured it the same way Daly did. Not one sent its first-string writer to cover the game. It deserved good coverage, of course, but the happenings at Cambridge, New Haven and Princeton took priority.

Harper, his quarterback, Dorais, and his captain and star receiver, Knute Rockne, had decided they wouldn't launch their passing attack early in the game. They'd test Army with their ground game and get an idea of the Cadet defenses. "We wanted to find out how quickly they could adjust," said Rockne.

Army kicked off and the Army crowd settled back to watch— as they assumed—the huge Army line contain the Irish. It did, too, stopping the first Irish running play and causing an Eichenlaub fumble on the second, which the Cadets recovered. The next time the Irish got the ball, Dorais fired a quick pass in the flat. The ball was overthrown. The sight of the ball in the air didn't seem to alarm the Cadets, but they were surprised they couldn't make any offensive headway against the Irish when they got the ball again and there was an exchange of punts.

Still, Notre Dame appeared to be taking a physical beating. It seemed only a question of time before they began to fold. In fact, Army coaches noticed that Rockne seemed to be limping and that he was only half-heartedly blocking the cadet tackle, appearing to sidestep him. But when Notre Dame received a punt, Rockne grinned at Dorais as they lined up and said softly, "Okay, let's show 'em something."

On the next play, Rockne put a crisp brush block on the Cadet tackle, knocking him off his normal charging stride, then burst out around him. The defensive back, who no doubt was aware that Rockne had been limping, wasn't even in the ball park as the speedy Rockne, no longer gimpy, shot past him into the open. He took Dorais' twenty-five-yard pitch perfectly over his shoulder and whipped over the goal line. The Army fans were in a state of shock. It was the first time in history that anyone had ever scored on Army with a forward pass.

The Cadets reacted with slashing fury. Hoge, Hobbs and Hodgson ripped the Irish line for huge gains, and scored late in the quarter but missed the point. Early in the second period, quarterback Vern Prichard directed another drive (with the aid of a pass, strangely enough) that took the ball to the Notre Dame 3. A holding penalty against Notre Dame set up an Army first down on the 1-foot line. Hodgson smashed straight ahead but was smothered for no gain.

Now the entire Irish line dug in and turned back the next thrust. A third assault was a bit wider, and Rockne and Jones wrecked it. On fourth down, Prichard beautifully faked a lateral to Hoge, wheeled, kept, and nipped low into the middle and scored. The point was kicked and Army led, 13–7.

"We still felt we could win," Rockne recalled, "but we honestly didn't think we could do it with our running game, good as we thought it was. Army was just too big and tough to move out of there. We decided we'd do it mostly through the air. We didn't think Army was quick enough or smart enough to adjust its defenses. It was time to put all our overhead stuff to work."

It took the Irish just four plays to get a message to Army . . . After the kickoff, which Rockne returned to the 15, Dorais daringly called for a quarterback sneak and ripped through for eleven yards. There were a few seconds short of two minutes left in the half. And in those days time was not taken out when a first down was registered.

Dorais sent Rockne straight downfield and two of the Army secondary converged on him. Dorais flicked the ball right over the line to Joe Pliska, who got thirty yards before he was downed. On the next play, Rockne whizzed between two defenders on a slant-in and Dorais hit him high, right in the hands, for twenty more. On the next play Rockne angled for the sideline as Dorais stepped back and dodged two Army linemen. Rockne broke to the inside and

Dorais fired. An Army back hit him, but he was down to the 5-yard line. Army, befuddled, was sure it would be a third straight pass, but Dorais coolly pulled the string when he saw the cadet ends and tackles spaced wider than usual, and sent Joe Pliska barreling between guard and tackle for the touchdown. At the half it was 14–13, Notre Dame.

Early in the third period, Army mounted a punishing drive that Notre Dame simply couldn't handle. It went right up the middle, because the cadets had found they simply couldn't turn the flanks guarded by Rockne and Fred Gushurst. Army blockers would pound at the 155-pound Rockne, and he would nimbly fight them off and either nail the ball carrier or contain him to the inside. But the Army onslaught up the middle carried to the Irish 2. This was it. This was where the Irish would crack; the floodgates would be open and not only would the cadets score but their momentum would dominate the last half.

On the first down, Rockne pinched in on Hodgson and threw him for a two-yard loss. The entire Irish line smothered the next play. Then, dramatically, Vern Prichard ripped a page from Dorais' book and faded back to pass. He flipped the ball to the corner of the end zone, where Lou Merillat reached greedily for the sure touchdown. Like a ghost who wasn't there a split second ago, Gus Dorais bounded upward, in front of him, and intercepted.

After that, the picture was one that was etched forever on the memories of knowledgeable critics of the game.

Harper, Dorais and Rockne unleashed the full beauty and precision of their passing game. Thirteen times in the last half, Dorais put the ball in the air. For ten completions, seven of them to Knute Rockne, one each to Gushurst, Pliska and Finegan. Short. Long. Over the middle. And never to a stationary receiver. Befuddled, Army tried to spread their defenses, but the backs were confused. There was no way to contain the Irish aerial pattern that used the entire field in its flawless plan. And how do you cope with a 5'9", 155-pound slippery target like the left end named Rockne, who always took the ball in his outstretched hands, on the fly and in full stride?

When the cadet defense gambled too recklessly and dropped

back too far, Dorais sent Pliska or Eichenlaub through the gaps for five, eight and ten yards at a crack. Never had Eastern sportswriters seen a defense so demoralized.

When it was all over, it was 35–13, Notre Dame, with Ray Eichenlaub getting the last two touchdowns on blasts through the Cadet line after passes had set up the scores. The next day, the Sunday New York *Times* ran a very appropriate headline: NOTRE DAME OPEN PLAY AMAZES ARMY. And followed it up with the note that "the Westerners flashed the most sensational football ever seen in the East."

It was, indeed, just that. Princeton's famed Bill Roper, later the Tigers' coach, had umpired the game. "I've never seen the forward pass used with such stunning perfection," he said.

The stats for the day showed Dorais fired for 14 completions in 17 attempts, and 243 yards. It was undoubtedly a collegiate record to date. And one of the things the press buzzed about was the length of some of Dorais' efforts—perfect spiral tosses of thirty-five yards and longer, which no one had ever seen before.

There was yet another bit of Dorais flimflammery that impressed the viewers. Rules of the period didn't recognize deliberate grounding of a pass. Dorais, nimble though he was, couldn't always avoid a rush. At the last instant he'd peg the ball into the ground a few yards away from him and not only avert a loss but have his next down at the same scrimmage line. Other quarterbacks were quick to pick up the trick, and in a few years the rules committee put in a deliberate grounding law.

The Army players, awed in their total defeat and humiliation, crowded around Dorais and Rockne after the final gun, pumping their hands. A story bandied about for several years after the game —and lingering to this day—was that Army invited Dorais and Rockne to stay over for a couple of days to teach the Cadets some pass patterns and, incidentally, Rockne's trick of snaring the ball with open, relaxed hands while on the dead run. Nothing to it. Just another romanticized legend surrounding that historic game. Besides, Jess Harper had to get his tired heroes back to South Bend, work them out for three days and return East again for a date with Penn State.

But Cadet coach Charley Daly developed instant religion. After spurning the pass as a major weapon—even after the rules had opened up its possibilities just a year earlier—Daly proved that imitation was the sincerest form of flattery, and the following week started putting together an aerial offensive patterned after the Irish. With Prichard at the controls, and throwing mostly to Merillat, an exceptional athlete, the cadets went on to beat a fine Navy team with the pass. The Notre Dame game turned out to be the Cadets' lone loss for the season.

Years later, in his autobiography, Rockne would write: "That victory gave the greatest impetus yet to the development of the Notre Dame spirit. Among other things, it brought out more boys for varsity football—and began attracting high school players who might have gone elsewhere."

On Monday morning, when the train pulled into South Bend, the entire student body and virtually every priest on the faculty were there to greet the squad in the noisiest demonstration yet witnessed in that town, complete with brass band, rockets and fireworks.

Just one more item remained to be reported on the team's return. According to the tale told by Bunny Larkin, a substitute halfback, it had been almost a perfect iron-man performance by the Irish. For fifty-nine minutes, Jess Harper had used only his eleven starters. With a minute to go, Sam Finegan broke a shoelace. Harper told Larkin to give Finegan his shoes. Larkin refused. He figured he'd sat on the bench long enough. Harper smiled, shrugged, and told Larkin to take his shoes into the game on his own feet. That, too, may be part of the legend, but Larkin always insisted it was true.

One thing was incontrovertible, however. A new dimension had been added to the game by Dorais-to-Rockne and the 35–13 rout of the Cadets. Old-fashioned football had been delivered its death blow.

At the end of the season, Gus Dorais was prominently mentioned as All-America. Knute Rockne was honored with a third team selection—the smallest end since Yale's 140-pound Frank Hinkey, twenty years earlier.

6

The Assistant

*"Once when Rock was a young playground direc-
tor in South Bend, a guy much bigger than him
was smoking near some little kids, and challenged
Rock to make him stop. Not another word was
exchanged. Just a beautiful right cross from Rock,
and that was that."*

—Chet Grant,
old-time Notre Dame QB

Suddenly it was all over—the four years of college that had been
so sweet, so enlightening, so successful for Knute Kenneth Rockne.
Graduation Day, June 15, 1914, had provided him with marvelous
memories and a degree in chemistry. He had graduated with a
four-year average of 93, magna cum laude, and with honors not
only in chemistry but biology and bacteriology. But what to do
now? What direction to take? Where might he fit into the American mainstream and fulfill the immigrant dream of success?

The times were temperate and salubrious. The nation was excited over the impending opening of the Panama Canal. Woodrow
Wilson, the ex-Princeton professor, familiar in *pince nez* glasses,
was doing well in the White House, and most jobs in the U.S. were
plentiful.

The Boston Braves were deep in last place in the National
League and anyone who would predict they were about to surge
to the top and win the pennant and World Series would be carted

away to the Funny Farm. Virtually on the day Knute Rockne received his diploma, some burning-eyed youths named Gavrilo Princip, Vasco Cubrilovic and Trifko Grabez, and a few others, were conspiring darkly in a Serbian coffeehouse, planning a bloody reception for Archduke Francis Ferdinand, heir to the Austria-Hungarian throne, who would be coming to Sarajevo on a state visit.

On that balmy June 15, 1914, Knute Rockne finally knew what he wanted to do. He wanted to become a doctor. He had the instincts for it, the sensitivity, the love of people, and he wanted to put all that chemical knowledge to work. It had been in the back of his mind for a few years now, replacing the idea of opening a drugstore, and even though he had graduated at the advanced age of twenty-six he was willing to embark on that long, tough road to a medical degree.

Notre Dame had no medical school so he got in touch with St. Louis University. They said they'd take him. But first, Harper helped him line up a job as a high school coach to pay his tuition and support himself.

He reported early, in St. Louis, to get cracking on his coaching job, checked in with the medical school and was thrown for an immediate loss. They told him, flat out, that he couldn't take the medical course while coaching.

Confused and disappointed, he resigned from the high school and went home to Chicago. Almost immediately he heard from Harper. There was a coaching job open at St. Joseph's College in Dubuque, Iowa (now Loras College), and Harper urged him to apply. He had also suggested the same thing to Gus Dorais. The ex-teammates wound up the final two candidates. They looked at each other and smiled weakly. "There was only one thing to do," Rock recalled. "I don't remember whether it was Gus's idea or mine, but we decided to flip a coin."

It was a fateful coin toss for Rockne. He lost. He went back to South Bend to readjust his thinking and explore other possibilities.

Jesse Harper was a wise and ingenious man who knew what he wanted: Knute Rockne as an assistant coach. He liked Rockne's analytical mind and his knowledge of the game. Notre Dame was ready to blossom as a football power. It was a perfect place for the right kind of football attitude and growth. There were no fraternities or coeds, no class distinctions. It was close-knit student body. The young Rockne would know how to develop a great school spirit that would translate into great football teams.

But Harper didn't think Rockne would sign on merely as an assistant football coach. There was pitifully little money in it—too little for a young man with an eye on matrimony. Harper knew that Rock was in love.

He took Rock aside. "I've been talking to Father Nieuwland in the chemistry department," he began. "I think he needs an assistant and you can get the job." He paused as Rock looked at him indifferently. "If you get it, I think we can also sign you as an assistant football coach . . .

"But just talk to Father Nieuwland about chemistry," Harper suggested evenly. "We'll settle the football part of it later."

Harper grinned. Rock had his signal.

Father Nieuwland was delighted with his candidate. He wasted little time. "Knute," he said, "you have every qualification to become an outstanding chemistry teacher. If you want it, the job's yours."

Then Harper went to Father Cavanaugh, president of Notre Dame, and sold him on the idea that the school had a chance to hire a man who could bring in two great talents. Cavanaugh had always admired Rockne as a student and an athlete. He said he'd allow Rock to wear two hats. Father Nieuwland wasn't quite as enthusiastic when he found out. He had envisioned Rock putting all his time and intellectual gifts into a brilliant career in chemistry. Subsequently, on occasion, he would grumble to Rock that football was an abominination, an impediment to science, but Rock would merely smile and nod cheerfully, and Nieuwland would grin back in defeat.

So, for Knute Rockne, the magic, elusive key had been turned. The wellspring of some unspoken, inner desire had been tapped. And not a moment too soon. A year earlier, while working at Cedar Point, he had met a lovely, warm, animated girl from nearby Sandusky, Bonnie Gwendolyn Skiles. One month after his graduation, the following note was placed in the records of the parish church of Sts. Peter and Paul in Sandusky, Ohio: "To whom it may concern: Knute Kenneth Rockne and Bonnie Gwendolyn Skiles were married by the Rev. William F. Murphy on July 15, 1914. Witnesses were Charles Dorais and Marie Valzarina." Bonnie had become a Catholic just months earlier, and although she didn't ask Knute to convert at that time he readily consented to have their children raised as Catholics.

Between his chemistry teaching and football coaching he would receive a bit less than $2,500 a year. Not for an instant did he consider whether he and Bonnie could make it financially. As he confided to Gus, he was sure he would have the best of two worlds, and nothing else mattered.

As an assistant under Harper in the fall of 1914, he found coaching was tougher than playing. Here were kids he'd been lining up with just a year earlier against Army and Penn State, and now he was telling them what to do on a vastly different plane. There was very definitely an emotional and psychological gap.

Two weeks into the season, Charley Bachman, a guard, disregarded some blocking advice Rock had given him and listened, instead, to a teammate whose technique he considered superior to Rock's. When Bachman blatantly refused to do things Rock's way, the young assistant coach brusquely told Bachman to turn in his suit. By that evening a current of uncertainty was moving through the squad. Could an assistant coach fire a varsity man or was that only the prerogative of the head coach? Jesse Harper soon put everyone straight. If Rock said Bachman was through, he'd back up his assistant coach. Bachman came around, apologized to Rock, returned to the team and became an outstanding lineman. Using Rockne's techniques, of course.

Harper's new assistant made one other major contribution that first season. When Notre Dame went east to play Yale at New Haven, the Irish got slaughtered, 28–0. It was the first Notre Dame loss in four seasons and everyone was unhappy. Harper decided to make a big change in his attack by putting in a jump shift out of the tight T. Stagg had tinkered with it and so had Minnesota's Henry Williams, but Rockne offered something new. "Let's work on the timing," he said, "so that our backs are away on the snap so fast that the defense won't be able to adjust."

Rock had still another gimmick. Out of it would come the famous and completely refined Notre Dame shift. "Let's flex the ends along with the backs," he continued. "Put one or both of them out two, three or four yards as needed. It will mask our real point of attack, give us more momentum and get as many men as possible to that point on every play."

Rock went on to explain how they could concentrate on the weak points in the defense. With the offense in a set T formation the defense had a chance to move in against the offensive team's strength. But with the shift, the defense wouldn't be sure where the blow was coming. After the Notre Dame backs had made their shifts, the ball could be snapped at the very instant the shift had ended, and although the defense might try to compensate they really wouldn't have enough time to do it properly.

Rock also added a couple of moves he had dreamed up as a player to help a smaller end move a heavier defensive tackle. With the ends flexed wider on the line of scrimmage, the new techniques would have an even better chance because of the improved blocking angle.

Actually, this was not Rock's first experience as a football coach. When he was dumped as a freshman by Shorty Longman, Rock was approached by a raffish downtown club team called the Huebners. The Huebners, most of whom were foreign-born and had never finished high school, were a boozing, smoking, carousing bunch who played for the sheer physical exhilaration of it, and didn't want to be limited by training rules. But they needed a coach.

Rockne made them change their habits in a hurry. "It was out of sheer respect," recalled Chet Grant, then a teenaged sportswriter for the South Bend *Tribune*. "It was amazing how he could command their attention—especially when he inserted himself into a game now and then and showed them he could *do* as well as coach."

(Chet Grant was later to become one of the most remarkable men in Notre Dame sports, and his recollections of Rockne would be among the most penetrating. After several years as a sports-writer, he entered Notre Dame and, at 5′7″ and 138 pounds, played quarterback on one of Rock's greatest teams. Today, still vibrant and steely-minded in his eighties, he is associated with the famous International Sports and Games Collection at Notre Dame's Memorial Library.)

"A year after Rock became an assistant under Harper," Grant remembered, "Rock got a summer job as a city playground director, where I first met him. "By coincidence I was back at the park a few days later and witnessed a scene in which a big, tough eighteen-year-old youth was annoying the younger children and a girl assistant director. When Rockne told him to shove off, the lout came at him with a huge stone. In a flash, Rock had him flat on the ground without even hurting him. Calmly, Rock said to me: 'Take that thing out of his hand.'

"Another time, some guy—also much bigger than Rock—was smoking on the playground near the little kids and challenged Rock to make him stop. There wasn't another word exchanged. Just a beautiful right cross from Rock, and that was that."

Rockne's playground experiences were a natural prelude to the career that would follow, and the relationships he would have with players and other people who would come under his direction. Once his Oliver Field baseball team was excitedly looking forward to a widely advertised game with the bearded House of David team of Benton Harbor, Michigan. A full set of uniforms ordered for the South Bend team was supposed to be ready in time for the game, but wasn't. The kids were disconsolate, realizing they'd have to face the famed visitors in ragtag civvies. Rock spirited the kids out to the Notre Dame gym and scrounged enough Notre Dame uniforms to outfit the team. He knew he had no right to do so and could have gotten in trouble had the administration found out, but Knute Rockne knew what his priorities were. He knew how important it was to this playground team.

With his intensity and drive, Rockne quickly became a distinct personality as an assistant under Harper. Unlike Harper, who was mild-mannered, Rockne quickly established his blunt one-to-one relationships with the players. He never issued a disciplinary threat to a player; he thought it would give the boy an excuse to think a warning didn't mean much. Instead, he administered the full punishment on the first offense. But off the field the player found that Rock was still his friend, amiable and relaxed. Rock's attitude quickly built great relationships between him and the players, and he found—with some small embarrassment—that they were starting to come to him rather than Harper, with personal problems. "When we'd complain about something to Harper," said one ex-player, "he'd quote long passages from Franklin or Burke on the virtues of frugality or patience."

On road trips Rock handled the money for Harper. At mealtime he'd take the squad to a modestly priced restaurant, select from the menu and pay the bill. One Sunday morning when their railroad car was sidetracked to allow time for the team to attend Mass, Rock gave each player fifty cents. "Have a good breakfast," he told them, "but don't overeat." After Mass, the players saw Rock enter a rather fancy restaurant. They followed him in and ordered big and expensive breakfasts, then turned over their checks and fifty-cent pieces to Rock. They said their half-bucks were really nothing more than tip money and suggested that Rock take care of the meal costs. For the first and perhaps only time in his life, Knute Rockne was speechless in front of his players. But he paid.

On the way East to play Army, Rock and some of the boys got off the train in Cleveland to stretch their legs. At the rear of the train was a private car. Through the window they recognized ex-President Teddy Roosevelt. He invited them in to talk football. One Irish player rousingly boasted they'd whip Army by several touchdowns.

Roosevelt winked at Rockne. "That sounds bully, Coach," he said.

"Yes, sir." Rock nodded. "Just plain bull."

He was right. Army smashed Notre Dame, 30–10, for the only Irish defeat of the year.

In 1913, because of his newly developed passion for theatrics, he was the prime mover and shaker in the founding of *The Monogram Absurdities,* a musical show put on by the Notre Dame Monogram Club. Even after he became Harper's assistant he continued to stage all its numbers, choreograph its dances and write most of the lines and gags. He attended every rehearsal and was as concerned about an overall smooth performance as he was in tuning up a football play. Often he took part in the show himself.

Once the students helping to write the script told him they were going to put in some lines sniping at him. If he didn't like the material, they said, they'd take it out. Rock insisted they leave the stuff in. When he looked at the finished script, he let go with loud, cackling laughter and told the student gag writers that they weren't gratuitous cracks at all, but the absolute truth.

The Rockne coaching character was slowly but definitely emerging. Before the Wabash game in 1916 Harper had a heavy cold and asked Rock to take over the team. Rockne knew it wasn't a big game but he was obviously edgy with Harper absent, fearing Wabash would regard this a perfect spot for a big upset.

It was the occasion for the first of dozens of fiery, emotional pep talks that would mark Rockne's career. He told his kids they had to prove how tough they were on the field. They were due for a rude shock if they didn't concentrate on execution and hit with everything they had on every play, offense or defense. It was a rapid-fire, nonstop Niagara of exhortation—a real screamer. He wound up by yelling: "Now go out there and crucify them!"

His players stopped just short of that command but smashed Wabash, 60–0. When Harper was told of the speech, he smiled and murmured he'd like to hear Rock someday himself. Later, he decided to let Rock do the chores again. He picked just the right game.

Notre Dame that year was ending its season with the first in a dramatic series of games with Nebraska, and Harper, having lost to Army, wanted to wind up on a blazing note of triumph.

Word had reached South Bend that Jumbo Stiehm, the Nebraska coach, had been making disparaging cracks about the Irish, some of which were aimed at promoting personal discord in the Irish ranks.

"I'd like you to talk to the men on Saturday," said Harper.

"Sure, Jesse. I'd be glad to," said Rock.

Rock looked out at the serious young faces before him, some of them really not many years younger than himself, and started slowly. He opened calmly and innocently about the new opponent the Irish would be facing today and on future schedules, and there was no great reaction in his players' faces.

Suddenly there was a clap of thunder, as though Jehovah Himself was cleaving boulders with the sound of his voice. The atmosphere sizzled and cracked, and mouths fell open and eyes widened as the Notre Dame squad listened, spellbound, to the young assistant coach. Rock pounded on, outraged, incensed over the Nebraska coach's pre-game polemics, which had questioned Notre Dame's fitness to play the game, and even included some supposed reference to Nebraska's "fish-eating" opponents.

"Okay," said Rock, winding up, "here we are on their own field, and we'll pound their words right into their own turf, right?"

Jesse Harper watched in awe as his troops tore out of the dressing room, on their way to an 18–0 shellacking of the Cornhuskers. "Nice speech, Swede," he said softly to Rockne, shaking his head. "I think you really fired 'em up."

The relationship between head coach and young assistant was building into a close and complementary thing. Harper quickly perceived that "the Swede" was more a partner than an aide, and more and more sought his advice and ideas.

There was only one semblance of disagreement between them. Rockne was slightly irritated over the fact that Harper never wore a uniform or work clothes while coaching. He dressed completely in civvies. Rockne, who wore a uniform without pads, vowed he always would so he'd be ready to demonstrate techniques on an instant's notice. It would become one of his trademarks.

Settling into married life and a commitment to the classroom as well as coaching didn't necessarily stifle Rockne's combative spirit and his very personal love of the game. Quickly he found an outlet for it.

In the three or four years prior to America's entry into World War I, semi-pro football had established a rather high profile in small-town life in Middle America. A great portion of the hinterland's football fandom had little or no college attachment; for them the local weekend warriors were the only show in town. It was natural that many towns of more than 5,000 population supported a local semi-pro club. "Supported" in many instances was a pure pablum word. What the locals did was live and die with their club.

If you couldn't identify with Michigan, Illinois, Notre Dame, Ohio State or Purdue, you sure as hell could with your hometown team—especially if a red-hot promotor hustled several former high school or college stars into his livery for $10 to $50 per game.

Although Bonnie didn't like the idea of Rockne continuing to play, she knew he felt it important to pick up a little grocery money and, at the same time, satisfy his still-flaming competitive urge. The one thing she wouldn't do, however, was accompany him on his Sunday junkets. Many of his appearances were with South Bend semi-pro teams (Chet Grant still cherishes a canceled $5 check made out to Rockne for playing with a club Grant served as business manager) and with a couple of teams in downstate Indiana.

It's a matter of record that Rock even journeyed as far as Massillon, Ohio, the acknowledged birthplace of pro football, to play two or three games with the old and justly famed Massillon Tigers. A certain mythology has surrounded Rock's confrontation with the legendary Jim Thorpe, who played for the neighboring Canton Bulldogs.

According to the myth, Rock tackled Thorpe a couple of times for little or no gain. Thorpe was supposed to have had no reaction. When Rock, a defensive end, braced himself to tackle the big Indian a third time, Thorpe roared right over him, flattening Rock like a reed in a cyclone. Returning from his touchdown run, Thorpe is supposed to have patted him on the shoulder, saying: "That was just a warning, Rock. People came here and paid to see Jim Thorpe run. You'd better let Jim run, huh, Rock?"

Rockne himself straightened out the story years later, although it still persists. "He never actually said it that way," Rock explained. "It was more like: 'I'm glad you're slowing down, Rock. Now the people who're paying to see me run can get their money's worth.'

"The fact was that Thorpe was still the greatest runner in the game and I no longer had the legs and stamina I thought I had. He was getting around me on almost every sweep and I decided right then and there that I was going to hang up my cleats for good. And I did. It was the last game I ever played—making Bonnie very happy."

By the end of the 1917 football season, Jesse Harper was certain he would not be returning for another year. His father-in-law, who operated a large ranch in Kansas, was ill, and every indication was that Harper would have to take over for him. Subsequently, he went to President Cavanaugh, told him he was leaving Notre Dame and bluntly suggested that his young assistant, Knute Rockne, be named head coach.

Father Cavanaugh got up from his desk and paced slowly, his hands behind his back. Harper waited for him to speak. Finally Cavanaugh looked over at him, his head cocked sideways. "I have some doubts, Jesse," he said. "In the first place, I think he's too young . . ."

Harper knew that would be an objection. He also thought that the administration had a tendency to look down on its own, and would prefer to hire somebody from the outside. From what Cavanaugh went on to say, Harper sensed that the president felt Rockne was too young to control players only a few years younger than he.

Harper, a shrewd, perceptive man who knew what made people tick, also perceived that Cavanaugh's true feelings might be somewhat the opposite of his spoken fears. Perhaps he worried that Rockne's will and determination might be a bit much for the administration to handle. But Harper had supreme confidence in Rock. If ever a man was destined for success, Jesse Harper knew Knute Rockne was that man.

He reminded Cavanaugh that he'd allowed Harper to sign Rockne as varsity track coach in Rock's senior year, that he'd done a fine job as a performer-coach before he'd even graduated. He reminded the president that the head of the chemistry department had taken Rock on as a senior to teach undergraduate classes. Was there a better acknowledgment of maturity by the administration?

Harper knew something else that Cavanaugh probably didn't. After almost four years as Harper's assistant, Rockne had been thinking of doing something more for himself. He and Bonnie already had their first son and early in 1917 had let it slip to friends that he was seriously thinking of leaving Notre Dame to take a job as head coach at Michigan A&M (later to be known as Michigan State).

He would make more money with the single job as head coach than he had been making at Notre Dame as assistant football coach, head track coach, chemistry teacher and South Bend playground director. To think that he could consolidate all his energy into a single job was, well, unthinkable. Who could be so lucky? Yet there was something about this place on the shore of lovely Lake St. Mary's, something that grabbed and tugged and held on to a man, making the thought of leaving it a haunting thing. It would happen again and again . . .

Harper told Cavanaugh about Rockne's interest in the Michigan job, and that seemed to make a difference—the fact that Rockne was an attractive candidate for somebody else. Cavanaugh said he would think about it. Such is human nature and the psychology of merchandising. Meanwhile, could Harper offer some alternative candidates?

Jesse Harper shook his head. Knute Rockne was his first and only choice to succeed him. Every other day or so, Cavanaugh would stop by and suggest somebody else, some other name that he'd thought of or someone who'd been recommended to him. Harper would be stubbornly evasive and unimpressed. Cavanaugh's candidate simply wasn't in the same class as the young Rockne.

Finally Jesse Harper could contain himself no longer. The next time Father Cavanaugh came by with another name, Harper revealed what he realized he should have said at the very beginning —that he had virtually promised Rock the job a couple of years ago if he retired in the near future.

Cavanaugh stared, and then a small smile broke on his lined face. "Well, Jess," he said gently, "if you promised it to him, we surely will have to offer him the job, won't we?"

In early March, 1918, Knute Kenneth Rockne signed a one-year contract to become Notre Dame football coach and athletic director at a salary of $5,000 a year.

He was exactly thirty years old.

7

Gipp

Not once did Rock hear a player grousing about working so hard in practice, keeping rigid training rules, laying it all on the line, while Gipp marched to the beat of his own drummer. To the rest of the squad—as to Knute Rockne—George Gipp was the exception—a football genius. Rock once put it in perfect perspective: "George Gipp was nature's pet, yet, as with many of her pets, nature punished him."

It was the season of 1920. World War I had ended two years earlier. The nation was heading into Warren G. Harding's "return to normalcy." It was also heading into what historians later would call "the Golden Age of Sport." A decade in which more towering sports personalities would emerge than in any other before or since. Knute Rockne, of course, would be one of them, along with Dempsey, Tunney, Ruth, Grange, Tilden, Jones, and others.

It would not merely be a sports boom; it would be an outright explosion. An explosion without end. It would be an era in which football would make its greatest headway, reach out for intense, popular acceptance. A decade when spectator attendance would be awesome as the huge, concrete college stadiums would rise all over the land to keep pace with alumni demand for bigger and better carnivals. A time that could produce a Yale coach—Tad Jones—who would say, in all solemnity, to his charges: "Gentlemen, you are about to go forth on the greatest mission of your lives—you are about to play Harvard in football." Given the temper of the times, they believed it.

Stagg, Yost, Harvard's Percy Haughton, Georgia Tech's John Heisman, and Carlisle's and Pitt's Pop Warner had already become national headline names among a college coaching fraternity, and the status of coaches was reaching a peak never dreamed of. The 1920's would produce others: Cornell's Gil Dobie, Illinois' Bob Zuppke, Alabama's Wallace Wade, Southern Cal's Howard Jones—and a rasp-voiced, balding genius at Notre Dame.

Rockne had had two years in which to discover what the job of head coach was all about, but 1918 and 1919 had been unnatural and unsettled seasons: one a war year with no official grid campaign to speak of; the other a year in which returning students were still picking up the pieces of an interrupted education and reestablishing themselves in a normal routine.

Knute Rockne's plunge into coaching was immediately marked not only by his technical skills but by his emerging philosophy, developed to fit his own psychic needs as well as the demand of the game he was fashioning. Nor did he have to go around spouting it overtly to his players; it was all there, evident in everything he did.

First and foremost, his players knew where they stood in his scheme of things. "An automobile goes nowhere efficiently," he said to a writer, "unless it has a quick, hot spark to ignite things, to set the cogs of the machine in motion. So I try to make every player on my team feel he's the spark keeping our machine in motion. On him depends our success and victories."

And as a corollary to that, he told the interviewer, "A coach's greatest asset is his sense of responsibility—the reliance placed on him by his players. Handling your personnel is the most important phase of coaching. The secret of coaching success can be reduced to a simple formula: strict discipline in your training program and on the field, combined with a high and continuing interest in all your other relationships with your kids."

"And remember this," he would say. "We can all be geniuses because one definition of genius is the infinite capacity for taking pains. Perfection in petty detail is most essential. Generalities don't count and won't help you in football."

Of course, he knew exactly what the prime ingredient should be for an ideal coach: "One who in his playing days had to fight for everything he got."

There was no denying that his own success was a reflection of his immigrant background and his dogged drive to make it despite his size.

Once, after a loss early in his career, a writer begged the question and asked him how he felt. Rock glared and then shrugged. "One loss is good for the soul," he said. "Too many losses are not good for the coach."

Later, he said: "Win or lose, I'm running this team. Nobody else has anything to say about its make-up, its plans, its type of play. It's my show. If I flop, let 'em pan me. If we're a hit, let 'em say anything they want. I worked hard around here as an assistant for many years, and seldom saw my name in print. Well, all I want now is the truth."

In the fall of 1920, Rock knew that many of his returning players, having been through a couple years in the military, would be older, tougher and more used to discipline—the kind of discipline he hoped to bring to the Irish football program. And when he saw the talent he had, he knew that in his first full year of "normalcy" he would be well ahead of a lot of the established national powers.

He had momentum at his back. In 1919, his first postwar season, despite the uncertainty of knowing who he'd have available, the Irish had swept to a 9–0 perfect season, scoring 229 points to 44, with big victories over Nebraska, Army and Indiana. Now, in 1920, he knew who his veterans were and how they could be used.

Rock also had some ambitious scheduling plans. He had told Father Cavanaugh: "My intention is to play at least six nationally known teams each year. We need that for the kind of recognition Notre Dame deserves."

Cavanaugh smiled. "And winning all six each year would certainly help." He put it more as a question, however.

Rock smiled too, gently. "I'm glad we think alike." A place among the elite of college football was Knute Rockne's driving desire. "I figure on getting off to a good start this year," he said as he got up to leave.

"Because of George Gipp?" Father Cavanaugh said. There was little that went on around the Notre Dame campus that he didn't know about.

"He'll help," said Rock. "Oh, he'll help, all right."

It is, of course, a familiar story. Oft-told, composed of equal parts gridiron legend, a few facts, runaway charm, and the dogged desire by all Notre Damers to accept the whole thing exactly as it has been handed down to them. The legend persists and demands a retelling: the way Knute Rockne discovered George Gipp . . . how George Gipp has died more often than Camille . . . whether George Gipp was for real . . .

He was. It should begin and end with that. Yes. He was for real.

It was shortly after practice, early September, 1916. Rockne, still an assistant to Jesse Harper, was the last person to leave. He glanced toward the opposite end of the deserted field and saw a tall, rangy kid in street clothes booting a ball to a third-string squad member who had not yet gone to the showers. The kid in civvies sent a booming punt more than fifty yards down the field. What Rock didn't realize at first was that the punt wasn't spiraling or twisting; it was spinning crisply, end over end. When the boy booted another, Rock did a double-take. The kid wasn't punting. He was drop-kicking. He put up two more. Straight down the middle. Then the kid punted one. Rock estimated it at sixty-five yards in the air.

A couple minutes later, the informal kicking session ended and the kid in civvies came off the field. Rock stopped him and asked his name and where he was from.

"Gipp," the boy said, in a rich, warm baritone. "George Gipp."

He was from Calumet, Michigan. Actually from Lauriam, a small town nearby.

Rock learned that the youth had come to Notre Dame because a couple of his friends were there, that he hoped to play baseball —his favorite sport. He had played some football but wasn't too interested in coming out for the team. (Later, it was learned that

Gipp had been a super baseball player in high school; football was a secondary sport because his town was so far north that cold weather prevented a season of more than six or seven games. It was also a small town that didn't play strong opponents.)

Rock urged the boy to come out for football but Gipp just shrugged.

"I don't know," he said vaguely.

He didn't show up for three days, but Rock had already briefed Harper. When Gipp finally appeared, he seemed slightly bemused by what was going on. Harper suggested Gipp kick a few. After a couple of punts and two or three drop-kicks, Harper and the varsity men were staring. What Harper and Rockne noticed in addition to Gipp's kicking was a lithe and feline grace in his movements.

"A natural halfback," said Harper, "if he's tough enough."

Something told Rockne to reply: "He'll be tough enough."

It was the beginning of a psychic insight to an athlete that Knute Rockne never again would have with another football player.

A few days later, after he'd learned some signals, Gipp was put into a freshman scrub scrimmage and repeatedly ripped the opposing team apart with slashing ten- and fifteen-yard runs. And he punted three times, far over the receiver's head.

At 6'1" and 185 pounds, and with fantastically fluid movement, Gipp was a great prospect. But Rockne worried about the youth's interest. He now learned that Gipp had gone out for his hall team —Brownson—and had quit after three days.

"We were sort of holding our breath," Rock wrote later, "but about three weeks after he started practice we had a freshman game with Western Normal of Michigan. I think it was then that George Gipp discovered how much a challenge football could be."

The game was tied going into the last three minutes. Gipp had piled up a lot of yardage, but Rockne noted that while he had a natural instinct for cutting back and slipping tacklers, he needed work on his blocking. With a couple of minutes to go, the Irish frosh had the ball, fourth down, on their own 48. "Let me try a drop-kick," Gipp urged, but the quarterback insisted on punting, to at least ensure a tie. So Gipp dropped back to his own 38 to punt.

But when the snap came back, Gipp dropped it to the ground, got his perfect rebound, and put his foot into a tremendous drop-kick that sailed sixty-two yards to win the game.

His teammates at first were stunned at his free-lance caper, then jubilantly pressed their congratulations on him.

"He accepted their congratulations calmly, almost without reaction," said Rock. "It wasn't quite natural. I wondered just how unusual the kid was, and what it would be like in the future, because there was no doubt he was going to be a world-beater— but a loner.

"A few days before the Army game," Rock went on, "Harper put Gipp on the scrub team working against the varsity. Harper wanted Gipp to play the role of Elmer Oliphant, Army's great All-America halfback. Jesse explained to Gipp how Oliphant used a lot of cutting, change of pace and stutter-step dodging. After three days of practice, Harper ordered up a scrimmage.

"The varsity simply couldn't stop Gipp. He raced through and around them, and even completed several passes on the Army option play. He was a perfect Elmer Oliphant.

"Only one trouble," Rock added dryly. "In the Army game that Saturday, Elmer Oliphant gave a perfect imitation of George Gipp and whipped us."

Freshmen were no longer eligible for varsity at Notre Dame, so Gipp's real debut was a year away. Meanwhile, he had come to Rockne saying he was finding college financially difficult. Could Rock find him a job? Rock said he'd try to line up something not too demanding, but Gipp shook his head.

"I want to *work,*" he said. "How about getting me a job waiting on tables?"

Rockne was startled. He would learn to expect the unexpected from Gipp. Kitchen and dining room work was as menial as it comes for college kids. Sweaty and tedious. But Gipp played it seriously for two years, earning his room and board. Rock once braced him, asking why he wanted that job. Gipp merely passed it off with no reply.

"I came to know a lot—and yet little—about George Gipp," recalled Rockne. "He lived quietly, had no single close buddy, nor even a circle of good friends. He rarely dated a girl. And, to our disappointment, he skipped study room more than Harper and I liked. Yet it was impossible for anyone not to like him and enjoy every moment spent with him. He was pleasant—but never cheerful. Friendly but never overtly congenial."

In the spring of his freshman year, Gipp went out for baseball. He was an outfielder with a tremendous throwing arm, and a great hitter. Once—being the original Gipp—he was given the bunt signal and instead powdered the ball over the fence for a homer.

"It was too hot to be running around bases after a bunt," he explained.

Nobody thought he was joking.

As a sophomore in 1917, Gipp didn't play regularly. It was entirely possible that Jesse Harper didn't understand this gifted athlete who seemed not to be putting everything into his performance. Gipp played for a few minutes in several games, but made no great impression.

The following year, Gipp joined the Student Army Training Corp and wasn't drafted. The 1918 grid season was declared an unofficial one, and Knute Rockne, who had taken over for Jesse Harper that year, was very satisfied with the way things worked out. The ruling would give George Gipp an extra year of eligibility. The one thing that startled Rockne in 1918, however, was that Gipp told Rock he was switching from the College of Arts to law.

"I knew that eventually he'd be a brilliant lawyer," Rock recalled, "even though his academic performance, on the record, hadn't been sparkling. But before he became a fine lawyer, I knew he was going to be a memorable football player."

During spring practice of 1919, Rock began drilling for what he expected to be the biggest Irish year ever. Then someone hurried over to him with sickening news. George Gipp, captain-elect of the football team, had been bounced out of college for missing too many Law School classes.

At first Rockne was furious with himself for having allowed the situation to develop. He should have been checking more closely on Gipp's habits. He knew that Gipp had a way of disappearing from sight, and cutting class was not new to him.

Gipp told Rockne that he had been ill on at least three of those cuts. He stared Rockne straight in the eye. "Rock, I know the material that's been covered. Let them give me an oral exam—as tough as they want to make it—and I'll prove it."

All sorts of important people in South Bend were appealing to the administration to give Gipp another chance, one way or another. Rock figured he wouldn't be out of line if he tried to preserve the youth's chance for a great senior season. He went to Reverend James A. Burns, then Notre Dame's president, with Gipp's plea for an oral exam.

Reverend Burns, an ex-Notre Dame baseball player, was sympathetic and finally said okay. Word spread swiftly about Gipp's second chance. The word also included the fact that there were no real football fans among the law professors who would sit in Gipp's judgment. It would be one helluva stiff exam. Gipp's classmates knew that he wasn't famed for the quantity or quality of the notes he'd taken when he did go to class. They told Rock not to be too hopeful.

The entire campus—and city, too—held their collective breath while George Gipp spent two hours before a battery of law profs.

Rockne, waiting outside the building, grabbed Gipp as he came out. "How'd you do, George?"

"Made it," Gipp said indifferently. Then, with a rare touch of feeling, as he started to walk away he said: "Thanks, Rock."

Gipp had astonished the profs with a brilliant performance. He'd been poised, confident and completely in command of his material. He'd passed with ease. The campus was elated, but with his natural calm and detachment Gipp showed nothing. Rockne actually found himself wondering whether Gipp hadn't been through—for him—a very natural act. Had it been a lark for Gipp to be tossed out of school so that he could reveal under great pressure that he was superior to more meticulous students?

Knute Rockne once wondered out loud what kind of football player George Gipp could have been if fully aroused: "He was in excellent physical condition, always, but there'd be times he'd come out of a game absolutely drained from exhaustion from putting out all he had. Yet he never allowed himself to lose complete control of his emotions. Perhaps if he were more emotional he could have risen to even higher heights than the incredible things he was able to do."

Gipp would seem to do things the easy way, although in essence he would be getting the job done superlatively. On defense he'd be content to shove a runner out of bounds instead of tackling him, yet he gave up no extra yardage. But when he had to make an open field tackle he did it with unhesitating and deadly force.

"I learned very early to place full confidence in *his* self-confidence," said Rock.

This was something Knute Rockne rarely did with a player. He knew these were just kids, and a kid's self-confidence could so easily be misplaced or be the product of unwarranted cockiness. But Rockne instinctively understood the precious gifts, physical, mental and spiritual, embodied in George Gipp and allowed him to chart his own course. Gipp loved playing in a game; he detested practice. Rockne let him get away with this attitude. He might have felt differently if Gipp had ever goofed on a signal, missed a tackle or allowed a pass to be completed in his territory, but Gipp never permitted those things to happen. Rockne was fully aware of what George Gipp could do. He wasn't sure what the result would be if he interfered with this blithe and free spirit.

Rock's feelings were buttressed by the attitude Gipp's teammates had toward him. Not once did Rock ever hear of a player grousing about working so hard in practice, keeping rigid training rules, while Gipp marched to the beat of his own drummer. To the rest of the squad, as to Knute Rockne, George Gipp was the exception—a football genius.

Rock once put it in perfect perspective. He said: "George Gipp was nature's pet, yet, as with many of her pets, nature punished him."

In 1919 Rockne put Gipp in the starting line-up. Opening against Kalamazoo, a softie, Rock didn't want to roll up a big score and told the officials before the game to call penalties very strictly against Notre Dame. Early in the first quarter, Gipp blazed seventy-five yards for a touchdown, but an official detected an Irish lineman offside and called back the TD. Three minutes later, Gipp raced sixty-eight yards for another apparent score but an official detected Notre Dame holding and nullified the touchdown.

Gipp by then was seething inwardly but Rockne said nothing to him during half-time. Early in the third quarter, Gipp fielded a towering punt and cut left, then back up the middle seventy yards for a touchdown. Holding on the line of scrimmage, said an official. No score.

As Gipp walked past the referee, he said plaintively: "Listen— from now on, give me one whistle to stop and two to keep going."

"I remember him against Morningside College right after that," Rock recalled. "It was a frigid 20 degrees, with a whistling wind. Gipp didn't even want to play but I thought he had an obligation to people who bought tickets. It turned out we really needed him for a while. The field was hard as a rock and we led by only two touchdowns. Anything could happen. Gipp asked to be taken out but I told him let's get one more score first."

Gipp took the next punt on the Irish 17 and raced it back eighty yards, only to be tripped up on the 3-yard line.

"On the next play," said Rock, "one of our backs fumbled, close to our sideline. Gipp looked over at me, pointed to a Morningside player hugging the ball on the ground, and shrugged his shoulders expressively. It was all I could do to keep from busting out laughing, but I took him out of the game."

It was this game that produced one of the most hilarious and probably most apocryphal of all Irish football stories. It was so cold that the Morningside coach equipped all his players with white cotton gloves. On one of the first plays from scrimmage there was a huge pile-up and, allegedly, the Notre Dame linemen came up wearing the white gloves.

"Not quite true," said Rock, "but a couple pair did change hands during the game."

Against Army, according to Rockne, Gipp displayed some of the quickest thinking he'd ever seen. "We were trailing, 9–0. With seconds left in the half, Gipp completed a pass to one of our ends down to the 1-yard line. The teams were just lining up and our quarterback hadn't even started to call signals when Gipp barked sharply to Fred Larson, center: 'Give me the ball!'

"Gipp, out of the corner of his eye, had spotted an official lifting his horn to blow an end to the half. Larson flipped the ball to Gipp, and while both teams were frozen in surprise, George dove over the goal line for a touchdown. The horn had sounded after the ball had been flipped, so it was a legal play. We went on to win, 12–9."

Nebraska, ever tough, ever feared, was a personal triumph of another sort for Gipp. The Irish were leading, 14–9, but were bone-weary and battered by the heavier Cornhuskers, with only a few minutes left in the game. Rock had few subs of proven quality and it was a question of time before Nebraska would push across the winning TD.

"Gipp put on the greatest stalling tactics I've ever seen," Rockne recalled.

It was Notre Dame's ball and Gipp started to engage the Irish quarterback in a gibberish conversation before he called signals. Up came the referee to penalize them.

"I thought it was a time-out," Gipp said in mock surprise.

On the next two plays, when the backfield would shift one way, Gipp would shift the other, incorrectly, and the backfield would have to do it over again, eating up time. The rules specified no maximum time allowed between plays, but the ref growled a warning to Gipp.

On the next play, Gipp allowed himself to be tackled after a short gain. When down he held on to the tackler while shouting: "Let me up!"

He urged his quarterback to stutter the signals on the line of scrimmage. Finally, forced to punt, he drilled the ball out of bounds in the corner of the field. In those days, time wasn't out on an out-of-bounds punt. Time ran out soon after, and Notre Dame won.

The disgusted Nebraska coach, Henry Schulte, stopped Gipp, grabbed his arm and glowered darkly. "I'd just like to know what the hell course you're majoring in at Notre Dame."

Gipp laughed. "I major in clock repair."

Knute Rockne and Gipp had led the Irish to a 9-0 season. The team was recognized as Champion of the West (which really meant Midwest in those days), but Rock was a bit miffed that he hadn't drawn more national attention. He was only thirty-two, but he was an impatient thirty-two, and there was a gleam in his eye and a new zip to his every gesture and command as he contemplated the 1920 season with a full-flowering George Gipp. Gipp had been stripped of his captaincy by the administration as penalty for his academic lapses of the previous spring, but that didn't dampen his ardor for the game.

In any estimate of college supremacy in 1920, only two teams merited truly critical consideration at the season's end: Andy Smith's undefeated "Wonder Bears" of California, who conquered Ohio State in the Rose Bowl, and Knute Rockne's unbeaten Irish of Notre Dame. The youthful Rockne was steamed at the end of the season at any suggestion that California rated an edge for national honors. The polls were not yet operating and it was all a matter of opinion. Opinion seemed to favor California.

There was little difference of opinion, however, on who turned out to be the nation's premier back. It was clearly the slashing, bold and larger-than-life George Gipp. No one could touch him in physical capabilities; none could match the luminous aura of authentic hero that surrounded him.

His gliding, mecurial running and his deadly spot-passing, his brilliant defensive play and his unerring gambling instincts, put him squarely stage center in every one of Rockne's ten winning conquests that year.

He was already in the spotlight when the Irish came east to play Army in the first big test of the year. For the first time, hotshot sportswriters from New York and elsewhere in the East came up to West Point to see Gipp and interview him. Gipp refused to talk to them before the game, or after. He was strangely uninterested in personal publicity, a leading man who never read his notices. Rock could never get him to pose for a photograph. Only one or two are available today. He was the only one of Rock's superstars with whom Rock never posed.

The New York writers, however, had no problem finding something to write about once the whistle blew in that Army game.

With a minute to go in the first half, fourth and five on his own 10-yard line, the Notre Dame quarterback called for a punt. Gipp dropped back into the end zone to await the snap. But before he did, he whispered to Roger Kiley, an end: "Forget the punt, and tear straight downfield. I'm going to throw it to you."

"I was too dumbfounded to say anything," said Kiley, who later became a Chicago judge.

Army, believing that Gipp had to kick from that dangerous situation, put on a nine-man rush. Kiley, racing downfield, had no defender to pick him up. Gipp side-stepped two Army men crashing in on him and tossed a perfect forty-five-yard pass. It hit Kiley right on the hands. For the only time in his life, Roger Kiley dropped a perfect pass.

"I just shook my head in sadness," Rock recalled. "It was so beautiful, so perfectly typical of George Gipp, that it should have succeeded. Luckily there was time for only one play left when Army took over and they didn't score."

George Gipp never felt he had to atone for anything he did. So it was perhaps just happenstance that in the second half he sliced the Cadet line to ribbons with his dazzling running, piling up 357 total yards for the game on rushing, punt returns and kickoff returns as he led an Irish comeback for a 27–17 victory.

The New York sportswriters called Gipp "the cool gambler responsible for the Irish victory." One writer asked Rockne if he approved of that kind of gambling on the football field. "I simply approve of George Gipp" was Rock's reply.

Within a few weeks, Knute Rockne was to learn that George Gipp was more of a gambler than he'd ever known. He'd often wondered how his star halfback, of modest background, with little or no help from home, who had worked in the dining room for meals and board, never seemed to be without spending money. It turned out that Gipp, a remarkable pool player and an astute poker player, often sneaked downtown at night to the Oliver and LaSalle hotels to take on—and beat—some of the best journeymen pool hustlers and card sharps from Chicago.

Only once did George Gipp ever set up a sticky situation for Rockne. Johnny Mohardt and Norm Barry were reserve halfbacks in 1919 who saw a lot of service. Both were talented and hardworking. In the spring drills of 1920, Mohardt knew that Rock was looking for a blocker for Gipp and doggedly worked on his blocking. Barry was probably the better runner of the two. When the 1920 season had opened, Rock decided to alternate them opposite Gipp. It made them intense rivals. Mohardt would look good on one Saturday; Barry would stand out on another. Inevitably, sparks began to fly between them and after the Army game they virtually came to blows on the practice field.

"I was upset with their attitude, though I tried to understand it," said Rock. "Finally I told them to turn in their suits. But just before the Indiana game I realized the punishment was unfair and reinstated them. My problem was to balance their talents for the benefit of the team."

Against Indiana, Rock started Mohardt along with Gipp. To Rockne's—and the Irish fans'—shock, the Hoosiers led, 13–0, at the end of the third period. Then Gipp hurt his shoulder.

"Get in there, Barry," Rock said.

Norman Barry, now an eminent Chicago judge, recalled the moment with a chuckle. "Rock told me it was my big chance and I should do anything I could to shake up the team. 'Insult them if you have to,' he said. I didn't quite know what he meant by that but I decided to concentrate on Johnny Mohardt.

"The first play was Mohardt off tackle. I blocked for him and cut down the Indiana end, and Mohardt ran for eighteen. On the next play, it was my turn and I said to Mohardt as we were lining up: 'You take out that end the same way or I'll flatten you after the game.' Johnny put a beautiful block on him and I went for twenty-five. We kept alternating and blocking like crazy for each other, and finally Mohardt scored.

"We put on another drive like that—Johnny and I ripping off the yardage—and then with two minutes to go I plunged down to the Indiana 2-yard line. I expected to hear my number called so I could score the touchdown. After all, I had earned it.

"Meanwhile, our fans had been yelling for Gipp. Suddenly I looked up and there was Rock sending Gipp in. Would it be for Mohardt or me? Well, I didn't have long to wait. Gipp came in for me.

"Gipp scored the winning touchdown but I didn't see it. I was so mad at Rock that I ripped off my helmet and threw it at him. I think it was the only time in history that one of Rock's players had ever been insubordinate. But I couldn't help it. The look of shock on his face was an inch thick but I didn't linger to enjoy it. I rushed out of the park—we were playing on a neutral field in Indianapolis—jumped into a cab and went back to our headquarters at the Claypool Hotel.

"When the team got there, Rock came up to me but I said: 'Don't talk to me!' He knew why I was upset, of course, and Monday at practice he came over and apologized for what he'd done. He never asked me to apologize for slinging the helmet at him. He knew where the guilt lay. Only a man like Rock could have taken that from a player."

It was a freezing, damp day that Monday as Rock began practice for Northwestern. The next day Gipp went up to him.

"I have a sore throat," he said. He also had a fever.

The coach sent him to the infirmary, where he was put to bed until his temperature came down. He left the hospital on Friday. The legend says that he sneaked out of the infirmary without permission and nonchalantly told Rockne that the doctor had said he was fit to play the next day against Northwestern.

Whatever the situation, Rockne reluctantly allowed Gipp to suit up but planned not to use him in the game. Then, with Notre Dame leading, 33–7, in the final period, Irish fans sent up a riotous clamor for Gipp. Rockne relented and sent him in for a few token plays. Moments later Notre Dame had won its eighth game of the season. On Thanksgiving they played Michigan State and won handily, 25–0. George Gipp had no part of that last game. He was back in the infirmary in South Bend.

He was there for three weeks. After the second week the prognosis grew grave. The entire Notre Dame community was aware how ill he was. Antibiotic drugs were a generation away, and Gipp's streptococcus infection ravaged his spectacular body, unchecked. Pneumonia set in. On December 14, 1920, even as hundreds of Notre Dame students were saying prayers for him, George Gipp died.

Two days earlier he had asked to be baptized in the Catholic faith. At his death he was twenty-five. Like Rock, he had entered Notre Dame at an advanced age.

Two weeks before Gipp died, Walter Camp had named him All-America fullback and had also called him the outstanding college player in America—and the Chicago White Sox had told him they were going to sign him to a baseball contract.

Except for a few students who were ill in the infirmary, every Notre Dame student attended services for Gipp and then accompanied his body to the railroad station for its trip home to Lauriam, Michigan. Because of a blizzard, it was said that George Gipp's body made the final five miles to Laurium by dog sled. For a hero it was a fittingly romantic touch.

"Football," said Knute Rockne, a quietly contained but inwardly broken man, "will never again see his equal—as a player or a person."

Knute Rockne had been at his bedside at the end.

It is fact and not legend that Gipp had mustered a tiny smile and told Rock that he wasn't afraid to die. Fact, not legend, that in a thin, barely audible voice he told Knute Rockne that someday, in a game that looked tough, Rockne should ask his team to win one for the Gipper.

Knute Rockne, despite his flair for the theatrical, with his long love affair with drama, never thought he could do such a thing. But he would . . .

8

Ambush –
and a Weird Affair

Rock felt he had to hype the gate for the game with the Haskell Indians, so he issued a press release pointing out that some of the Indian stars were direct descendants of Geronimo, Black Fox, Cochise, Sitting Bull and other early scrimmage foes of the White Man.

"You never know who might have believed it,"
said Rock, "and we needed the publicity."

Early Friday morning, October 7, 1921, Knute Rockne shepherded his team onto a day coach leaving for Iowa City. The next day he'd be meeting the Iowa Hawkeyes in the third game of the season. He felt comfortably at ease, and supremely confident that an expected win over the Hawks would be his opening bid for a second straight national championship. Rock was ready for another super year and very much in his mind was the vision of a Rose Bowl invitation which had escaped him the previous year. The Rose Bowl (then the only bowl game) would finally and dramatically establish Notre Dame as a continuing, national power—Rockne's true objective.

His optimism seemed justified. The Irish line, mostly veterans of the 1920 team, was awesome. Most of them would later become coaches of note: guard Hunk Anderson, at Notre Dame; center Harry Mehre, at Georgia; end Eddie Anderson at Iowa and Holy Cross; tackle Buck Shaw at Santa Clara. Roger Kiley, later a judge, was the other end; Hector Garvey, the other tackle; Jim Dooley, the other guard. The backfield was a slick unit headed by halfback Johnny Mohardt, fullback Chet Wynne and quarterback Chet Grant, a 5'7" 137-pound banty rooster who had been a young sportswriter for the South Bend *Tribune* before enrolling at Notre Dame. Grant's backup was Frank Thomas, later a great coach at Alabama.

How Grant ever managed to nail down the starting job was somewhat of a mystery to him: "I think I must have been the least versatile quarterback in Irish history," he recalls. "I'd had a knee operation at the Mayo Clinic that summer and I was slow and not very agile, and hadn't scrimmaged all season. I guess Rock had his special blend of faith in me. I also recall that for one of the few times in his career Rock gave no pre-game pep talk before the Iowa game. The only thing he asked me was how I felt. We had no way of knowing what we were getting into . . ."

The eight-hour trip didn't seem long or particularly restrictive. There was a lot of singing and jesting, and Rock even looked the other way when some of the kids got up a a penny ante poker game. The Irish were on a twenty-game winning streak and word had trickled out of Iowa that there was little local betting on the Hawkeyes, who had swamped little Knox College, 52–14, in their opener. But there had been no early-season reports that Iowa would have more than a respectable team. Experts picked them to finish third or fourth in the Big Ten.

Yet common sense should have been nibbling away at the Irish superconfidence. Going into the game, Rock had scheduled two straight breathers against Kalamazoo and DePauw, and the steamroller numbers (56–0, 57–10) shouldn't have impressed anybody. But the team was doing all that Rock had expected and he felt no great need to plead with his veteran troops to take caution.

Iowa over the years had been no threat to the lodge members of the Big Ten. Since its entrance to the league in 1900, it had enjoyed exactly one winning season in twenty-one years. But it had wound up the 1920 campaign with three straight wins and just about everyone was returning. Rock apparently thought Howard Jones, the Hawkeye coach, had just another bunch of guys named Joe.

Instead, their names were Duke Slater, a big, tough black tackle who had briefly left high school to take a job cutting ice on the Mississippi River in the wintertime; Gordon Locke, a pile-driving fullback; the brothers Devine—Aubrey, a slick running-passing quarterback, and Glenn, a blocking back; Les Belding, a great end, whom Rock surely knew had received All-America mention as a sophomore in 1919.

It was a classic case of a good football team neglecting to feel intimidated by a super team as it was supposed to. Aubrey Devine whipsawed the Irish with a devastating mix of running and passing. He slashed off tackle himself; sent Gordon Locke busting up the middle; flipped short tosses to end Les Belding. In the first quarter the Hawkeyes got a touchdown and a field goal. The Irish got a bad case of the frustrated frights but managed to score a touchdown on a pass from Johnny Mohardt to Roger Kiley. But Rock, on the sidelines, had a sinking feeling that he was watching a Greek tragedy unfold, helpless to do anything to shape this particular bit of destiny.

"Some awfully strange things happened in that game," Chet Grant later said. "We decided to come out passing in the second half. Well, we were wearing our regular dark-blue jerseys. Iowa was wearing their usual black. There was no such thing as home and road contrasting jerseys in those days. Everybody wore their school colors and that was it. Anyway, it was getting toward dusk in the final quarter and twice Mohardt fired passes toward a dark-blue Notre Dame jersey, and twice Belding, the Iowa end, in a black jersey, dropped off the line and intercepted the pass as though Mohardt were aiming for him."

(An hour after the game was over, Rockne resolved to order a set of bright-green jerseys for next year as a highly visible alternative to any other team's colors.)

"We kept coming on, piling up the first downs and yardage," Grant continued, "while Iowa just sat on its 10–7 lead. Twice we completed fourth down passes which fell one yard short of a first down. Four times we got inside their 10-yard line and four times we came up empty.

"We had a tackle eligible play off a double shift. We were right down there and had Iowa set up for it. Hector Garvey, our big tackle, was our trick play star. But a sub halfback had just come in. He's nervous and doesn't quite get the call. He yells for signals over. Naturally, Iowa gets suspicious, takes a good look at everything and smells out the play.

"Meanwhile, Garvey has been pestering me to call a split buck inside tackle, giving him a good blocking angle on the great Duke Slater. I've noticed Slater's tendency to protect outside, and I call the play and Garvey is all set on a great angle block and a big gain. Again somebody yells signals over, but by then the center has snapped the ball, there's a big mix-up and I've got it with no place to go. So I get smeared.

"With one minute to play, Frank Thomas comes in with a trick play from Rock. It's a fake halfback-to-halfback reverse, ending in a pass to the fullback in the flat. It came within one yard of winning the game for us, but Glenn Devine made an ankle tackle on Paul Castner and the game was over."

Grant admits, though, that Rock should have seen the handwriting on the wall early in the second quarter. Grant had sent Johnny Mohardt and Dan Coughlin alternating on a slashing march to the Iowa 6. Chet Wynne blasted to the 1.

"Then I got tricky on fourth down." Grant smiled thinly. "I called a pass to Captain Eddie Anderson off a fake split buck. I was supposed to pivot for fakes to a halfback and fullback. What a mess. A future newspaper editor at left half and a future surgeon at right half bumped heads with a future trial lawyer at fullback. I tried to get clear of the chaos, jostled somebody's elbow and the ball slid off my fingertips when I finally tried to throw it. Of course, I should have eaten the ball and tried to dive the one yard into the end zone. It cost us a score which we so desperately needed."

Suddenly it was all over, along with Irish dreams of an undefeated season.

"Rock never said a word to me," Grant remembers. "Never in the rare defeats he suffered at Notre Dame did he ever consciously blame anyone but himself. It was always a 'coaching loss.' He had allowed our mental attitude to get out of hand and so the loss was deserved. There was no bitterness afterwards. He left us sore at ourselves for having let him down, but with our confidence in his coaching unshaken."

That didn't mean that Rock had to enjoy losing. Leo Durocher made the famous quote: "Nice guys finish last." George Strickler points out that Knute Rockne said it thirty years earlier—in slightly different form, but in essence unchanged.

"Walter Meanwell, the famous Wisconsin basketball coach, had come down to Notre Dame for a brief visit," Strickler recalled. "He watched our practice, and afterwards Rock and I drove him to the railroad station. Meanwell was talking about a coach both of them knew, and was bubbling on and on with Rock being very noncommittal. Meanwell was saying what a fine coach the guy was and what a good and gracious loser.

"Finally Rock couldn't stand it any longer. 'Walter,' he exploded, 'you show me a good and gracious loser and I'll show you a failure!' "

The trip from Iowa City back to South Bend would be a nightmare for Knute Rockne. In anticipation of a fitting reward for the victors, he had booked his players into the luxury of Pullman sleepers for the overnight trip. Francis Wallace remembers it well. Wallace was one of the earliest of several bright young Notre Dame students whom Rock had hired and trained as campus football correspondents to handle Notre Dame football publicity.

"Rock went into a deep sulk," Wallace says. "He took refuge in his private drawing room to contemplate his first defeat in three years. He thought of the humiliation he'd feel when the team got into South Bend Sunday morning."

Even though his team had outplayed Iowa in every way but the score, Rock needn't have worried about his reception. But for the only time in his life he tried to hide his own bitterness in deception. As the train pulled in he was stunned to see a huge and cheering crowd up ahead. Virtually every student was on hand to welcome the team, even in defeat. Rock wanted no part of them and didn't hesitate in his next, spontaneous action.

Rock ducked off the opposite side of the train and tried to get away. Then he was spotted and several students hauled him back into the center of the cheering throng. He literally tried to fight them off, but they were blind to his reaction. He resented, as he later explained, that they were trying to make a hero out of him in defeat and would have much preferred to get away by himself.

The students' heartfelt gesture got to him, and two or three minutes later he was standing atop a trunk with tears in his eyes.

"I thank you . . . I thank you deeply," he was saying. "I can tell you that I'll never leave this place . . ."

It was a conviction he felt at this emotional moment, yet it would come back to haunt him . . .

But there were eight games to go. The eleven-game schedule was the longest the Irish had yet attempted. From then on, Rock and his troops breezed, with the exception of a close 7–0 win over Purdue.

There was even a period that year when Notre Dame, because of Rock's ambitious schedule-making, was to play three games in eight days. On November 5 the Irish disposed of Army, 28–0, at West Point. That night, Rock, forever hopelessly in love with the theater, took his team down to New York City to see the Ziegfeld Follies. The previous unbeaten season, plus the drama of George Gipp, had launched Knute Rockne into the national spotlight, and the team was cheered as they filed to their seats. Rock was in a box close to the stage. A young, storytelling cowboy star did a rope-twirling act while snapping off wisecracks and added a few *bon mots* about the Notre Dame team. His name was Will Rogers. Suddenly he flipped his lasso toward Rockne's box, neatly caught the bald head and hauled him to the stage for a bow. It was the beginning of a warm and close friendship.

The Irish Eastern junket was just under way. "We left the next day for Asbury Park, New Jersey," Rock recalled, "to spend a day or two at a seaside resort where we held two drills. Because on Tuesday we were going back up to New York for an Election Day game with Rutgers in the Polo Grounds."

Rutgers, a moderate big-time power in those days, was annihilated, 48–0. Then it was back to South Bend on Wednesday for two days of practice for a game on Saturday with the Haskell Indians, a school which in the previous two decades had won big headlines by scalping a lot of the White Man's resident football powers in the Midwest. Rock wanted to hype the gate for this one, so he had his campus correspondent issue a release pointing out that some of the Indian stars were direct descendants of Geronimo,

Black Fox, Cochise, Sitting Bull and other earlier scrimmage foes of the White Man.

"You never know who might have believed it," Rock said dryly, "and Haskell was the one gate we were worried about."

The Irish wound up winning everything after the Iowa debacle and in the finale against Michigan State (48–0) were being scouted by a dozen or more of the big-time schools Rock was trying to land for future schedules.

"They wanted to see whether we were as good as the press was touting," he said. "For some, the proof would be enough to give us a game; for others, it would be a signal to avoid us like the plague."

Rock also felt that a big win over the Michigan Aggies would convince Andy Smith, coach of California's "Wonder Bears," that he couldn't again avoid inviting Notre Dame to the Rose Bowl.

Despite the Iowa loss, which most of the press had by now discounted as just one of those things, the Irish were clearly the finest team east of California. They'd rolled up an astounding 375 points to their foes' 41, and five of the Irish had received All-America mention.

Andy Smith was in a bind. Notre Dame was the last school he wanted to dignify as a Rose Bowl invitee, but he had had two straight undefeated seasons and couldn't bear the thought that someone might accuse him of being afraid of a thirty-four-year-old coach and his rousing Irish-German-Slovenian Catholic janissaries. So Smith reluctantly dispatched a scout to Rock's final game with the Michigan Aggies. When it was over, Smith knew there was no way he could duck the Irish, and the word trickled eastward that in due course he would probably extend the invitation to Notre Dame for the New Year's date in Pasadena.

In the next few days, however, one of the most quixotic episodes in Knute Rockne's football career would come to Smith's rescue.

It would be known as the infamous "Taylorville Game," and for many years afterwards there would be a lingering ambivalence alternating between shocked tongue-clucking and tolerant amusement. For Knute Rockne it would be a sentiment nothing short of agonized betrayal . . .

*   *   *

It was almost incredible that Rockne and Bob Zuppke, the colorful coach at Illinois, should have been oblivious to what was building up toward Sunday, November 27, 1921, in Taylorville, Illinois.

It was billed as just another semi-pro football game between neighboring towns—the rural rivalry so much a part of small-town culture in that era. But the events of a few days in late November were to play a major role in changing the entire Midwest concept of semi-pro football, and even influence the pro game just being born.

Actually, Rock could have been expected to be somewhat more sophisticated and alert to the situation than Zup, because Rock had played some pro ball after he'd graduated, and he knew it wasn't unusual for a team owner to lace a couple of current collegians into his line-up. Under assumed names, of course. Rock knew it had been going on but obviously it simply never occurred to him that his very own Notre Dame players could be induced off campus on a Sunday for some extracurricular skull-popping. Rock had long since settled into Notre Dame psychologically and spiritually, and there could have been no way he'd entertain the most ephemeral thought that an Irish gridder would break the rules.

Though no less an idealist than Rockne when it came to college sports, little Bob Zuppke never paid much attention to the hard-scrabble semi-pro game flourishing in Illinois. His own feelings were that only a high school or college game was worth the price of admission, and he held at least a mild contempt for anything smacking of professional football.

A hearty, burly football coach named Grover Hoover was turning Taylorville, Illinois, into the scourge of the territory. By 1916 he was not only leading the town team but was advisory coach at Christian Brothers College in St. Louis and commuted to that post three or four days a week. Once he pulled off the picaresque stunt of scheduling his own Christian Brothers club for a road game with his own Taylorville, "Hoover Institute," his program name for the town team that day. His "Institute" beat his college team, 28–0.

By 1920 Carlinville, Illinois, was into the town team whirl and challenged Taylorville to a game. Carlinville, a much smaller town but with heroic-sized ambitions, put together a club that whipped Taylorville by a touchdown. There wasn't much Taylorville betting money dropped, however, because the Taylorville locals were pretty much tapped out from a defeat three weeks earlier by the Decatur Staleys (who two years later moved to Chicago and became the Bears).

But revenge burned deep, up and down Main Street in Taylorville, in the cigar store, the pool hall, on the outlying farms and down deep in the coal pits.

At any rate, for Rockne and Zuppke, the two college coaches, November 27 would be just another Sunday the week after the last game on their 1921 schedules. Rock busied himself around his office, catching up with administrative odds and ends. Zup, as usual, put in a few hours in front of an easel with his beloved oil paints. (He was quite good.)

This bizarre football game was virtually inevitable. Taylorville for years had dominated Illinois downstate semi-pro football. In seven years they'd won fifty-eight games, lost only five and had scored 2,167 points to their opponents' 94. Everyone in the Midwest had heard of them. Hoover earlier had led Taylorville High School to several undefeated seasons, and his Taylorville semi-pro club was at first made up mostly of his ex-high school stars plus a few big, tough local miners and farmers. They played such towns as Moline, Auburn, Decatur, and the winning team took home the entire gate in addition to their winnings on bets, which everyone made.

It was the betting which was the danger in this genre of football. With their fierce loyalties and pride, local businessmen and farmers often got in over their heads. If he didn't have the cash, a farmer would wager a cow or horse—maybe several. Rent money was always in jeopardy during the autumn months. Local bankers could always tell it was Friday because of withdrawals made on savings accounts to cover a bet on Sunday.

In 1921 Taylorville challenged Carlinville to a game in Taylorville on November 27. It would be for blood and money. Taylorville had seethed for twelve months over the deflating they'd taken from the tank town upstarts in 1920. Two ends from the University of Illinois, Roy Simpson and Vern Mullen, had begun playing on Sundays for Taylorville. Zuppke, of course, oblivious to it all.

Simpson and Muller would return to practice every Monday afternoon with multiple abrasions and discolorations, and teammates were curious. Finally the two varsity ends admitted to some of their teammates that they'd been picking up $35 a game every Sunday with Taylorville, more money than the average college boy saw in a month. Other Illinois players asked to be cut in. Every Sunday another Illinois player or two joined the ranks until a half-dozen were beefing up the Taylorville entry—and fashioning a very nice winning streak.

No dummies, they, at Carlinville. They figured their rivals would be strengthening their club for the 1921 return match but didn't realize quite how it would be done. So, just to be on the safe side, the Carlinville coach had a talk with Mike Syfrit, a Notre Dame end, who had played a couple of games for him. Would any other Irish gridders be interested?

A week before the game, Grover Hoover in Taylorville stared at an unsigned letter and was all shook up. "I have close friends in both towns," the unknown writer declared, "and I don't want either side to arrange an edge. So let me warn you that you'll have to play just about the whole Notre Dame varsity next Sunday."

Hoover sent a master spy to ferret out more information in Carlinville. He learned that not only would Carlinville field virtually the Notre Dame varsity, but more than a thousand Carlinville fans, sensing a betting coup, had chartered a special Illinois Central train of sixteen coaches.

Grover Hoover and his backers quickly went into a huddle and called the only possible play. Notre Dame, had been undefeated and national champions in 1920 and had lost only in an upset to Iowa in 1921. Going up against that kind of talent was folly, unless . . .

Hoover had only one course. He phoned Roy Simpson at Illinois. Hoover thought he had a good enough front line but he could use a couple of Illinois backs as subs. Simpson, an Illinois end, laid it on Hoover a bit stronger. "If Carlinville is bringing all these

Notre Dame guys, maybe I should bring our whole backfield and a few linemen, too. Just to play safe, in case your own guys have trouble in the first half. We could even use our own signals and plays."

Grover Hoover was not one to fumble an opportunity. He told Simpson he'd employ anyone who could come over.

About ten Illinois players piled into three autos early Saturday morning, and by 10 A.M. were into a signal drill, in Taylorville, acquainting Hoover's guys with Illinois plays.

Saturday night in Taylorville was abuzz with speculation as the local sports turned to the pool hall and an illegal grog shop. The big question was whether their spy had the right dope on the Notre Dame ringers. There wasn't too much comfort in knowing that Grover Hoover had prepared a counterpunch with his Hessians from Illinois. After all, Illinois that season had won exactly one Big Ten game. And even though it was a monumental upset victory over Ohio State, depriving the Buckeyes of the conference title, the record still didn't point to the Illinois imports as the answer to Taylorville's prayers.

Finally an outrider appeared with the word: Saturday night reservations had been made in a Springfield hotel for twelve people arriving on a train from Chicago, probably via South Bend. Notre Dame.

On Sunday morning, Carlinville fans poured into Taylorville—headed by their betting committee, which had collected thousands of dollars in Carlinville money. The committee made for the back room of a cigar store where their opposite numbers were socked in with a collected Taylorville bundle of their own. An off-duty Carlinville constable rocked slowly back and forth on his heels as he kept a protective eye on the fiscal matters.

With a few lights and a camera, a movie director could have made an American Gothic scene that would have put Hollywood to shame. It would even have drawn cheers from that thwarted thespian, Knute Rockne, back in South Bend, if it hadn't been for the *dramatis personnae* involved. Had he known what was going on, however, he wouldn't have needed a train to get to Taylorville. He'd have exploded there on one shot.

By 10 A.M. on Sunday the Taylorville field was jammed with close to 10,000 fans who had poured in from at least three counties. The streets were a mini Mardi Gras. The 1,600 grandstand seats had long since been reserved, and the overflow ringed the sidelines or stood atop parked cars.

Thin, pale sunlight cut through the brisk 35° air as three officials met at midfield with the team captains. (There were never any more for these lusty, semi-pro frolics, and what went on unobserved up front in the trenches often bore little resemblance to what the rules allowed.)

The Carlinville talent was impressive. In addition to two or three bona-fide hometowners there were eight or nine of Knute Rockne's finest, including All-America ends Roger Kiley and captain Eddie Anderson. Another star on hand was Chet Wynne, Notre Dame's mighty fullback.

Grover Hoover started most of his regular, home-grown heroes, waiting for the psychological moment to insert his Dragoons from Champaign-Urbana. At quarterback was a hard-bitten character destined to make headlines in a few years as a big league baseball manager: Charlie Dressen.

For virtually the entire first half it was all Carlinville, with Notre Dame's Chet Wynne ripping through the line for huge gains but no score. Finally Taylorville blocked a punt and a couple of Taylorville linemen kept stumble-footing the ball along the ground toward the Carlinville goal line—all in good clean innocence while trying to pick it up until it got to the 1-yard line, where they decided their innocence had been demonstrated long enough. There they fell on it. After two running plays had been stacked up for a yard loss, Dressen got tricky and waltzed around end on a bootleg play to score.

Taylorville had been outplayed, but they were still ahead. The 7-point half-time lead didn't look too good to Grover Hoover, however. Carlinville was having trouble because the one Notre Damer they didn't have was a quarterback. So they weren't able to use the Notre Dame shift. Hoover was afraid Taylorville would get squared away in the second half, jeopardizing his local supporters' money.

Hoover made his move. Into the game for the second half went the Illinois varsity, headed by quarterback Joe Sternaman, halfback Laurie Walquist and fullback Jack Crangle. Up front were at least six Illinois linemen.

Hoover had his new unit take a warm-up signal drill before sending them out. Taylorville fans and the Carlinville team resting on the sidelines stared. There was something different about the quarterback. Heck, that wasn't flat, monotone Charlie Dressen. The new guy was belting out the numbers like firecrackers. Suddenly the mystery, as far as Carlinville was concerned, was cleared up. A Notre Dame kid recognized one of the Illinois-Taylorville players as somebody he'd played with in high school.

Taylorville completely dominated in the second half. The Illinois backs took Carlinville apart, and although they failed to get across the goal line, they romped into field goal position often enough for Sternaman to boot three of them for a 16–0 victory.

Taylorville fans swarmed out of the stands and off the truck tops to mob their imported heroes. One fan sat down and cried, mumbling over and over: "They saved my store. They saved my store . . ." He had mortgaged his business to get $2,000 down on his team.

Tug Wilson, who had recently graduated from Illinois and was about to embark on his distinguished career in athletic administration, recalls the game clearly: "Never had there been such a wild, intertown affair, and never such insane wagering. When it was all over, it was as though everyone sat down and realized what a monstrous thing they'd gone through, and what damage they'd done to their families. More than $35,000 was supposed to have changed hands, and I don't doubt it to this day.

"From that day on, as word of the Taylorville affair got around, the fierce betting matches between neighboring towns just seemed to lose steam and die out. A good thing, too. It was bad for everyone concerned, including college players who'd been junketing all over the countryside."

The game also was instrumental in shaping the new National Football League. One of its first rules was that college players were not to be approached while they still had eligibility left.

But no impact on any one was equal to that which hit Knute Rockne a week after the game. Ordinarily he might never have heard of the affair but the ramifications of this one were too immense to contain. It was the worst-kept secret in South Bend and when it reached Rock it was like a blow in the gut. He called in every one of the Notre Dame players involved and asked for their admission of guilt.

There was nothing he could do about Anderson, Kiley, Wynne and a couple other seniors; they had used up all their varsity eligibility. But he fired as least three underclassmen and told them not to report next fall.

Norman Barry, one of his stars of 1920, later commented: "I'm amazed that Rock never was aware of the situation. After all, he'd played semi-pro ball over in Ohio right up through his first year as head coach, and he knew what was going on.

"Why, just the year before the Taylorville affair, right after the Purdue game, a bunch of us Notre Dame guys drove two hundred and fifty miles to Rock Island, Illinois, arriving at two A.M. for a semi-pro game on Sunday. Among others there were Hunk Anderson, Dutch Bergman and me. Bergman fractured a leg in the game. Many on the opposing team were Illinois players, too. Each team bet a thousand dollars and we played for all or nothing. As I recall, we won that one."

There were people on campus, and downtown in the South Bend pool halls and cigar shops, who figured Rock was more upset over the fact that his Notre Dame–Carlinville ringers had lost the game to the Illinois-Taylorville troop than he was over the busted eligibility rules.

Rockne was now faced with a soul-wrenching decision over the Rose Bowl invite he knew would be coming from California. He felt that ethically his team was tarnished by the Taylorville incident and was no longer eligible for the Bowl assignment. Deeply disappointed personally, he nevertheless let it be known to the University of California that Notre Dame would not be interested in an invitation. He didn't bother to give reasons and the matter was dropped. (The Bears invited undefeated Washington and Jefferson, a small school team from Washington, Pennsylvania, with big-time credentials. The Rose Bowl game ended in a scoreless tie, the only such in Rose Bowl history.)

For Rockne and Notre Dame the season had ended on a sour note. But some sweetening would not be far off.

9

The Shift

By the mid 1920's, college and high school coaches, awesomely impressed by the Notre Dame shift, rushed to install it. There followed one of the strange phenomena of football. Nobody else could make it work . . . It was forever a mystery why the Notre Dame shift and box became so stilted and ineffective when used by Rockne imitators.

On a chilly November Saturday in 1921, Rockne's Irish had a 14–0 half-time lead over Army. As the teams came off the field, Charley Daly, the Cadets' coach, complained bitterly to the referee about the Notre Dame shift. It was the first time Daly had seen it and he complained that the Irish had an unfair advantage because their backs were actually in motion when the ball was snapped.

There was nothing yet in the rule books to cover the shift the way the Irish were using it, and Ed Thorpe, the ref, didn't know what to do. So Rock went over to Thorpe and said: "Ed, just so you won't be embarrassed any longer, we won't use the shift at all, for the rest of the game."

Army, which had made only one first down in the first half, got only three more that day. Using a short punt formation and an occasional tight T, the Irish got two more TD's for a 28–0 win.

If there was any single thing—no, make that two—which marked the particular genius of Knute Rockne as much as anything else, it would have to be two concepts which he developed to an art form. Certainly that was the light in which it was viewed by fans and coaches throughout the nation. "The Notre Dame Shift" was not just a football formation. And Notre Dame's "Shock Troops" were not just another tactic. Both elements were pure Knute Rockne. Both added an aura of excitement to the game, becoming a prime focus for fans and critics alike. In fact, the shift would become the *cause célèbre* of college football tactics of the 1920's.

By 1921, Rockne had developed his shift to choreographed perfection. The backs would line up in a T, with the quarterback up front, about two yards behind the center. The quarterback would call his signal, giving the play and direction in which the backs would shift. If to the right, the lead man—the right half—would make the loud count: "One, two, three, hip!" If to the left, the left half would call it out. There would be three crisp steps, sometimes crossover steps, left leg over right or vice versa, and then on "hip" there would be the final hop that sent the four backs into a box formation just as the ball was snapped.

Nothing was haphazard or out of sync. Every motion was to the count, not a glimmer of movement wasted. When the arm of one player moved, the arms of the others had the same sweep and timing. A foot made contact with the ground at the same time as that of the other three men. Four sets of shoulders swung in unison. Four heads shake as one. Everything absolutely on count, and with the final hop into position the ball would be snapped and the defense had no time to determine ball carrier, direction, hole or any variation off the final set.

In working on the shift in practice, Rock aimed at drama, color and precision. Like the stage director he innately was, he'd sing out softly: "That's marvelous . . . lovely . . . beautiful motion . . . sweet. You've got it . . . you're ready for opening night."

The ends did or did not shift out wider, according to the play called. "We aim for maximum deception," Rock explained. "Seeing our shift going to the right, the defense will go to its left, but the odds are the defense will shift too far, not far enough or not quickly enough. No matter which, our offense has strategic points of attack opened up for it. In concentrating its strength to its left, the defense leaves its right greatly weakened, and before it has time to figure out where we're going the ball has been snapped and the play is gone.

"And if they overshift to our strong side we'll just come back with weak-side stuff and catch 'em where they ain't. I just hope they challenge us that way."

Bill Ingram, Navy's coach, recalled the situation exactly as Rockne had discussed it: "All summer I'd made up my mind to stop that shift to the strong side. I worked on it for weeks and in our game that year I stopped it cold. That's what I thought, anyway. Rock came back with stuff to the weak side and killed us."

(A more common complaint by rival coaches was that half the time a Notre Dame opponent couldn't locate the ball following the shift. The other half, when they did locate it, it was already past the line of scrimmage.)

Thus was power assembled to one side or other, still retaining an option of coming back on a reverse. And with his system of man-for-man blocking angles he didn't have to tie up two of his blockers on one defensive player, freeing more of his men for downfield blocking.

In essence, it was a dynamic mix of speed, precision and deception, and nobody else could approach Rock's brilliance in perceiving its effect and in teaching its execution. Failure of his imitators and their frustration in acknowledging it proves the point.

His players responded to Rock like the cast of a musical, perfecting their rhythm not only for tactical needs but because they shared Rock's intent for its effect on both the defense and fans in the stand.

The defense often found themselves almost mesmerized by the count and by the ominous threat of what could come of it. It took tremendous discipline to play defense against a Rockne team and not many opponents were up to it. In the stands, spectators found the shift a delightful part of the show.

By the mid-1920's, college and high school coaches, awesomely impressed by the Notre Dame shift, rushed to install it. There followed one of the strange phenomena of college football. Nobody could make it work. Years later, as the T, the winged T, the I formation, the veer, the wishbone and other attacks became popular, dozens of teams used them effectively if not brilliantly. But it was forever a mystery why the Notre Dame shift and box became so stilted and ineffective for Rockne imitators. Not even his disciples, who played or were trained under him, could perfect it as coaches. There was nothing wrong with the system. More likely other coaches could not get out of their players what Rockne could get through the magnetic force of his personality.

Notre Dame used the shift with such devastating brilliance that there was only one way to stop it—by legislation. Until the first limitation was put on it, the shifting backs didn't need to come to a full stop before the ball was snapped, and their momentum carried them right into the play with blazing speed. So, the rule makers, by the mid-1920's, said the backs had to come to a full stop before the snap.

But Rockne had taught his backs to take advantage of shoulder, head and torso movement, while coming to a split-second stop, with the residual movement still giving them some kind of edge.

Next the rules called not for just a brief stop but a full one-second stop. Finally, by 1929, the rule mandated a full, one-second stop without upper torso movement.

Rockne, upset over the gradual downgrading of his beloved shift, grew more bitter with every restriction. "If they ever take it away completely," he warned, "football will lose a lot of its color and will revert to an old-fashioned game. And if they ever rule it out all the way, it will be like taking the feinting out of boxing and leaving only the slugging. I'll just pick out my biggest eleven men and prove I can still win with set formations.

"But that's not my idea of football and I think I'd give up the game if that's what it came to." He did not, of course, and proved with his last two teams that he could be just as devastating under the limitations.

By the end of the 1921 season Rockne knew that one particular strategem he'd been toying with, somewhat indifferently, should now become a solid and even dramatic part of his game. Not only did it fit into his physical and tactical plans but the psychologist in him told him he would be adding a dimension of brilliant proportions.

He never really liked the label which sportswriters would be laying on it but he was enough of a writer and public relations man to grudgingly go along with them.

He invented his famed "Shock Troops." The phrase was applied directly as a result of Prussian military tactics in World War I, and with that bitter struggle still fresh in people's minds Rock was once asked whether he liked the idea of his clean-cut Notre Dame kids being compared with the Huns, one of whose favorite Western Front tactics had been to launch an attack with second-string troops, and then mop up with veterans. The shock troops took most of the early casualties but softened up the Allied positions for the experienced units which followed.

"Just because the Kaiser called them shock troops," Rockne growled, "doesn't mean we can't apply the principle to the football field. You call 'em anything you want. We like what happens."

What happened was a direct result of Rockne's perception of the amount of talent he sensed would be attracted to Notre Dame. That, plus his complete confidence in his ability to train and mold players to his system.

Rockne had first hit on the idea in 1920, though he used it sparingly. In essence he would open with a group more talented on defense than offense, but he made certain it included a good punter. The punter was particularly important because under the current rules a player could be in the line-up only once per quarter and he wanted to be sure he had a kicker in there who could bail him out when necessary.

His shock troops were just as tough and no less dedicated than his regulars, but they were just a cut below them in natural athletic ability, and a step slower. But Rock didn't start them just to wear down the opposition. "I start the game with them," he said, "so that my regulars have a chance to study our opponents' formations and analyze their strengths and weaknesses."

More importantly, Rock would have an arm around his regular quarterback as they both studied the enemy, with Rock spewing forth a steady stream of comment. He'd pop questions at him from all angles. "Did you see who made that tackle on our guy? Did you see where he came from?" And, "Who made that block on our end? Who was leading the interference?"

If the enemy defense performed as Rock presumed from his scouting reports, Rockne and his first-line troops on the sideline merely corroborated what they'd prepared for, and Rockne was more content to be more of a spectator. But let the foe show something just a bit different and his regulars would be swarming around him, soaking up his instructions. When the shock troops came out, he had a whole new campaign ready.

Generally, by the time he began using shock troops as a regular procedure, Rockne would insert his regulars near the end of the first quarter or early in the second. By the mid-1920's, when he'd begun swinging into the tough schedules he'd lined up, he was constantly faced with the necessity of saving his starters and he frankly admitted that his second team acted much in the capacity of a shock absorber for his regulars. "We know by experience," he said, "that both we and our foe always hit hardest in the first quarter, and with everyone primed to knock us off we had to give our first string the best possible shot at 'em."

The tactic was particularly valuable with the Four Horsemen. They were so light that Rock's shock troop backfield saved them from some of the bruising, violent whacking they normally would have absorbed in the first quarter.

By the mid-1920's, with his system in full operation, and with Rockne's unique ability to psychologically capitalize on a good idea, many of his players were persuaded that it was a distinct honor to perform with his shock troop brigade, and some actually came to Notre Dame with that ambition. "I can vouch for that," says Edward (Moose) Krause, Notre Dame's athletic director, who arrived in South Bend at the tail end of Rock's career. "I actually heard guys saying: 'If only I can make the shock troops . . .'"

There was yet another reason for deploying shock troops. Strictly psychological. As Rock once put it, "The varsity on the sideline, watching the shock troops performing their function, became keyed up unconsciously, getting their combative juices flowing, and just itching to get in there. It was as though I had a leash on them and suddenly unsnapped it."

Although it took a few years for opposing coaches to imitate Rockne, the tactic rarely met with anything more than lukewarm success elsewhere. For one thing, others lacked Rockne's depth and, more importantly, their squads never seemed to generate the spirit the concept demanded. Incidentally, the flattery of imitation bothered Rockne on one count. High school coaches all over the nation, trying to ape his methods, particularly the shift, sent a barrage of mail his way, asking his advice on how to operate the shock troop tactic on the prep level. Rock didn't think it could be handled, at all, in that arena. There simply wasn't enough maturity and physical strength on prep squads and he was fearful that coaches would be exposing their kids to unnecessary injury.

Once when Doc Spears brought Minnesota to South Bend, neither Spears nor Rock gave any indication of their starting line-ups. Spears was content to wait to see what Rock was doing. And Rock was perfectly willing to let him wait. The final, quick look which Spears flung at Notre Dame showed that Rockne was tuning up his shock troop backfield. But he neglected to look at Rock's line. Spears sent out his own shock troops. Within three or four minutes, before Spears was able to get them out of there, Rockne's regular line had ripped the Gophers to pieces and opened the way for the second-string backs to take a 7-point lead. "A little deceit took us a long way today," Rock rasped hoarsely after the game. The first period TD was the only one the Irish got in a 7–7 tie.

Over the years, Rock's use of shock troops depended on the type of team he met and the material he had. There were, in fact, a few times when he'd open the game with his regulars and put in the shock troops after getting a two- or three-touchdown lead. Or he'd get the shock troops back in there late in the third quarter or the first two or three minutes of the fourth quarter of a tough game, while his regulars rested and got cranked up for a furious and often game-clinching final period.

His manipulation of resources and the response they would make to his psychological demands were, perhaps, as much responsible for his success as any other factors anyone could list.

As far as the public was concerned, however, Knute Rockne's success was signed, sealed and catechized by a date with destiny: the arrival of the most glamorous, the most famous backfield in the history of football—the Four Horsemen.

10

The Four Horsemen

" 'Okay,' Rock barked, eying the horses narrowly.
"You can put the boys aboard but God help you if
they fall off and get hurt . . .' So I put Harry
Stuhldreher, Don Miller, Jimmy Crowley and El-
mer Layden, in full uniform, each holding a foot-
ball, and mounted them on those nags for a pic-
ture. I doubt if any one of them had ever been on
a horse in his life."

—George Strickler,
one of Rockne's early student publicists

It was Saturday afternoon, October 18, 1924, and the whistle had just ended the first half of the Army–Notre Dame game in the Polo Grounds in New York. There was an animated buzz as dozens of sportswriters in the chilled press box watched the two teams troop off the field under a cold, leaden sky. Some of the writers were shaking their heads in wonderment, expressing their awed views of the visiting Irish from South Bend.

George Strickler, Knute Rockne's twenty-one-year-old student correspondent from Notre Dame, had been to a movie in South Bend the Wednesday night of that week. It had been the film version of Blasco Ibáñez's great novel *Four Horsemen of the Apocalypse,* starring the famed Rudolph Valentino.

Someone in the press box said: "What a backfield. They're going to absolutely destroy Army."

The young Strickler nodded and suddenly recalled the film he'd seen three nights earlier. "Just like the Four Horsemen," he said innocently enough and let it go at that.

Three feet away from him, Grantland Rice, the top sports columnist for the New York *Tribune,* looked up sharply, glanced at Strickler, then leaned back in his chair, staring out at the field . . .

Said Strickler, many years later: "There was no way I could ever know what would come from my simple remark. But the next morning, I picked up the *Tribune* and stared in dumbfounded delight at Rice's lead. I can quote it to this day, complete with date line:

> Polo Grounds, New York, Oct. 18.—Outlined against a blue-gray October sky, the Four Horsemen rode again. In dramatic lore they were known as Famine, Pestilence, Destruction and Death. These are only aliases. Their real names are Stuhldreher, Miller, Crowley and Layden . . .

"My first thought was that it was a great lead. My second thought shook me with amusement. Several sportswriters must have heard my comment. What if three or four had decided to use the same reference. Could I have taken credit or blame? But then another thought hit me that erased everything else. I mean *really* hit me.

"I telephoned my father in South Bend and told him to get in touch with a livery stable and hire four horses to be standing by at the practice field at three P.M., Monday. I also told him to call a photographer friend of mine and tell him to meet me there.

"At three o'clock I was there with the photographer and the horses. I told Rock what I wanted to do and he just stared at me, like he couldn't believe it, and who could blame him? I talked fast, telling him what a great publicity stunt it would be. Well, when it came to public relations and what was good for Notre Dame, Rock had real sharp instincts.

" 'Okay,' he barked, eying the horses narrowly, 'you can put the boys aboard, but God help you if they fall off and get hurt.' Or something like that. So I got hold of Harry Stuhldreher, Don Miller, Jimmy Crowley and Elmer Layden, in full uniform and helmet, each one holding a football, and mounted them on those nags. I doubt if any of them ever had been on a horse in his life, but they went along with it.

"What a picture! I knew what we had, and I peddled it to the press, where it appeared in hundreds of papers throughout the country."

What Strickler had was one of the all-time great sports pictures, which, along with Rice's famous Four Horsemen lead, created the most glamorous backfield in football history. It also made a tidy bit of pocket money for Strickler, who peddled the photo to hundreds of Notre Dame students for 50 cents each.

In 1921 they were freshmen, and neither Knute Rockne nor anyone else at Notre Dame could possibly dream of the glory and romance ahead of them.

Not one of them had been the object of a heavy recruiting campaign. Stuhldreher grew up in Massillon, Ohio, the cradle of pro football. He'd been one of dozens of kids who'd worshiped the early pro players and who'd tried to sneak into the games on Sunday. Once, one of the stars, sizing up the situation, had allowed young Harry to carry his helmet and bag into the park, telling the ticket-taker, gruffly: "This kid's with me." The player was a baldish, tough-looking end named Knute Rockne.

Harry Stuhldreher's older brother had gone to Notre Dame, but Harry's high school grades weren't good enough for admittance. He'd been a pretty good schoolboy quarterback at Massillon, and was noted for his cool head and agility. He decided to go to Kiski Prep in Pennsylvania for a year to bring his grades up. When he came to South Bend a year later, he was just another freshman quarterback, and not a very big one at 5' 8" and 155 pounds.

Don Miller, from Defiance, Ohio, was the younger brother of Red Miller, great star of the 1909 Irish team, and of Ray and Walter, who had preceded him to Notre Dame. Don, a star at little Defiance high school, simply never thought of going elsewhere. He was 5' 10" and 163 pounds.

Jimmy Crowley, 5' 11" and 165 pounds, had been a standout at Green Bay, Wisconsin, high school. He planned to go to college but had no particular school in mind. But there was a guy in town who had organized a pro team called the Green Bay Packers, fellow named Curley Lambeau. Lambeau had played one year at Notre Dame but then dropped out of school. He recommended it highly to the young prep flash.

In Davenport, Iowa, the bright star was a swifty who could also punt the hide off a football. Elmer Layden had leaned toward Iowa but allowed his father, a Notre Dame fan, to point him toward South Bend.

When the foursome reported as freshmen in the fall of 1921, they were unexpected and unheralded as far as Knute Rockne was concerned. Crowley was the only one who'd been preceded by a personal recommendation. Curley Lambeau had written Rock a letter saying he thought Crowley might be good enough to play.

Don Miller almost didn't even get to the practice field. When two hundred freshmen turned out, Miller was near the end of the line as the uniforms were passed out. There was none left for Miller and one other kid. The other kid said to hell with it and never came back. Don Miller came back every day for a week until he could scrounge something to wear. The ripped pants came to his ankles. The jersey was full of holes. The socks were unraveling and the shoulder pads were held together by tape. When he appeared on the field, he was more of a Mack Sennett apparition than a football player.

"My God!" said Rockne, almost convulsed. "That's Red Miller's kid brother, isn't it?" He turned to an aide. "Get him an old pair of varsity pants before somebody sees him. This is *still* Notre Dame!"

Normally, Rock paid little attention to the frosh, but this group he watched like a hawk. He didn't interfere with the freshman coach but was aware that he had started Layden as a quarterback. By the end of the season, however, Layden and Crowley were alternating at left half, Miller was at right half and Stuhldreher was alternating at quarterback with a couple others. Two other frosh were sharing the fullback slot.

There were also some good frosh linemen. One was Adam Walsh, a fine center. There was also a chunky tackle from Canton, Ohio, named Rip Miller. Miller insisted on playing without a helmet and taped his ears back to his head. (It took Stuhldreher six weeks to make him get rid of the tape.) Noble Kizer, a 160-pounder who later would become a great coach at Purdue, was a guard.

Still, that frosh team had an indifferent record, winning four games and losing two, being whipped by the Michigan Aggies and —incredibly—Lake Forest Academy.

The young players were subject to the usual freshman strains. Elmer Layden became terribly homesick and went back to Davenport two or three times to see his girl friend. The freshman coach was afraid Layden might drop out.

"Do you think he'll be back next year?" he kept asking Rockne.

"He'll be back," Rock said grimly. "I'll talk to him."

Coming off his great season of 1921, Rock and his freshman coach made some intensive notes on the kids as Rock planned for 1922.

Stuhldreher: probably has most promise . . . sounds like leader . . . fearless blocker . . . quick and brilliant thinker in emergency.

Layden: 10-second speed . . . but punting ability seems best asset.

Miller: not bad blocker . . . could be outstanding ball carrier.

Crowley: shows little except for his wit and occasional flash of open field running.

In spring practice in 1922, Rock thought his chances looked bleak for the coming fall, but there was something about those freshman backs that intrigued him. He kept wondering whether he was using them at the right positions. Frank Thomas and Paul Castner, his varsity quarterback and fullback, were out for baseball so he was taking a long look at his new kids.

He noted they were working harder than any frosh he'd ever had. He installed Stuhldreher as temporary number one quarterback. He put Miller at one halfback and Layden shared the other with a varsity reserve. Two other kids continued to split fullback.

Jimmy Crowley didn't participate in spring practice that year. The irrepressible Crowley, involved in a ten-cent dormitory crap game, was chucked out of school for breaking university rules. But not wanting his family to know, he went down to Indianapolis and got a job as a drugstore soda jerk, wrote letters to his mother and sent them to a buddy on campus who then relayed them to his parents in Green Bay.

He made up his missed work in summer school and reported to Rockne in the fall, in good standing. Rock, who knew about the escapade, lifted an eyebrow, said not a word of reproach, and worked Crowley's tail off.

When the season opened in 1922, Miller was the only starter.

That fall, the Irish jumped off to four straight wins, with all four sophomore backs seeing considerable action. Miller was the only one to sew up a regular job when he raced for three touchdowns in the second game against St. Louis. Then came a memorable game against Georgia Tech, in Atlanta, which was to convince Rock that he had a Team of the Future. It was the game in which he was to read the phony telegram from his son, Billy. It wasn't the only Rockne psychological ploy of the day.

"We went to Atlanta with goose pimples," Stuhldreher was to recall. "This was deep Dixie and we'd heard about that dreaded rebel yell and wondered what it would do to us when that cheering section let go. Probably scare us witless, we thought privately, and Rock didn't help any by warning us it was coming.

"The dressing room was directly across from the stadium. The windows were open and we could hear that awful rebel yell already going up from the Tech cheering section. The dressing room was small and the sound seemed magnified inside. We didn't know it then, but word had leaked to Atlanta that Rock had warned us about the devastating effect that yell could have on us. Tech made capital of that knowledge and really poured it on. It was working perfectly with Rock's plans.

"We had to cross the street through a gantlet of spectators pressing in close to see us. We expected any instant they'd break into the yell, right in our faces and ears.

"We found out later that Rock had arranged this group to give us a psychological baptism, so to speak. When we entered the stadium and a big rebel yell went up, we hardly heard it. It kept up right into game time but we'd really licked it by knowing about it and hearing it in advance."

Against Army the following week, Jimmy Crowley gave the first evidence of the wit and whimsy that would help keep his mates loose for three years. It was a rock-'em, rugged game all the way and appeared headed for a scoreless tie. Late in the third quarter the Irish had a first down on the Army 3. Crowley, alternating at halfback, hit the line and fumbled. The Cadets recovered. His teammates, hoping to restore his spirits, patted him on the back and mumbled all the right things. "Don't worry about it," Crowley said cheerfully. "It can happen to anyone."

The game ended a scoreless tie.

Rock was still mixing Stuhldreher, Crowley and Layden with veterans when the Irish played Butler the following week. Just before the half, regular fullback Paul Castner went out with a broken hip. Rock sent in a substitute and wasn't happy with the result.

Over the weekend, a bit of intuition bloomed and flourished as he toyed with a notion that had buzzed fitfully inside his head all autumn. At midnight, working in his den, he brought his fist down hard on his desk. He knew that what he had in mind was absolutely on target. Everyone would be wondering which of two or three fullback substitutes he'd be using for the injured Castner. What he was about to do was going to shock everyone.

He took Elmer Layden aside before practice on Monday. "Elmer," he said casually, "you're moving to fullback."

"But Rock," Layden protested, "I'm a halfback. I'm no fullback. I could never crack those big lines. I just don't have the heft and power."

"That's where we're going to fool them, Elmer," Rock replied easily. "Everyone is used to a straight-ahead plunger at fullback. I think we can come up with a new type of game with you. With your speed we're going to make you a slicing and quick-opening fullback."

It just might have been the first time anyone ever used the phrase "quick-opening."

But Rock's intuition had been working overtime that weekend. He made an even more dramatic decision on Monday. He would stop spotting Crowley and Stuhldreher. He would use all four of his promising sophomores in the same backfield. They were so adaptive, so nimble and had such excellent timing that he mentally kicked himself for not having thought of it sooner.

Stuhldreher went to quarterback, replacing veteran Frank Thomas. Miller and Crowley lined up at halfback and Layden was the fullback. The first signal drill convinced Rock he'd hit it right. He held a brief scrimmage (unusual for him) and was sure of it. They looked as though they'd been performing together all fall.

Sportswriters from the big Chicago papers came over, half curious, half amazed. Nobody could recall any major college team ever starting four sophomores in the same backfield.

That week, as Rock prepared his new unit, the Irish were to launch a great intersectional rivalry with Carnegie Tech, coached by Judge Walter Steffen, a one-time Stagg star at Chicago. (Years later, after the Horsemen had graduated, a Tech game would provide one of the most stunning highlights of Knute Rockne's life.)

When his sophs performed flawlessly in a 19–0 romp, Rockne knew that something exciting had happened. What's more, the element would be a constant for two more years. It didn't even upset him, terribly, when Nebraska handed the Irish their lone defeat of the year, 14–6, in the season finale at Lincoln. It was a Cornhusker team that outweighed Notre Dame more than fifteen pounds per man, and although Rockne, who never had a stomach for a loss and was one of the game's worst (but not ungracious) losers, was thrilled at the battle his young kids put up. And by then four of his starting linemen were sophs, too.

An era was launched. Only Rockne himself was fully aware of it.

By their junior year, in 1923, the unit was ready to lead the Irish toward national recognition. Their timing was beginning to reach split-second perfection with a smoothness that not even Rockne could find a flaw with. "We had immense respect for each other," remembers Don Miller, "so our timing was something that was spiritual as well as physical. We *sensed* each other. We knew each other's physical gifts. We could anticipate, compensate, all that sort of thing. There was no jealousy, no doubting. Lord, how we meshed."

They were completely different in style. Layden, a ten-second man, was the fastest and ran with low but spearlike velocity. He could accelerate instantly to maximum speed. Miller, the next fastest, was a hard runner with high knee action. Crowley didn't have good speed but was the shiftiest of the three, with a lot of hip action and fakery. Each, however, was a constant threat in his own fashion. Stuhldreher wasn't much of a runner but was a natural leader, a fine passer and punt returner.

In his desire to get more speed out of Crowley and Stuhldreher, Rockne provided them with lighter stockings, lighter thigh pads and lighter shoes. "Finally," said Stuhldreher later, "with his obsession for speed, Rock made me discard the thigh guards completely, telling me I'd simply have to run faster to protect my health."

All four were excellent defensive men in the diamond defense which Rockne used with Crowley backing up the line, Miller and Layden at halfback, and Stuhldreher at safety.

"They were all deadly tacklers, which delighted their teammates and me immensely," Rock once said. "With all the publicity the Four Horsemen were getting, it was important that they prove themselves all-around players. And I'll add this: they had the same fluid, coordinating instincts on defense as they did on offense. And because they were such great pass defenders they made our six- and seven-man line work."

Rockne thought his 1923 team would mature as juniors and had every reason to contemplate an undefeated season. There were six straight victories, including a string of four against tough opponents like Army, Princeton, Georgia Tech and Purdue. By now even the Eastern press was beginning to acclaim Rockne as a "miracle coach." He hated the description. "Baloney," he growled. "I've got some pretty good players who are willing to listen to me and do as I tell them. Of course, maybe *that's* the miracle, in view of the demands I make on 'em."

The backs were taking turns starring. Miller had TD runs of fifty-three yards and twenty-three yards against Georgia Tech and another of eighty-nine yards called back. Layden was splintering enemy lines for five and six at a crack. Crowley was a slippery runner who also was adept on the option pass. Actually, he passed more than Stuhldreher.

Nebraska was coming up. The Cornhuskers had been beaten by

Red Grange's Illinois team and tied by Missouri and Kansas.

"Frankly," Rock told the press, "I'm worried about Nebraska. They've had only a fair season but they're working up a mean streak for us. I hear they'd trade next year's corn crop to get our hides."

Nebraska outplayed the Irish in every way and nipped them, 14–7. Rock hadn't minded the earlier loss to Nebraska because his stars had only been sophomores, but the loss in their junior year cut deep. They'd been flat, with no drive. Rock was afraid they were beginning to believe too much in their burgeoning national publicity. He vowed never to let publicity beat him again.

Don Miller was named an All-America halfback by Walter Camp at the end of the season, yet as far as Rock was concerned it had been a tarnished year. He looked forward to 1924. But he already was enjoying this bunch immensely.

Crowley, the established wit, was a fey creature whom Rock found exasperating at times, but the actor-stage director in Rockne appreciated Crowley all the more. He often told of the time Crowley came into his office to recommend a hot shot from his hometown, Green Bay.

"Really good kid, eh, Jimmy?" Rock asked.

"Awfully good, Rock."

"As good as you, Jimmy?"

Crowley hesitated. "Well, perhaps not that good." He grinned. "But awfully good, Rock."

Rockne appreciated Crowley's light-hearted approach to life, and tolerated Jimmy's antic notions more than he conceded he should have. "But Jimmy kept us from getting tense and taking ourselves too seriously. He was a reminder that college and even football should be fun. If anything, he was our team's unofficial spokesman."

In more ways than one. On the way home to South Bend after a road game, the train would often stop for a few moments in small towns. Sometimes there would be a small crowd at the depot. Crowley would appear on the train's observation platform, look out at the crowd commandingly and then break into an impromptu speech on taxes, immigration, prohibition or whatever popped into his nimble mind. As often as not, the train would pull out in the middle of a sentence. The crowd would be puzzled at first but invariably would break into loud applause.

Once, on the train returning to South Bend after an unconvincing win over Northwestern, a drunk stumbled into the Notre Dame car. He had no ticket. The conductor irritably asked the drunk where he thought he was going.

"I guess nowhere in p'tickler," mumbled the drunk.

"That's okay," Crowley said quickly to the conductor. "He's one of the Four Horsemen. They've been going nowhere all day."

Crowley, much later, would enjoy his own version of how Rock, in the locker room, would announce his first-string line-up for a game: " 'Collins, you and Hunsinger, at end, and for heaven's sake, be careful you don't get sucked in too far on defense. Miller and Bach, the tackles, and I want to see a little more drive in there today; Kizer and Weible, the guards, and when you pull out I want to see some real snap. Walsh, center, let's have some quicker blocking after the snap. Stuhldreher, quarterback, and be sure you don't call too many wide sweeps. Miller, halfback, and don't forget to come up fast on defense. Layden, fullback, I want you hitting in there a little faster today.'

"Then there would be a slight pause. Rock would look at me and say: 'Okay, Jimmy, you go in at the other halfback and give us your usual superlative game.' "

It is Crowley's favorite story about Rock and it gets him a lot of mileage in his banquet speeches. Actually, the only favoritism Rockne seemed to show the Four Horsemen came when he announced the line-ups. He'd use last names for the linemen and then wind up, casually, matter-of-fact, when he got to the backfield, saying simply: "Harry . . . Don . . . Jimmy . . . Elmer . . ."

Rock, however, could blister any of his stars if necessary. Against Princeton, Crowley broke into the clear but didn't seem to be going all-out and was dragged down from behind by the Tigers' Jake Slagle. As the Irish trooped in for Rock's half-time message, Crowley mentioned casually that he'd made a mistake; he hadn't realized Slagle was that fast.

"That wasn't your mistake, Crowley!" Rock roared. "Slagle just didn't know who you were! Your mistake was in not showing him all the press clippings you've been saving, telling the world how great you are. If he'd have seen them, he wouldn't have dared come near you!"

Crowley never loafed again. Incidentally, his nickname, "Sleepy Jim," had nothing to do with a penchant for sacking out. As the team would line up, just before going into its shift, Crowley would seem to slouch indifferently, too lazy or bored to be concerned. His eyelids would appear to droop. When the ball was snapped, it would be an entirely different Jimmy Crowley, but the nickname stuck with him all his life.

Don Miller, now a judge in Cleveland, recalls Rockne as "absolutely masterful at handling us, no matter what the situation. I was the only one of our group that didn't have a scholarship. All I had was the job as prefect at my dorm for two hundred and fifty dollars a year, and had summer jobs that took care of the rest of my needs. After my junior year, when I'd made All-America, I complained to Rock that there were guys on the bench who had scholarships, but I didn't have one. It just wasn' fair.

"Rock just nodded absently—maybe agreeing with me, maybe not. As it turned out, he simply had no more scholarships to hand out, but he called me in the next day and said I could have the football program concession for my senior year and could keep a big hunk of the money for any ads I sold. He knew damn well I could sell ads. I made fourteen hundred dollars that fall— but I was still the only guy on the first team without a scholarship."

"I recall how Rock once psyched me out of my sox," said Harry Stuhldreher. "It was before an Army game in New York. Apparently I had bruised a nerve in my throwing arm the previous week. The pain was terrible. My arm was virtually dead. Rock was very concerned, of course. But he said he knew a doctor in New York who'd developed a special liniment to loosen dead nerves and we'd apply it just before the game. So, an hour before the game Rock handed one of our student managers a brown bottle with some pale-green liniment. The manager rubbed my arm and put a hot pad on it for fifteen minutes.

"I was all excited and went into that game and threw passes as though nothing had been wrong with the arm. But immediately after the game it felt numb again.

"The next week, practicing for Princeton, it refused to come around. Again, before the game, Rock applied the same liniment treatment and I had no trouble with the arm. It was like that for the rest of the season, and finally when the year was over Rock smiled and told me the magic liniment invented by the fancy New York specialist was the same stuff we used at Notre Dame, with a little coloring added. He put it in a different bottle so I wouldn't recognize it. He knew the excitement of the game would be the only healing agent I'd need."

But Rockne never let himself appear to hold his great backs in more esteem than his linemen. By 1923 he knew the backs would get all the public attention in the press. It was then that he began, subtly, to manipulate his custom of having a lineman elected captain. Rock never interfered with the team's election but he was a master at conveying private thoughts which he never even uttered. The squad soon knew how he felt—that he would prefer a lineman as captain. When the time came to choose a leader for 1924—the looming year of Irish supremacy—they elected Adam Walsh, their center. "Not one of us in the backfield felt slighted," said Miller. "It was a fitting choice. Adam was a great guy, a terrific football player and a fine leader."

It was Walsh, who later that year, would put into sharp focus the tolerant amusement the line felt for the inordinate publicity the backfield was receiving, and Rock was always fond of the story. On a whim, Rockne put his great backfield behind a second-string line to start a game. The backs got nowhere. The holes weren't opening. Their frustration was obvious.

After about eight minutes Rock sent in the first-string line, which by now was calling itself "the Seven Mules." Just before the snap on the next play, Walsh looked back as he hunkered over the ball. "What's the matter?" he inquired good-naturedly. "You guys having a little trouble finding a hole? Well, let's see what we can do about it . . ."

"Nobody had to explain it to us," Miller grinned. "What a difference it was, running behind those guys."

By now they understood each other, and appreciated the contributions each was making. This team had jelled and was ready for greatness.

11

Picking the Roses

When Rockne heard that Stanford was limiting him to 18 Rose Bowl players, he told George Strickler, his student correspondent, to get Pop Warner on the phone. "Tell him the game's off!" he howled. "He'll pay for 35 players or we won't show up!" Strickler complied. With Warner on the line, Strickler had just started talking when Rockne grabbed the phone. "Wait!" roared Rock. "I'll tell him myself!"

The 1924 season was a season of unmatched brilliance in that golden decade of college football. It produced the incredible feats of Red Grange, the most famous running back in football history. Grange's pyrotechnics against Michigan, when he raced for four long touchdowns the first four times he touched the ball, undoubtedly was the most remarkable individual effort football had ever seen. He had already electrified the nation with his performance as a sophomore the previous year.

But perhaps even more impressive in 1924 was the impact made by Knute Rockne's team headed by the Four Horsemen. Their first two seasons, sparkling though they were, were just a prelude to the awesome perfection of 1924. Following tune-up romps against Lombard and Wabash, Rock was scheduled for seven straight top-rated teams: Army, Princeton, Georgia Tech, Wisconsin, Nebraska, Northwestern and Carnegie Tech.

The momentum generated by the split-second timing of the shift was unstoppable and the deception coming off the shift was unfathomable. Knute Rockne had something truly new in football. Together with mastery of the physical techniques of football he mixed improvisation, imagination and intelligence. His theory on brush blocking proved sound. His one-on-one blocking angles were drafted and executed to geometric perfection. Rarely were there huge, crude pile-ups when the Irish were on offense. The hole was there and a back would come slicing through, needing only a crack of daylight.

"But as often as not," Layden once said, "the hole would be wide and beckoning and we'd laugh in pure enjoyment as we blasted through—just as Rock would be doing on the sideline. He could sure appreciate those quick, sudden holes our linemen would make for us. I think he got more kick out of that than anything else, because flawless line play was the heart of his football philosophy."

Nearly every game stood out in a brilliant victory string which saw the Irish score 258 points to 44. "Nebraska," said Rock, "probably gave me my most personal satisfaction because they'd handed us our only defeats in 1922 and 1923. Especially after they'd scored first and seemed on their way to repeating our 1923 disaster. They looked as though they were toying with us. We couldn't seem to get any of our backs more than two yards beyond the line of scrimmage. So Harry Stuhldreher, knowing what I had in mind, suddenly took to the air. With one lightning move he hit Jimmy Crowley on an eighty-yard touchdown pass play and it so stunned Nebraska that we went on to a 34–6 victory."

It was not surprising, of course, that something which happened before the game would have an effect on the result. Nebraska had an open date the previous Saturday when the Irish were playing Wisconsin. When Rock heard that several Nebraska players had come up to see the game, he met them and urged them to say hello to his players after practice on Friday.

Rock knew the Nebraska kids would say more than hello. They'd handed Notre Dame its lone losses the previous two years, and Rock counted on the Cornhuskers to exercise some strong bragging rights and put their overconfidence on display. As usual, Rock was right on target. His kids got all steamed up and could hardly wait for the opening whistle next day.

For Jimmy Crowley, it was the Wisconsin game that provided a big lift. Playing at Madison, Don Miller and Elmer Layden were carrying the ball for big yardage but no scores. Crowley took Stuhldreher aside:

"Harry, you know I live in Green Bay, don't you?"

Stuhldreher nodded.

"Then you realize," Crowley continued, "that more than five thousand people from Green Bay are here to see their favorite son play, and I haven't had my hands on the ball yet."

"We'll take care of that, Jim," said Stuhldreher.

Crowley got the ball and raced for more than one hundred yards as the Irish rolled to a 38–3 victory.

Years after the Irish had defeated Princeton that season, Charley Caldwell, who played in that game and later became a great coach of the Tigers, recalled: "Never in my life had I experienced such a frustrating time. Notre Dame could have made the final score anything they wanted, but I was more impressed by the way they handled me while I was backing up our line.

"We thought we had a great team that year but Notre Dame just toyed with us. I didn't make a clean, unassisted tackle all day. I'd get set to nail a ball carrier and someone I never saw would crack me out of the way or just nudge me out of the play. I was so sold on Knute Rockne's football that I decided that very day that I wanted to be a coach."

Returning from the Princeton triumph, the Four Horsemen were now national property and Rock knew it. He was also wise enough to let it happen, knowing that the intensive exposure in the press was good for Notre Dame—for both the team and the school. He turned down no requests for interviews, either for himself or with members of his famous backfield. It got to be pretty silly and finally a big paper assigned a woman reporter to try for a different angle. She had tried unsuccessfully to catch up with them by phone, mail and telegram. Finally she came out to South Bend unannounced and cornered Crowley after practice. Crowley was trapped but politely answered all her questions.

When she finally left, a teammate asked Crowley who she was.

Crowley looked after the departing woman. "That," he sighed, "was the Second Horsewoman—Pestilence."

Against Northwestern, the Wildcats led by two field goals, but the Irish went ahead, 7–6, late in the fourth period. Elmer Layden sewed up things by intercepting a Northwestern pass and flying down the sideline fifty yards for a TD. Rock remembered it well: "An official marked a spot where he thought Elmer had stepped out of bounds, but quickly changed his mind and let the play stand. Elmer had missed the line by at least two inches."

In the season finale against tough Carnegie Tech, the Irish were tied, 19–19, at the half. Rock followed the team inside the dressing room and marched stonily to the blackboard. "They've got the best spinner play I've ever seen," he snapped, "but that doesn't mean we can't stop it." Furiously he scrawled his X's and O's, then turned to Adam Walsh, who backed up the line. He gave Walsh unshirted hell for sloppy play, and ordered him back into the line for a seven-man front.

Then Rockne pulled a telegram from his pocket. It was from a Notre Dame representative on the West Coast. "This came this morning," said Rock. "HAVE LEARNED THAT GAME WITH STANFORD IS OUT IF WE LOSE TO TECH."

The game with Stanford would be the Rose Bowl. Rock put the telegram away. "I've got enough money to pay my own way out there to see whoever Stanford plays," he said. "If you guys want to go it's up to you."

In the second half Stuhldreher went to the air. Between him and Crowley the Irish completed fifteen of nineteen passes, twelve of them in a row, on the way to three TDs and a 40–19 win. Walter Eckersall, covering the game for the Chicago *Tribune,* wrote: "Not only did Notre Dame win the right to be rated the strongest football team in the country, but it gave an exhibition of forward passing never before equaled by any team."

Yet it was the Army game, earlier in the season which first alerted the nation's fans to the perfect machine put together by Knute Rockne at Notre Dame. That was the game, of course, that drew the immortal lines from Grantland Rice, creating the legend of the Four Horsemen.

As usual, Rockne started his shock troops the first quarter. He and Stuhldreher studied the Army defenses, then he opened the second period with his first string.

Calling his own plays at the line of scrimmage, Harry Stuhldreher was a little Napoleon, a master strategist, deploying speedy troops wherever and however needed. If Army defenses were spread to stop Miller and Crowley wide, or off tackle, he'd send Layden spearing up the middle. If the secondary closed in on the middle, Miller would race wide or Stuhldreher or Crowley would flip passes into the gaps.

It was perfect coordination between backs and line, each man doing what Rock had designed for him. Although the score was only 13–7, with the Cadets putting up a blazing fight, it was the impeccable yet slashing versatility and execution of the Four Horsemen that made the difference.

Grantland Rice's lines labeling the four backs for life were not to sweep the nation for a few days—not until after George Strickler's classic picture had provided the impetus. But by season's end Knute Rockne was the most famous and most successful football coach in America. If there were any doubts, some New Year's Day events in Pasadena, California, would sweep them away.

After the great 1920 season with Gipp, Rockne had yearned for the Rose Bowl invitation but it had slipped away, instead, to undefeated Ohio State. Although the Irish undoubtedly were a better team, Rockne did not yet have the force of personality that would have made him—and his team—the hot ticket in Pasadena. And in 1921, with his great season tarnished by the hanky-panky at Taylorville, he had personally removed Notre Dame from any consideration.

But for New Year's Day, 1925, there was only one possible choice for the visiting team, and the whole nation, including Pop Warner of Stanford, knew it. Warner, with a great, undefeated team, led by the incomparable Ernie Nevers, was the West Coast host. He knew he did not dare pass up Knute Rockne and his Four Horsemen or there would be a howl of national rage and disappointment.

So, late in November 1924, Notre Dame received a telegram

inviting the Irish to the Rose Bowl. A week later Knute Rockne was furious. He had requested that 2,000 tickets be set aside for Notre Dame fans. Now he learned that the seats would be in the student section behind the goal posts, at $1.50 each. Rock fired off a telegram to let Stanford know what the real score was. The Notre Dame demands would be met or there would be no game. A day or two later there was an even greater eruption from Rockne, as reported by George Strickler, then his student correspondent at Notre Dame. "I was in Rock's office," said Strickler, "the day the formal contractual arrangements came in the mail. Rock read it and exploded. 'What's this baloney about our being allowed to bring only eighteen players!' he howled. Then he turned to me. 'Call Warner on the phone and tell him the game's off. He'll pay for thirty-five players or we won't show up! Remind him I've signed no contract.'

"Apparently no Eastern team had ever been allowed to bring more than eighteen men," said Strickler, "but Rock's attitude was that a Rose Bowl trip should be a fitting reward for the kids' work all season, and he wasn't going to jettison several players who had contributed so much. Especially when he knew Warner would have a full complement of forty or fifty players.

"So I called Stanford, got Pop Warner on the phone and gave him Rock's message. I'd barely started talking when Rock grabbed the phone out of my hand, yelling: 'Here, I'll tell him myself . . .'

" 'Warner,' he roared all the way across the country, 'the game's off. You can play anybody you want but we're not coming out there!' Then he hung up.

"For the next sixteen hours or so, I was the only reporter in the nation who knew the Rose Bowl game between Stanford and Notre Dame was canceled, because I knew Rock meant it. But I sat on the story, and its lucky I did. Next morning Pop Warner called and said Rock could bring his thirty-five players. By the way, we also got our fair allotment of good tickets, and through local donations Rock was able to take a squad of forty-five players."

If there was any doubt that Knute Rockne was now a personal as well as artistic force in college football, it was now dissipated.

And if there was any doubt that Rock didn't have the best football team in the nation, *that* disappeared in the warm, dry air in the newly built Rose Bowl in Pasadena. Aside from the Rockne system, which featured the notorious shift, Pop Warner's style was the only other famous system in the game. It featured a double wing back assault that made use of a lot of reverses and spinners, mixed in with a tricky passing attack off a fake spin. And in 205-pound fullback Ernie Nevers the Indians had probably the greatest player in the nation. He had speed and terrifying power. Even though he had played most of the year on bad ankles, nobody had ever completely harnessed him. Nor would the Irish . . .

On New Year's Day, Rockne started his shock troops, as usual, to see what Stanford was all about, but it took him just two or three minutes to realize that he had to get his first-stringers in there immediately or the Indians might jump out to a lead. And in an emotional situation like this, that could be the ball game.

The Pasadena affair was the only Bowl game around in those days. It attracted 100,000 people and generated great fanfare. This year, with two super undefeated teams, the game would clearly establish a national champion.

Stanford had driven forty-three yards to Irish territory and Murray Cuddleback had just barely missed a field goal for the Indians. Rock was taking no chances. In went the Four Horsemen and the Seven Mules.

Don Miller promptly fumbled on the first play from scrimmage. Stanford recovered and a moment later, on fourth down, Cuddleback tried again for the field goal, this time successfully, and Stanford led, 3–0.

The Irish marched right back with Stuhldreher picking apart the Indian defense with a beautifully balanced mixture of running and passing. Suddenly the Irish were on Stanford's 4-yard line, fourth down. Stuhldreher, disdaining the sure field goal to tie it up, called a pass which was incomplete. He was sacked on the attempt and hurt his foot. The pain was intense, but he shook it off and told no one about it.

The Irish roared right back again after Nevers had punted out, and reached the Indians' 7-yard line early in the second quarter.

Two plays later Elmer Layden speared over for the touchdown. It was to be the only TD scored on the ground that day. The rest of the scoring—and there'd be a lot of it—would be pure pyrotechnics.

Stanford, on its next series, drove to the Irish 31. Then, on fourth and six, quarterback Fred Solomon flipped a pass in the flat, intended for Ted Shipkey, the Indians' star end. Elmer Layden raced in, cut in front of Shipkey, snagged the ball in full stride and was off. He got key blocks from Jimmy Crowley and Ed Hunsinger and sped seventy-eight yards for the longest pass interception yet seen in the Rose Bowl. Crowley missed the point-after but the Irish led at half-time, 13–3.

Stanford's big backs—Nevers particularly—kept pounding at the Irish line, putting on drive after drive which penetrated to the shadow of their goal posts but no further. And time after time Elmer Layden boomed Notre Dame out of trouble with lofty, spiraling fifty- and fifty-five-yard punts.

Finally, midway in the third quarter, the Indians' safety man lost one of Layden's boomers in the sun and fumbled. Ed Hunsinger, racing in to make the tackle, scooped up the ball instead, and under the rules of the day, kept going with it into the end zone.

The safetyman, still kneeling on the turf, pounded his fists on the ground. "What a dope . . . what a dope I am!" he moaned.

"You're right about that," Crowley said cheerfully as he passed by. "Nobody's gonna disagree with you."

Four minutes later Stanford got back in the ball game on a TD pass to Shipkey. Now the score was 20–10. Early in the final period Stanford intercepted a Crowley pass and returned to the Notre Dame 31. Nevers hurtled into the line four times, getting to the 6. The beleaguered Irish looked toward their bench, hoping Rock would send in a sub to tell them what to do. By the rules, however, he'd have to wait until one play had been run off before he could talk. Sure enough, onto the field came big John McMullen to replace Rip Miller. Nevers smashed into the line again. The ball was on the 2. Now the Irish pounced on McMullen.

"What did Rock say?" Adam Walsh, the captain, said hoarsely.

McMullen was noted for stuttering when nervous or excited. His

face contorted. "R-Rock s-says the t-t-trouble with you g-guys is
—you c-c-can't stop N-N-Nevers . . ."

Stanford would have two more chances. Everyone in the ball
park knew Nevers was coming. He smashed over guard for one
yard. The ball was two feet from the goal line.

"We knew there'd be no trick stuff," said Harry Stuhldreher.
"He'd be coming again. All four of us backs were virtually on the
line. Nevers came, all right. There was the damnedest crash of
bodies I'd ever heard. When the ref dug everybody out, there was
Nevers on the ball and the ball was four inches from the goal line.
Later, Nevers swore he'd been robbed, that he'd gone over, but I
told him he was wrong. I knew because I was sitting on his neck,
which was over the line, but the ball was under his chest."

"It was the play of the game," said Rock. "The greatest goal line
stand any team of mine ever made because the toughest line
smasher in the world was coming at us. If he'd scored it would have
given Stanford terrific momentum and, quite possibly, the ball
game. But then Elmer Layden got us out of trouble again with the
greatest punt of his or anybody's life. From back in the end zone
he kicked that ball seventy-five yards in the air and it finally rolled
out of bounds on the Stanford 17."

But Stanford wasn't through—and neither was Layden. With
about five minutes left in the game the Indians again mounted an
assault that carried to the Irish 35-yard line. With a minute remaining Ed Walker flipped a pass toward Shipkey in the flat. But there
was Layden again, streaking in, plucking the ball virtually out of
Shipkey's hands at the 30. He raced seventy yards for the final Irish
TD and it was all over.

"We were spent," said Rock, "emotionally and physically. It
had been a very warm day. Stanford was used to the weather but
we suffered. Jimmy Crowley even had to go to the hospital after
the game, dehydrated and exhausted."

"That would always be my favorite team," Rock would later
reveal. "I think I sensed that that backfield was a product of
destiny. At times they caused me a certain amount of pain and
exasperation, but mainly they brought me great joy. I suppose
they'd been brought together by accident but it was no accident

that had made them into great players and a great unit. That was design and hard work."

It was a fitting end to a great year and a crowning climax to the careers of the Four Horsemen and Seven Mules—Knute Rockne's most famous and glamorous team. Stuhldreher, Miller, Layden and captain Adam Walsh, at center, had been named All-America, and if the coach-of-the-year polls had then been in existence, Knute Kenneth Rockne clearly would have been the choice.

12

Making It Mesh

"Rock was inimitable on that practice field. Whenever he was stopped or stumped, he'd slap his hands on his hips and spit. If something went beautifully, he'd spit. Spitting was his punctuation. It was also his way of being silently evasive or of stalling, or just acknowledging that you'd beaten him."

—Chet Grant

"Okay, everybody down!"

It was the famous command, barked out in that inimitable voice, that launched every Notre Dame practice at 3:30 P.M. It signaled the fifteen-minute calisthenics session over which Rock would preside in the center of a huge circle. Individual players often arrived earlier to work out on their own: passing, kicking, receiving, hitting a blocking dummy. But when Rock showed up precisely at 3:25 everything fell into a rigid routine that never varied.

Calisthenics wasn't just a *pro forma* thing with Rockne. With his broad understanding of the human body, based on prodigious research in medical books (which he read as avidly as his whodunits), there wasn't a muscle, a joint or bone Rockne didn't understand in terms of function and physical limitation, and he designed his calisthenics to provide a very serious warm-up. Players rarely took them lightly. Once a great halfback in the circle behind Rockne decided to loaf. As though he had eyes in the back of his head, Rockne swung around at that instant and halted the drill.

"Our Mister Famous Halfback," he barked, "seems to have lost the proper rhythm. I think he should demonstrate that he can restore it . . ."

The halfback was summoned to the middle of the circle, and then Rock lay down on his back, crossed his knees in comfortable position, plucked a few blades of grass to chew on and ordered the All-America back to do a solo drill, double-time, for two minutes.

"Excellent," Rock announced. "Mr. Famous Halfback has proved he can do the same thing the common people do."

The fifteen-minute calisthenics period would end on the dot and Rock would yell, "Everybody up!" Then he would plunge into the business of working with individuals, while others practiced their specialities with his two assistants.

He was a bug on teaching kids to protect themselves. Regulars and reserves alike would go through repetitious drills. A boy would be taught to bob his head to avoid a slap by an opposing lineman. Rock might keep the boy in a head-bobbing session for five minutes at a time. There could be as much as twenty minutes on a tackling machine, with Rock himself teaching correct torso position and leg dynamics for charging and contact.

"Learn to love that ground!" he would bark. "Keep those legs spread and grip that good earth for hard contact, both before and after contact."

"Use all the power in your hip and thighs!" he would bellow. "That's where nature placed it."

Rockne always claimed that any other football skill could be conquered, but that it took a special type of player and person to become an excellent blocker.

"Love to block and let them know you like it!" he would yell.

Not only would Rockne deliver impeccable instruction for the correct stance and contact for each blocking position but he carried it further by showing how the movements and blocking angles could vary depending on how and where the play developed. He demanded instant compensation and adjustment from his players, both on offense and defense; his intellectual criteria were so high it was said he often passed over much bigger, stronger and even tougher players for one who was not as big or tough but was lightning-quick and demonstrably smart.

"Football," he said over and over, "is a game played with the arms, legs and shoulders but mostly from the neck up."

Bert Metzger was one of Rockne's famous "watch-charm" guards, so called because they seemed so small. Metzger never weighed more than 149 pounds yet made All-America. He explained how he managed it: "People could understand how we might get by on offense, because we depended on speed in pulling out to block and in hitting our defensive man before he could get set. But they often wondered how we survived on defense where we had to go against 215-pounders, and bigger. Well, Rockne showed us such exquisite angle play that we never presented a full target for the blocker. He taught me to charge and drop a shoulder at the same time, so I could get under or slip past. He made sure I wasn't presenting too much leg or thigh to be hit. The man used to coach in inches. It was the scientist in him, I guess."

Operating in an era of single-platoon football, with never more than two or three assistant coaches to aid him, Knute Rockne, wearing a sweat shirt, baggy pin-striped baseball pants, and nothing on his balding dome, was a *teaching* coach who believed in showing *how*.

"Rock was a natural for teaching blocking angles," recalls Rip Miller, one of the Seven Mules. "He'd played end himself, and because he only weighed 155 he'd had to make a study of blocking angles, leverages and all sorts of tricks, in order to move the bigger guys on defense opposite him. He was simply a master tactician and strategist and he was right in there, at practice, getting down without pads, smacking into us, hitting us with shoulder, hip, upper arms, everything that was legal. 'Come on, I won't hurt you,' he'd yell at the guys, and they'd get mad and really come at him.

"Feet were important with Rock. He'd have us refine that first step, getting shove-off power into it, and always barking to us about balance and keeping our charge ferocious from the instant we came off the ball. He'd made such a study of blocking that he was the first to use a sort of brush block on certain plays. You could neutralize your guy without trying to grind him into the dirt, and get a chance to continue on downfield and hit another defender. He showed me the best reverse body block I'd ever seen in football."

Rockne could be ferocious when demonstrating combat tactics. "Once he was upset by my execution of a half-spinner sneak play," Chet Grant recalled. "Rock took it himself on the next play and gained five yards. He just turned back and looked at me as if to say: 'There! That's how it's done!' I just looked back at him with a look that said: 'Hell, I expected you to go all the way for a touchdown!'

"Rock was inimitable on that practice field. Whenever he was stopped or stumped, he'd slap his hands on his hips and spit. If something went beautifully, he'd spit. Spitting was his punctuation. It was also his way of being silently evasive or of stalling, or just acknowledging that you'd beaten him."

It was a personal demonstration that produced one of the most memorable Rockne photos. As Frank Wallace remembers it, Rock's effort, especially when blocking or tackling, always showed up in a fierce, distorted facial expression, his eyes ablaze with competitive effort. Wallace thought a picture of Rock in a moment like that would make a great picture, but figured Rock would never go for it. Still, he arranged for a photographer from the Chicago *American* to make the shot with Wallace screening him from Rock's view. "The next day," wrote Wallace, "the *American* used the photo almost full-page. The Chicago *Tribune* insisted that Rock pose for a similar shot for them. Rock always hated both of them."

Rockne demonstrating his techniques, incidentally, was one of the best shows in town, but only a few privileged witnesses were there to see it. Rip Miller recalls that Rock had to make a special effort to curb some of his more colorful expressions when priests were within earshot. "But though he cussed a lot, and you knew who he was swearing about, he never swore *at* you, if you know what I mean. He could use subtle anger, wit or sarcasm with equal effect. He knew the temperaments of every kid on the squad and picked his approach accordingly."

Harry Stuhldreher, the quarterback for the Four Horsemen, explained Rock's painstaking work with centers: "Rock impressed upon our centers that they had to snap in perfect synchronization

Knute Rockne in the early 1920's.

Beginnings: The town of Voss, Norway, where Rockne was born *(below)*, and the ancient church in which he was baptized *(right)*, as they appeared in 1965.

Knute at age six with his sisters, shortly after the family arrived in Chicago *(left)*. *Below,* he poses jauntily with a tennis partner at sixteen and more seriously a few years later.

Student: Rock was a member of the track team, played the female lead in a student theatrical and excelled at football during his student days at Notre Dame.

Coach: After graduation, Rock coached track and football, and also taught chemistry. *At left,* he poses solemnly with a winning track banner. *Right,* in his early days as head coach, he wears a full uniform as he holds the ball for a kicker and hands the ball off to a running back.

STUHLDREHER   LAYDEN   CROWLEY   MILLER

Within a few years, Rockne was receiving national attention. His great backfield, christened the Four Horsemen, got their picture on every sports page in America in 1924. Rock still demonstrated at practice *(below)*, and his grimace at the moment of contact also made the papers.

Shown here at practice (with All-America halfback Jack Elder), on the sidelines (with assistant coach Hunk Anderson) and at the blackboard, Coach Rockne brought fame to himself and new status to the coaching profession as a whole.

Family: Rock poses with his wife, Bonnie; with his two younger children, Jackie and Mary Jean; and with his three sons, Billy, Jackie and Knute Jr.

The Office: *Above,* Rock dictates to his secretary, Ruth Faulkner, answering a huge stack of correspondence. *Below,* his desk in the athletic department at Notre Dame, a far cry from the luxury of modern coaching quarters.

Friend of Celebrities: *At right*, Rockne gets measured for a hat by haberdasher Babe Ruth. *Below*, he poses with matinee idol Rudolph Valentino. *At bottom*, he attends a game with his friend Mayor Jimmy Walker of New York.

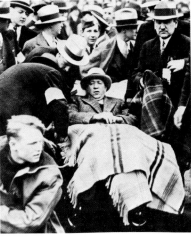

Illness: Rockne's serious bout with phlebitis in 1929 caused him great agony and seemed to age him prematurely. A platform, complete with public address system, was erected so that he could run practices. He was carried to games in a specially built car and rolled onto the field in a wheelchair.

Tragedy: *At left,* Rock plays in the Florida sand with his youngest son Jackie in early 1931. Then came the headlines of April 1 (this one from the New York *Journal*). *Below,* the twisted wreckage of the plane in a Kansas field.

UPI

NOTRE DAME MEMORIAL LIBRARY

KNUTE ROCKNE AND EIGHT KILLED IN PLANE CRASH

DEAD IN PLANE CRASH

COACHING ANOTHER GAME

EXTRA
ALL ON BOARD DIE AS SHIP SMASHES

UPI

Thousands came to the South Bend railroad station when Rockne's body arrived from Kansas, and hundreds wept inside Sacred Heart Church on the Notre Dame campus during the funeral.

UPI

IN MOURNING . . . . . . By Artigue

Tributes and Memorials: Editorial pages in newspapers from coast to coast reflected the shock and sorrow at Rockne's death. These cartoons appeared in the Los Angeles *Express (above)* and the Chicage *Herald & Examiner (below)*.

TIME OUT

Copyright, 1931, by
The Chicago Herald and Examiner.

To
KNUTE ROCKNE
• • •
In grateful memory of the man whose standards of fair play are an immortal inspiration to the youth of America, and whose many contributions to the great sport of football will never be forgotten.
He developed the Forward Pass on this strip of beach at Cedar Point.

NOTRE DAME CLUB
OF CLEVELAND

•KNUTE ROCKNE•
Født her 4. mars 1888

GIANT OF AMERICAN FOOTBALL
•KNUTE•ROCKNE•
Was born here March 4, 1888

DEDICATED 1962

Rock's memory was perpetuated by the Liberty ship christened in his name in 1943, and by plaques in such diverse places as Cedar Point, Ohio, and Voss, Norway.

Though he was overtaken by illness and tragedy, the image of Knute Rockne that persists is this one: baggy pants, torn sweat shirt—and the unmistakable aura of command.

with our shift, because the ball was coming back at the precise split second our shift ended and the backs took off. But there was more to it than that. The center had to be familiar with each back and his peculiarities. They liked different kind of snapbacks; very fast, medium, or even sometimes a sort of float. A back with high knee action didn't like a low snap because he might stride into the ball and fumble. Some backs were faster starters than others and needed a bigger lead. Rather than change a back's natural style of running, Rock felt it was easier for the center to give him the kind of snap he needed. And the way our shift operated, left or right, with a direct snap going to any of the four backs, our centers had to be letter-perfect. Under Rock's eagle glare they sure learned to be."

The last forty-five minutes of practice were devoted to signal drill and dummy scrimmage designed to prepare for the next opponent's characteristics. Four teams would be going through their drills, with Rock and his two assistants working with three of them and a scrub team working on its own. Yet Rock managed to keep an eye on all of them.

Often, neither players nor coaches would be aware of him until they suddenly heard him barking:

"Tom, you were late pulling out and you went back too shallow . . ."

"Call that play over again, Jimmy. Smith was supposed to lead the play but blocked straight ahead. We've got to correct our mistakes . . ."

"Your signal count isn't fast enough, Jimmy. Speed it up a bit. And I WANT TO HEAR IT!"

"I doubt," said Stuhldreher, "if there was ever a thirty-second period during practice when you couldn't hear that voice all over the field."

Much of Rockne's system was predicated not only on deception and skill but on getting the ball carrier to the point of attack as quickly as possible, with the greatest amount of interference, even if it was only brush blocking. He paid critical attention to his backs' speed. If they were slower than he liked, but were working behind a fast-charging line, he'd bring his backs closer to the line to ensure proper timing in getting the back through the hold. If he had extremely fast backs, with a somewhat slower charging line, he'd reverse the procedure, moving the backs two feet further to the rear so the linemen would be sure to precede the back through the hole.

Rock, ever intent on precision, once bent down in practice to closely scan the grass. Then he looked up and growled to a fullback: "You should have come back another five inches. There's the evidence." He pointed to cleat marks in the turf.

When practice first started in the fall, Rockne turned his field into a kind of laboratory, working out his "experiments" from a practical standpoint but with a nonscientific dollop of gut instinct. He would keep moving the players around, from team to team, first to second, second to first, second to third, third to second.

"He liked to keep the kids guessing," said Stuhldreher. "It kept them on their toes. There might be three hundred out for spring football but after three weeks of fall practice they'd be reduced to fifty or fifty-five at most. Natural attrition. Rock never cut anybody. Then there came a time when the first three teams were pretty much intact, except for a rare move here and there.

"The way Rock saw it, the best eleven men *as a team* and not the best eleven players would make the first team, and so on. You'll have to think about that for a while to get what I mean."

Perhaps the most colorful part of Knute Rockne's coaching technique was invisible to the press and general public. Every day at noon, Rock and his varsity squad would hurry through lunch and then report to a lecture meeting.

In these lectures, each position would be examined from a strategic point of view. Rock would ask a question, practical or hypothetical, and demand a quick answer. Technical situations would be clarified. Then Rock would put several players through an inquisition. A player might have to conduct a lecture himself and then submit to questions from the rest of the squad.

"A player had to think on his feet," Don Miller recalled. "And nobody wanted to mess up his chance."

At least twice each spring and twice in the fall, Rockne would give a written exam on everything covered during a particular week and then personally grade each paper so he could tell who was doing what kind of thinking.

So clear and exciting were his lectures that no one dreaded his exams. "In fact," recalls Francis Wallace, "one day when I was Rock's publicity correspondent he invited me to take the exam, too. I did, and got the second highest grade, right below quarterback Harry Stuhldreher. I was flattered and proud as hell." It must also have pleased Rock that his football teaching even got through to a nonathletic layman.

He loved to set up an offensive situation against a particular team coming up that week and demand that his quarterback handle it. Sometimes he'd call on a guard, tackle or end, to provide the answer, on the theory that everyone had to constantly think like a quarterback. "God, how we loved that," Rip Miller recalled with a laugh. "Some of us linemen always thought we were as smart as the quarterbacks anyway."

At least one quarterback, Chet Grant, managed to have a little fun at Rockne's expense in these sessions. "He'd pop something at me in front of everyone and I'd make a show of deliberate consideration. Instead of rushing into an opinion I might say: 'I'm sorry, Rock, but I don't think I have enough facts to go on. The situation is too risky for preliminary or immature judgment.' That would always throw him, and after he tried to stare me down for three or four seconds, he'd sort of cough and hesitate and go on to something else. I always loved it. I think I got away with murder with Rock."

From the very first, Rockne impressed upon his squads that his quarterback ruled the field. Even the team captain was subordinate to the signal caller. Rock would hammer that into all his quarterback candidates: "You are the boss. You run the show. You are to maintain discipline. You are to develop the feeling that you are never wrong in what you call."

To buttress this feeling of superiority and confidence, Rockne would go to devious lengths.

"During spring training," recalled Frank Carideo, probably his greatest quarterback of all, "Rock would put a green kid into a scrimmage to quarterback the varsity—he did this with me, too, incidentally—and then frame him. Rock would take a veteran lineman aside and tell him to pressure a bum steer on the kid.

"Sooner or later the veteran would come up to the kid after a play and say something like: 'I know you're the boss, Joe, but this is the perfect spot to run R-24. I've got my man ready to be taken.'

"The kid probably had something else in mind, but if the veteran had an idea the play might break it big and the kid quarterback would look good. But the play goes bad, the veteran pretends he's been out of town or something and the kid is there with egg on his face. But the kid has learned not to let somebody else call his plays. If it happens more than once, he's in trouble with Rock."

Carideo recalls that Rockne had sublime confidence in his field generals: "All Rockne quarterbacks called their own plays. They had no messengers coming in on every down with a play from the bench. Rock simply trained us to think the way he did and to react the way he would to every changing situation.

"The best way to put it—without sounding immodest—is that Notre Dame quarterbacks were an extension of Knute Rockne himself."

Both Carideo and Stuhldreher agreed that Rockne put intense pressure on his quarterbacks.

"We got to feeling," said Carideo, "that unless we understood and carried out his principles of field conduct, football would never succeed at Notre Dame.

"First of all, Rock would say: 'I want you cocky at all times. *At all times!* Without letup. For several reasons. First of all, it shows the other team that you have complete confidence and you know exactly what you're going to do next. There's no doubt in your mind.'

"He even wanted us to be mindful of our facial expressions, so we could indicate we not only knew what we were going to do but that we were going to pull it off successfully no matter how they try to stop us."

"I'm not asking you to put on phony airs," Rock told them. "You're just playing a role. It isn't you personally who I want to be cocky. It's you the Notre Dame quarterback. But be wise enough to know a limit. Don't get your own teammates soured on you. But you can irritate the opposing team all you want—the more the better."

Next was the quarterback's voice. Rock wanted it clear, staccato and incisive. There were no huddles, and plays were called immediately at the line of scrimmage. Rock wanted that voice to be that of a commander taking his troops to his objective—and a voice recognized by the opposition as one that would lead to that objective no matter what.

Rock would not even use a huddle. He wanted to eliminate all possibility of debate and discussion. He wanted the quarterback to study the defense calmly, then call a play so confidently that the command left no room for doubt.

"Another principle," said Carideo, "was that we constantly observe which defenders were making tackles and which were not, and to look for weaknesses in the secondary, especially on passes. No coaching from the bench was allowed. It all happened with signals we called at the line of scrimmage and Rock wanted us to have all information possible."

Rockne also wanted his quarterbacks to be on the alert for any little advantage. Once Carideo noted that an opposing tackle looked punchy and that a sub was talking to his coach near the bench:

"It was fourth and a foot at midfield, and normally a Notre Dame quarterback punted or Rockne might have his hide. But I knew Rock would go along with my call this time. I called a play over the groggy man for a first down before his replacement could come in.

"We actually had a map of Rock's field, divided into five zones, each of twenty yards. From our own goal line to our twenty was the danger zone. If we got out of it, we had to do it with simple power stuff—no intricate ball handling or passing—often punting on second down if our first play didn't succeed.

"From our 20- to 40-yard line Rock had what he called our transitional running and kicking zone. You normally started from here, anyway, if you'd received the kickoff, so we used feeler players and punted on third down. But no passing.

"Next, there was Rock's transitional running and passing zone from our 40 to the opposition's 40. If we passed, it was usually deep —just as good as a punt, if intercepted. And we could wait until fourth down to kick. From the opponent's 40 to their 20 was our scoring or trick play zone. From their 20 to the goal was the zone of intense resistance. Rock said that's where execution counted the most. No matter what the play, our superiority of execution had to overmatch the enemy's desperation on defense."

Rockne provided a whole education in football, but it was all directed at practical use—on game day. Not only did the players give their best performances then; so did the coach. It's a shame it took another four decades to perfect the tape recorder. Rock on the sidelines during a game was a symphony of sound, complete with movement and his own orchestration. He was all-seeing, all-knowing, immersed in every flowing facet of the game developing before him.

Since he didn't have an offensive coordinator, a defensive coordinator, a specialist coach for each position common today—since he didn't have three assistants manning telephones in the press box, linked to sideline coaches roaming the sideline—since he didn't have somebody snapping ten-second Polaroid shots of enemy defenses—since he didn't have five or six other assistants making their own personnel changes throughout a game—Rock's grasp of the overall situation had to be total and incisive. Offense and defense. No matter. Down and distance, time, injuries, broken plays, defensive lapses—everything crackled onto his pre-computer wavelength for instant decision. His two assistant coaches would be next to him, ready to offer advice, alert to catch something he might have missed. But he seldom did.

Rockne never ran out with his squad when it bolted through the dressing room door after his pre-game pep talk, the way today's coaches do. Instead of trying to keep up with that rushing tide of green jerseys, he simply trickled after them, as it were, with his short, jerky-quick steps, wrapped in his long, wide-lapeled topcoat, his roundish, inelegant fedora plopped squarely on his balding head, looking more like a detective sergeant than a coach. All the more so when he lit up one of his favorite ten-cent cigars.

A student manager unfolds a canvas camp chair (often described by others as a "director's chair") in front of the Notre Dame bench. This is where Rock will spend much of the game, except for brief periods when he leaps to his feet in frustration or anger, or when he wants to bawl out something to an official.

He has already gone into a brief huddle with the starting team, clapping a shoulder here, a butt there, as he snaps off final instructions or warnings.

Once the game starts, only his assistant coaches and his second- and third-string quarterbacks are at arm's length. In front of him, but not underfoot, sits a student manager nursing a stack of play charts and a large pad.

"Once the game started," said Harry Stuhldreher, his Four Horsemen quarterback, "Rock seemed to be calm enough, but what he was, was the eye of the well-known hurricane. The most visible thing about him was that damned cigar. He'd twirl it between his thumb and index finger. Often it'd go out and he wouldn't know it. He'd draw on it anyway. And then there was his constant chatter. A running comment, not loud, sometimes barely audible, but the student manager sitting at his feet had to be ready, because Rock wanted certain comments to be jotted down so he could refer to them later."

For those within hearing distance, Rock's running commentary was as much a show as the action on the field. Rockne was never a man who could make an observation in a neutral, documentary tone. Whatever he said was tinged with emotion—sarcasm, mock surprise, anger, disappointment:

"There's Miller losing the rhythm on the shift . . . Maybe we ought to buy him a few dance lessons . . ."

"What'd that official call there? Interference? He said it was *interference?* Don't listen to him, Smith. Ask him if he's been to his eye doctor lately, but don't let him hear you . . . Great block Tony, but you hit the wrong man . . ."

"Good end play there . . . good drifting wide with the runner . . . Okay, NOW! Now you've got him . . . NAIL HIM . . . Ah, son, you waited a tenth of a second too long and you hit him too low . . . slipped away from you, didn't he . . . Attaboy, Jimmy, that's backing up . . ."

"All right, let's lay back, now . . . *Lay back, lay back,* this is where they like to pass . . . Probably the long one . . ." And when it turned out to be a run: "Well, they had their chance . . . He coulda been a hero with the right play . . . Had us set up for it . . . We'll have to go over that one between the halves . . ."

"They'll have to punt now . . . And let's not just be *thinking* about a good rush . . . no time to *think* about rushing . . . THAT'S what the kind of rush I like to see, Tommy . . . Almost got it, didn't you . . . If you hadn't eaten that extra muffin last night, you'd have gotten it . . ."

"Weak-side spinner coming up, Frankie . . . This is how we talked about it all week . . . You're calling it that way, I hope . . . Well, okay, I like the reverse, too . . . Success always makes you look smart, Frank . . ."

Jimmy Crowley once said, "Just knowing Rock was there on the sidelines was inspirational enough. The opposition might have us down on our own 5-yard line. Suddenly, there would be Rock standing there, hands on hips, at a point just opposite the line of scrimmage. Those were the days when a coach wasn't limited to an area of the sideline. The team would look up, see Rock standing there. Then they'd dig in and hold. It happened again and again."

"Before a game started," said Frank Carideo, "we always knew Rock's game plan, his tactics, which always got us through. At a final skull session the quarterbacks were given a quota of plays to be used, and no others were permitted without permission from Rock himself. Any change in tactics during a game would be decided at half-time, or brought in by a sub. In one opening game we used only four different plays.

Harry Stuhldreher once said he was sure Rockne was the first coach to set up play-action passing and other deceptions so that the quarterback could hide the ball from the defense for that vital extra second when he was throwing. This allowed the Irish to devise more intricate pass patterns. "The fans loved it," said Stuhldreher, "and often other coaches wanted to cut their throats when they saw our stuff work."

A case could be made for Rockne executing more perfect plays than any coach of his time—or afterwards. Often as many as six defenders had to be taken out of the play completely in order for the play to work, and it was common to see all six flat on the turf while Irish backs were scoring.

And watching it, with complete satisfaction almost bordering on a smirk, Knute Rockne would slap a rolled-up program against his thigh or puff a cloud of cigar smoke skyward to punctuate the perfection he'd just witnessed.

He was once quoted as saying that a perfectly executed play would result in a touchdown every time. When asked to confirm the quote, he denied it. But he did aim for a kind of perfection that would bring big gains often.

Rock's could be as caustic during a game as he was in practice. The dart seldom failed to reach its mark. In a game against Northwestern, Rip Miller was having trouble blocking a big Wildcat lineman and generally having a bad day. Rock sent in a sub for him.

"I sat there on the bench for a few minutes," Miller recalled, "knowing it was only a matter of time before he said something. Sure enough, he finally sauntered past me and, without even looking at me, said: 'Anytime you're ready to take off your tuxedo and silk hat, Rip, we'll consider putting you back in the game.'

"Well, hell, I knew exactly what he meant. Rock could do things to you, or for you, with a word, a phrase or sometimes just a look. He could give you mental poise or inspirational drive, whichever he thought you needed most at that moment in the game."

Rock's treatment was sometimes more than just merely caustic. A highly regarded sophomore halfback was hot-dogging it early in a game and clearly revealing he liked to run with the ball but was lax in blocking for somebody else. Rock yanked him after one such episode. The boy came to the sideline furious. The game was being played near his hometown.

"You've humiliated me in front of my friends," he snapped, adding irrationally, "For two cents I'd turn in my suit."

Rock just stared out at the action on the field, rolling his big black cigar in his mouth. "I'll be glad to supply the two cents," he said calmly. "Do you want to take it off right here or in the locker room?"

By his senior year he was one of Rock's best backs.

Rock also had some strait-laced ideas of sportsmanship, in a day when the word was freighted with sincerity and a coach could use it without raising a bored eyebrow in the back row. "One man practicing sportsmanship," he would say, "is far better than a hundred teaching it."

Rock required enthusiasm and hard hitting, but he abhorred deliberate rough play and would yank a kid at the first sign of it. Once a Notre Dame halfback on defense piled into an opposing ball carrier near the Irish sideline and applied an extra ounce of deterrent with his fist. Out came the halfback. He was a sophomore and perhaps hadn't yet absorbed Rock's full philosophy. He couldn't figure out why he'd been taken from the game and at least expected a pat on the back for a hard tackle. But he had the temerity to ask Rock why he'd been yanked.

"That tackle," Rock growled, "could have cost us fifteen."

"Aw, Rock," the kid said breezily, "the ref didn't see it."

"But I *did,*" Rockne snapped, "and that's enough for me. If I see it again, it'll cost you your suit!"

Until very late in his career, Rockne, the frustrated medico, didn't even have a doctor along on road games. He was his own doctor, trainer, and bruise and tape artist. In his earlier days he didn't even want a trainer because he thought his players would develop all sorts of imaginary ills.

Jimmy Crowley remembers Rock preparing his own soaking solution and spending an hour the morning of a game soaking and ministering to Crowley's bad wrist. George Vergara, a crack end in the Four Horsemen era, and later mayor of New Rochelle, New York, recalls Rock doing the taping, himself, on a strained knee or ankle. "We knew he knew his stuff," said Vergara. "We had no doubts and we trusted him completely."

Then, along about 1924, a wiry little kid of about 125 pounds cracked up his leg badly trying to play football for Rock. Although he couldn't play again, the kid, Eugene Young, asked Rock to take him on as a "rubber." "Well," said Rock, "maybe you can do us some good inside the dressing room." He arranged for a small scholarship for the boy and gave him the nickname "Scrap-Iron."

"We had two rough pine tables, varnished and scarred," said Young, who remained as Notre Dame's trainer for many years. "There were a couple of shelves of liniments that Rock concocted himself, and some tape and bandages and some iodine. No heat lamps, no whirlpool baths, no diathermy. Just Rock and me. He taught me; I read some medical books he gave me, and we kept the guys together and ready for action.

"The man was a marvel at understanding athletic injuries and what the doctors called 'etiology' and 'kinesiology,' which are the study of the causes of disease and injuries and the study of movement of the joints and muscles. He could manipulate a knee joint and tell if there was a ligament or cartilage tear. He could examine a rib and tell if it was broken or cracked. Naturally, if he ever suspected surgery or radical treatment was required for anything, he got the boy to a hospital, quick.

"I remember one day the Mayo Clinic sent down one of their orthopedists—a new man who knew very little about Knute Rockne, but who was told to talk to Rock on the subject of athletic injury. He spent two hours with Rock—I was there, too—and when he was through, Rock asked me to conduct the doc on a tour of the campus. We'd no sooner stepped out the door when the Mayo doc said: 'What a remarkable clinician, what a complete grasp of his field.'

"And then he said: 'What medical school did he attend before he became a football coach?'

"When I told him Rock had never set foot inside the doors of a medical school, he stopped dead in his tracks, speechless. Couldn't believe it."

Getting ready for a road trip, Rock left nothing to chance. "He supervised everything," Don Miller recalls. "He even supervised our packing, regulars as well as subs. He personally inspected everybody's gear before it went into the trunks and was always going around muttering, 'I just know somebody's going to forget something. It could cost us a game.' He even packed our medical supplies, tapes and bandages, himself."

He also had some rather negative notions about the quality of drinking water found in such noncivilized communities as New York, Baltimore, Los Angeles, Atlanta, Pittsburgh and wherever the autumnal tourism took him. "Can't trust it," he'd grumble. "Could cost us a game." And his student managers would jug up one hundred fifty gallons of South Bend *aqua pura,* for drinking purposes only.

"What about our showers, Rock?" Harry Stuhldreher once inquired with a grin.

"It only hits your skin, son," Rock quickly replied, "and that Dutch hide of yours is thick enough to repel anything Satan can come up with."

As methodical and rational as Rockne was, he could also be superstitious. He took his flute with him on every road game as a good-luck piece. In order for the charm to work, he'd tootle it for a couple minutes on the train or in his hotel room. Arriving at the South Bend railroad station for one departure, he discovered he'd left his flute at home. He rushed a student manager into a cab with instructions to go back for it. With a straight face, one of Rock's aides asked the stationmaster to be prepared to hold the train for five minutes, if necessary. "Coach Rockne has forgotten a very valuable piece of equipment," he said.

Once, when he tried to counteract a bit of superstition, Rockne succeeded only in strengthening it. When no member of his team consented to wear jersey No. 13, Rock wore the number to practice every day for weeks. Finally a committee of players came to him pleading that he abandon the jersey. Grudgingly, he did. The Irish lost their next game—whether because he had worn the number or because he had given it up, no one ever figured out.

A Notre Dame road trip was more of a carnival, an Event, than a grim battle campaign. In New York City, before the Army game, the most glittering date on the Sports Social calendar, after it was shifted there from the secluded plains up the Hudson, the press and newsreel cameramen descended on the Irish contingent in waves. At first Rockne put up his entourage at the old Vanderbilt Hotel not far from Grand Central Station—which merely seemed to become an extension of that famed depot, with the press, gawkers, gamblers and local coaches piling onto the scene. After a couple years of that, Rockne realized privacy for himself and team was impossible and shifted his headquarters to the posh suburban Westchester Country Club, where he drilled his team on the adjacent polo field.

Sometimes he was welcomed on the road with a reverse twist. Once, Rock and his team arrived late at Indiana. The stands were already packed. His team hurried through the gate, but Rockne, bustling up behind them, was stopped by an attendant.

"Ticket, please," the gatekeeper demanded coldly.

Rock glared at him. "I'm Knute Rockne. That was my team that just went through there. Do you mind if I join them?"

The official, stony-faced, said, "If you have no ticket, you'll have to see Pat Page, our coach."

"What's the matter!" Rock roared. "Wasn't he expecting us?"

Only then did Rock notice the gatekeeper was trying to suppress a huge grin. "Okay," he growled. "You can tell Mister Page he made his point. We'll be on time from now on."

Rockne even paid attention to the other team's business when he was on the road. Arriving in Lincoln, Nebraska, on Friday, October 17, 1919, to play the Nebraska Cornhuskers the following day, he noted the playing field was soggy from a heavy rain the day before. The Nebraska maintenance men had spread a thin layer of wood shavings and chips on the field to provide more solid footing. So they said.

Rock examined the field. He looked up at the sky. Then he decided the field would be in better shape the next day if the sun's rays were allowed to work on it.

He summoned two of his student managers and handed them $25. "Get down to a hardware store," he ordered, "and buy forty brooms."

Within a few minutes, Nebraska students and officials stared, silent and slack-jawed, as Rock, his assistants and thirty-five varsity football players spent two hours sweeping the wood shavings off one hundred yards of football turf. The sun did its job. The next day the Irish beat the Cornhuskers, 14–9, in the key victory in Rock's first unbeaten season.

The minute Rock would get to town with his team, everyone who was anyone would use his influence or position in jockeying for scarce tickets. To Rock it was a nuisance, but it was part of the price he had to pay for his success.

"I remember coming into Pittsburgh," said Scrap-Iron Young. "An aide of a big steel executive approached me in the lobby and said he needed four tickets and money was no object. I went to Rock but I told him we had none left.

"Rock sighed and pulled four tickets from his pocket. 'Here, he's an important fella. But he's gotta pay for them.'

"I came back from the hotel lobby a few minutes later and stood there in front of Rock with a fistful of money. He stared at the money for a moment and then said quietly: 'Just give me twenty dollars for the face value of the four tickets.'

"It was my turn to stare. 'You mean I can keep the other three hundred and eighty?' I said.

" 'As long as you can convince me you didn't use a gun,' he said. He shook his head. 'My God—four hundred dollars for four football tickets. What's this world coming to?' "

13

A Very Personal Day

When word got around about Rock's baptism, some of his players came to him and said they'd like to be at the services. Rock was touched but he shook his head. "I appreciate your interest," he told them, "and I know you mean to honor me with your presence, but this is a deeply personal matter and I don't want to feel I'm some sort of star at a show."

Men driven in pursuit of careers—men consumed by the need to make it to the top, the perfectionists, the compulsively demanding ones, the men who tolerate no competition for their time in the rat race to success—are too often blind to their own needs or those of people who depend on them.

Knute Kenneth Rockne could never have been that kind of man. No matter what pinnacle of success he might climb, there was no way he could short-change his family, friends or his human obligations to his players.

Although Rockne was never paid more than $12,000 a year at Notre Dame, it was fairly comfortable money in those days, and as he became famous he supplemented his coaching income with his syndicated writing, his speaking engagements and his coaching school appearances.

The family lived first in a small house on St. Vincent's Street, with three bedrooms and a single bathroom, and later in a slightly larger English Tudor house on Wayne Street, with four bedrooms, a den and two baths.

His daughter, Mary Jean Kochendorfer, now married to an oilman in Oklahoma, remembers very well the famous and peripatetic father of her childhood:

"He was certainly the most active father on the block," she says. "He was an avid gardener and he'd spend an hour before going to his office, or after getting home from spring football practice, planting, cultivating and tending his good-sized backyard plot. He won prizes for his tomatoes, beans and cauliflower at the County Fair and he was as proud of those blue ribbons as he was of his All-America football players.

"In some ways, though, he wasn't so handy. I remember Mother kept badgering him to put up the screen door when summer came, and finally he did. When he stepped back in triumph, he saw he'd hung it upside down and inside out. He just flung away his tools and walked off, shouting to Mother to call in a handyman.

"He was constantly telling us stories—especially if one of us was sick. He often played his flute for us and we wouldn't let him stop.

"He'd take the entire family to the movies—all six of us—and would wind up holding the sleeping Jackie in his lap. Afterwards, he'd recite nursery rhymes to us before we'd fall asleep. One of his favorites wasn't exactly a nursery rhyme but we loved it. It went like this:

> *There is an old boarding house,*
> *Far, far away,*
> *Where they serve ham and eggs*
> *Three times a day.*
> *Woe, woe, the boarders yell,*
> *When they hear the dinner bell,*
> *For they know the eggs will smell,*
> *Far, far away.*

"In the evening during the off-season," Bonnie Rockne once recalled, "he'd read to the kids for an hour, and then he'd disapear into his den for more reading of his own. He loved biography, history, science, philosophy, and detective mysteries. He had this strange trick of keeping three books going at once: a detective thriller, a biography and something else. He'd read a certain number of pages of each and could pick up the thread of each book wherever he left off."

Rock was also particularly fond of his giant German shepherd named Noxie. The dog would follow him from room to room. In 1928, when Rock was seriously ill, Noxie would greet visitors at the front door and escort them upstairs to Rock's bedroom. When they left, Noxie would escort them downstairs again, then return to Rock's bedside.

Rockne often spoke to his family on the radio when his success made him a star attraction on the new medium. It was usual for him to preface his speech or his first words on a show with: "Hello, Bonnie and all the children . . ." The morning of a road game he'd always telephone them before going to the stadium. During the summer months, when he began getting involved with coaching schools, he'd often pile Bonnie and the kids into the car and take them with him if it weren't more than a few hundred miles away.

If it could be said that Rock had a favorite among the children it might have been Mary Jean, the lone girl. In the late 1920's, when he signed his first movie contract, Rock took the money and bought Mary Jean a baby grand piano.

"Once," recalls Mary Jean, who would have been nine or ten at the time, "he said he was going to bring me something for my neck. Naturally, it would be a necklace. When he came home, he handed me a small package with a smile. I opened it—and there was the 'necklace.' A bar of soap! I got the message."

His sons, Billy and Knute Jr., were constant visitors to the practice field, and Rock often had to yell at his players to stop tossing a football with his kids and get back to work. But it was his youngest son, Jackie, who brought out the most visible display of paternal emotion regarding any of his children.

Just before one game, Jackie started to choke on a peanut that had stuck in his throat. Frantically, Bonnie Rockne tried to dislodge it and finally had to rush him to a hospital, where it was removed in the emergency room. Rockne was not told of the incident until after the game. He grew white and seemed to have trouble controlling his voice. Finally, openly upset that his aides had kept the news from him, he said in a strained voice: "Thank you, but don't ever hold news like that from me again. I'll pass up a football game for my son anytime."

Even when towering fame came to him, Rockne remained a highly visible neighbor on Wayne Street and maintained strong relationships with people not connected with football or the university. He joined the Elks Club and was a faithful member of their bowling team. Although he was a good athlete, he could never raise his average close to 200 and it bothered him. It was the same way in golf, which he began to take up in the mid 1920's. Turned out in tan, tweed knickers, a snazzy sweater and cap, Rock flailed away in the high 90's and cursed the little white ball with the best of them.

Most of the time, however, Knute Rockne was a terrible dresser. His contemporay, Heywood Broun, the writer, was described as looking like an unmade bed. Knute might have resembled the inside of a laundry bag—with the laundry in it.

His shirt collars were invariably too big. The knot of his tie was seldom where it belonged. His suits were too loose-fitting and never hung right. The pants were always rumpled, a stranger to the pressing machine. He wore those terrible, roundish, misshapen fedora hats, which only accented his pudgy potato face. And in the middle of that face, nearly always, was a big fat cigar, the blacker the better.

For the millions of fans who had wondered what Knute Rockne could do for an encore after his Four Horsemen spectacular, the answer was laid out for all to witness. Coaching colleagues, fans and even critics (who had insisted his success was built on a fortuitous assemblage of material) now agreed that the Norwegian immigrant with the acid-tinged tongue was football's most luminous image.

But there was just enough toe-stubbing on his part—the occasional loss—which kept him in perspective as mere mortal, and there was as much fan interest in wondering whether Notre Dame *could* lose as in the Irish march of victories.

There were no potential "Horsemen" or "Mules" pawing the turf of Cartier Field in the next few years, and there were a couple of seasons that turned out to be the gray areas of Rock's career. A hundred other coaches, a hundred other alumni associations, would have been delighted with the same results, but the home-grown Irish fans and Rock's burgeoning national constituency had become heady with success.

There would be two solid defeats by Army and Nebraska in 1925, the Cadets ripping the Irish, 27–20. But as the season progressed, it was clear that things were changing for Rockne. He was becoming a national figure. And closer to home, his job with Notre Dame was changing, too.

He still operated from a small second floor-office in the rear of the Main Building, which reared its Golden Dome high above the Notre Dame campus. His view from two small windows overlooked the university bakery. The office, about twelve by twelve feet, uncarpeted, without a single furnishing or fitting that couldn't be bought at Sears, Roebuck, or even a Salvation Army second-hand shop, could have been called spartan, or spare, if you wanted to be charitable.

It was never locked. Its main feature was a battered, dark oak roll-top desk dating back to . . . the McKinley era? On it was the standard black stand-up telephone, nested in a cheerfully spreading pile of correspondence (opened and unopened), hand-scrawled memos, messages, bills and an errant laundry slip or two.

Against the opposite wall was a varnished but scarred wooden table, heaped with out-of-town newspapers, football posters, a few books and other oddments, all in an unorganized mess that would have defeated anyone who had to pick out something needed on the spot. Anyone, that is, except the man who presided over the office.

Knute Rockne was truly a one-man band, and he was just as talented and just as interested in one instrument as in another. At age thirty in 1918—and for many years thereafter—he was varsity football coach, track coach, athletic director, intramural supervisor, athletic business manager, and director of ticket sales, in which he handled tickets for all games in all sports and took care of the advanced sale. (And still teaching chemistry, don't forget!)

In the early years he worked without a secretary. If the phone rang, he answered it. If he wanted to make a call, he placed the number himself. When he wanted to write a letter, he either dashed it off longhand or, on rare occasion, pecked it out on a battered typewriter. He never bothered with carbon copies.

Interspersed with the incredible volume of official Notre Dame business was the personal mail he received—all of which he answered. It might be three weeks later but anyone who wrote to Rockne got an answer.

Often enough he would return to his office late at night and hand-scrawl an answer if it didn't need more than a paragraph. For instance, he received the following from a thirteen-year-old:

> Dear Knute:
> I'm writing to you to ask if you'll give us permission to name ourselves the "Rockne Colts." If it's okay with you, please write to me. We are pretty husky and snappy and would like to have a capable, honorable man and coach to play for. If you would suggest a better name I'd like to have it; also send some plays and hints. Please answer as soon as possible.

Rockne wrote: "Sure thing! Go ahead! Here are two good plays." Usually he signed his letters "K. K. Rockne." Once in a while he merely scrawled his surname. "You would look at that name and signature," a sportswriter said, "and you got an almost physical impact from it. Damnedest feeling I ever had. I doubt if Calvin Coolidge's name on a letter to me would have had the same effect."

A day in Rockne's office was a study in informality. Since he had no secretary to make appointments, he seldom bothered with such amenities. People just dropped in: visiting coaches, South Bend aldermen, sportswriters, football players, chemistry students, track men, the director of the latest student theatrical—and, once in a while, a timid emissary from Father Cavanaugh's office who just wanted to check on an administrative budgetary problem (Rock never paid much attention to these things).

Because he was also the ticket director, Rock, according to Francis Wallace, his student publicity man at the time, despite the fact that he never locked his office door, often kept a roll of bills in his desk drawer for weeks and even months, usually from the sale of tickets he often dispensed right out of his office or from collections he made for tickets sold downtown at hotel cigar counters.

If there was something he wanted to look up, he went to a closet where all the Notre Dame athletic archives and business records were kept in a pack rat's nest of disarray, and fished around until he found it.

He didn't believe in contracts. Tug Wilson, athletic director at Northwestern in the mid-1920's and later Big Ten Commissioner, recalls that the phone would ring and it would be Rock.

"He'd say how about a game next fall, second Saturday in October, or whenever, and I'd say, 'Sure, Rock,' and he'd say, 'I'll write you a letter to confirm,' but there was never a contract. He knew what part of the gate we'd give him, and we knew he'd show up for the game, and it was all very informal."

Wilson also remembered Rockne as a track coach, as curious and dynamic as he was on the football field. Rock almost didn't get the chance to mature as a coach of any kind, thanks to Wilson.

"The incident occurred in the spring of 1919, my junior year at Illinois," Wilson recalled, laughing and shaking his head. "Notre Dame had come down for a track meet—and I was in the stands, with some of my fraternity brothers. I had a cast on my left leg from an operation for a football knee injury.

"The javelin was a rather new event in American track and field, and out there on the turf the Notre Dame javelin throwers were struggling to hit 130 feet, which was pretty poor.

"I turned to my buddies and said: 'I can toss that thing farther than they can, even with this cast on.' I was a pretty good athlete but naturally my buddies started jeering and putting the needle into me. Next thing I knew they were actually egging me on. Somebody pointed to a javelin lying on the ground at the foul board, right out in front of us. 'There it is—why don't you try it?' he said.

" 'I'd better not,' I said, gesturing downfield where two or three

meet officials and coaches were standing. 'I might hit somebody.'
They cracked up at that and said I wouldn't get halfway there.

"Well, that was too much of a challenge, so I walked over,
picked up the javelin, hefted it a couple of times, took a couple
short hops on my gimpy leg, cast and all, and let fly. Just as I did
so, I recognized two of the men downfield even though their backs
were turned. They were Harry Gill, the Illinois track coach, and
Knute Rockne, the Notre Dame coach. I froze in horror because
I saw the javelin was going to reach them.

"Just then, they both turned around. As Rockne turned, that
steel-tipped javelin whizzed right by, not more than six inches from
his throat. He didn't even have time to react. He just stared upfield
at me, still standing there, still frozen.

"Gill rushed at me madly, his arms flailing, screaming at my
stupidity. Rockne was just a step behind him, but his approach was
much different. Instead of being furious, he grabbed me by the arm,
excitedly. 'Hey, son,' he said, 'how did you throw that thing? I
mean, just what did you do with it? Can you show me?'

"I must have done something right, because the following year
I made the U.S. Olympic team—and I guess Rock was entitled to
an assist on that."

As a teacher Rockne was superb. He was in complete command
not only of his subject but in his classroom presence and his students. He would pace back and forth before the blackboard, rolling
a piece of chalk between his two hands, his students' attention
caught by his voice, his eyes, his dynamic gestures. His lectures
were spiced with wit and charm, so much so that his classes became
so popular they attracted non-chemistry students who frequently
dropped by just to enjoy his style.

"There was never a boring moment in his classes," said Roger
Kiley. "Rolling that chalk between his fingers, jabbing a finger at
a formula on the board, coaxing the perception out of us, making
the merest detail sound important—we knew it wasn't an act. The
man knew how to reach a boy's mind and the boy would react
positively."

One day he was demonstrating an element in an experiment he

was conducting when he glanced over at a student who looked a bit bewildered. He jabbed a finger toward the pupil and shouted: "Did you get that? Like heck you did! I can tell! It bounced right off your dome!" The class broke up in gales of laughter. Suddenly Rock caught himself and the blush rose all the way to his balding scalp as broad smiles broke out all over the room. In his pedagogic eagerness he'd completely forgotten that he was working with a class of teaching nuns in a summer school course.

Few students flunked Rock's chemistry courses. They were simply challenged too deeply not to make it. Better to succeed than risk Rock's scorn and sarcasm. "He had us on our mental toes all the time," said Kiley. "Just as he had us that way on the football field."

No football player, however, enrolled in a Rockne chemistry class with the idea of staking out a snap course for himself. "You run your own interference here," he once warned a player, "and if you get sloppy you're out of the game—for good."

He not only taught two classes a day but handled two afternoon labs a week. Many was the time he was late for football practice because a shaky but sincere student needed some extra help after class. Rock felt he could no sooner abandon the boy than he could withhold extra blocking practice from a lineman who needed it.

Finally, toward the middle of the decade, President Walsh realized there simply was too much for Rockne to do. Football had made Notre Dame nationally known and the sport demanded all or most of Rockne's time. Reluctantly, he gave up coaching the track team—and, even more reluctantly, Father Nieuwland accepted Rock's resignation as a chemistry teacher.

Then two things happened that had his close friends kidding him about going big-time. Rock was able to appoint a young man named Arthur Hailey as business manager for routine work, and he also got a secretary. Up until then, the few secretaries employed by Notre Dame were either seminarians or part-time students. There wasn't a female secretary on the grounds.

Leave it to Rockne to shatter precedent. He hired the first female secretary ever seen at Notre Dame, a young, charming local girl named Ruth Faulkner who could type and take dictation, and within a matter of weeks Knute Rockne became an organized man.

"But not too organized," said Robert Cahill, the current business manager who goes back almost a half-century in the Irish athletic department. "Some farmer fan gave Rock a bushel of potatoes," Cahill recalled, "and put them in the trunk of Rock's car. Two months later I asked him what the awful smell was. He couldn't figure it out until he opened the trunk. He'd completely forgotten the potatoes, and they were on their way to becoming a mess of raw alcohol mash."

Just a year after Rockne's great success with the Horsemen crowd, word filtered out of South Bend that he was making news of equally dramatic—and more personal—nature. It was learned that Rockne, the Norwegian-born Lutheran, with his family rooted for generations in that religion, was about to be converted to Catholicism. He had made no previous announcement of his plans. It was something he had discussed only with his wife.

It had been impossible, of course, for Rockne not to have been a close observer of the religion which surrounded him at Notre Dame. Bonnie was Catholic, and their four children were being reared in that faith, but never did she pressure him to convert. Shortly after they'd been married, Rock had impulsively told Bonnie that it might be a good idea if he'd accept the Catholic faith, too. But Bonnie, thrilled though she was, suggested that he wait a while.

It didn't happen right away. There were the constants in his life: the coaching, the classroom teaching, the interminable duties as athletic director. But the idea, though tucked away in a distant priority system, apparently was never far from mind.

Then one day in the spring of 1925 Rock decided. "I'm going to do it," he told Bonnie. "Right away, before I get sidetracked. It's right now."

It was typical of Knute Rockne that he would look over the roster of priests at Notre Dame and pick one who would empathize with him, someone who would understand him in many different ways. He picked lean, vigorous Father Vincent Mooney, who had played football and baseball at Notre Dame.

For several months, at least three nights a week, Rock cleared his desk and his mind of all other considerations and sat down with Father Mooney for a series of spirited and zestful sessions that often found Rock reaching into football for analogy.

Mooney asked him, once, what he thought of the controversey between Fundamentalists and Modernists—a controversey then raging in many parishes throughout the country. Rock was ready: "According to what I've read on the subject, I think both teams are offside and both should be penalized half the distance to the goal."

Mary Jean Kochendorfer recalls how serious her father's original decision had been. "I remember my mother telling me what an intellectual approach my father took to his conversion," she said. "It would have been simple for him to do some of the reading and merely make most of the sessions with Father Mooney. But he never missed a night. He could have accepted everything at face value quite dutifully and with a minimum of extra time spent. After all, he was a terribly busy man."

Mrs. Kochendorfer paused. "But Daddy was too curious and too sensitive for that. Every time Father Mooney got off onto some new bit of religious philosophy, Daddy insisted on doing as much reading as possible on that phase of it. He'd come home with all sorts of big books, even during the football season, and wade into them because he wanted to know all the underlying thoughts and subtleties connected with whatever discussion was lying ahead. Then he'd go to Father Mooney feeling that he was better able to understand the precepts and dogma he was being asked to accept."

Finally, during the 1925 football season, Father Mooney was satisfied that Rock was ready—that, moreover, he was just about the best-prepared convert he'd ever instructed—and he told Rockne that he was setting the baptism for 2:30 P.M., November 20, in the old Log Chapel. Rock's First Communion would follow the next morning.

Rockne registered the dates in his mind and said nothing. If he would have preferred other dates, he gave no indication. If Father Mooney had given it any thought, perhaps the dates would have been different . . .

Word got around. Some of Rock's players came to him and said they'd like to be at the services. Rock was touched but he shook his head. "My wife is the only outsider who's going to be there," he told them. "I appreciate your interest and I know you mean to honor me with your presence, but this is a deeply personal matter and I don't want to feel I'm some sort of star at a show."

Rockne didn't even want his children to be there, or to know about it until he'd had a chance to tell them in his own way.

But on even so solemn an occasion, the impish element in his nature bobbed to the surface. Eying the preparations for the baptism, Rock rubbed his bald pate and quipped: "They won't have to pour much water to reach the skull, will they . . ."

Then he watched as the single candle was lit for the baptism and nodded toward the six candles at the altar. "Aren't those going to be lighted, too?" he inquired of Father Mooney.

The Father smiled and said that only one would be required.

Rock grinned. "You're being a little tight with the wax, aren't you, Father?"

Rockne's decision not to tell his children beforehand, says his daughter, gave rise to a very touching incident. "The way it was told to me," she said, "my father was to make his First Communion at St. Edward's Hall on the campus, the day after his baptism. By coincidence, my brother, Knute Jr., was to make his First Communion there. Seeing his father, my brother naturally thought: 'He's come to see me make my First Communion.'

"It had been arranged by Father Mooney that little Knute would be at the end of the procession which would move toward the altar. Father Mooney had also signaled my father to step in and walk beside his son. It would be a lovely thing. But the instant Daddy fell in alongside him my brother was shocked, and tugged at his father's sleeve.

" 'Daddy,' he said, 'you know you can't come up there with me. Only Catholics can receive communion!'

"My father realized immediately that Knute was entitled to an explanation—and immediately. But, thinking quickly, he brushed aside Knute's warning and whispered: 'Don't worry—Father Mooney will tell you all about it.'

"Then they knelt together at the rail, and when Father Mooney approached, bearing the ciborium, my brother stared at the priest and then back at Daddy. I'm sure Father Mooney caught on right away. He was a quick thinker, too. He bent slightly and whispered: 'It's all right, son. Your father was baptized yesterday.' "

Knute Jr. wasn't the only happy person in South Bend. Father Matthew J. Walsh, then Notre Dame president, was all smiles. Jesse Harper, the man who had first put Notre Dame football on the map, had been a Protestant. Knute Rockne, who had made his team the most preeminent in the land, had also started out as a Protestant. Father Walsh thought things had been brought into proper perspective.

Some of Rock's players, waiting outside St. Edward's, came over to congratulate him, and it was their expression of a feeling of new kinship which most visibly touched him. Deeply, inwardly pleased, his lumpy face broke into broad joy as a couple of big linemen took his hand in theirs.

There would come a moment, however, just a few hours later, when Rock—being typically Rockne—would use the solemn occasion to wonder whether he'd done the right thing. He would put it only as he, and none other, could put it . . .

When Father Mooney had established November 20 for Baptism and the following day for Communion, Rock never let out a peep to Mooney that on Communion day Notre Dame would be playing a very tough Northwestern team just a few hours after the rites, only a couple hundred yards away from where they had been held. He was determined that a football game would in no way be intrusive on his time or thoughts. "If we're not ready that morning," he had growled to his assistant coaches, "we're not going to be any more ready three hours later."

But at half-time Rockne wasn't very pleased with the way things were going on the football field. The Irish trailed, 10–0.

Rock said nothing for the first few minutes in the dressing room. Then, suddenly, scowling darkly, he jammed his fists into his coat pockets. As though reconsidering something, he quickly took his hands out of the pockets and planted his fists on his hips. He glared at his players.

"As you all know by now," he barked, "I received my First Communion this morning . . ." A finger probed the air in the direction of the chapel. "And obviously this is a helluva religion I've gotten myself into! Losing to a bunch of Methodists out there . . ." The finger jabbed toward the field. (Northwestern, of course, was a school founded by Methodists.)

"I don't know if I've made a mistake"—and now the voice began to rise, the typical Rockne blast on the way—"but I do know a lousy, gutless performance when I see it on a football field. You've quit out there—and if you can quit, so can I! I'm through with you. I'm going up in the stands and get as far away from you as I can!"

He stomped out. His players sat stunned. But one of them, fullback Rex Enright, was seen to smile faintly as he looked after his departing coach.

When the Irish took the field, Rock was nowhere in sight on the sideline. He had, indeed, abandoned them for a seat in the stands.

Rex Enright led a furious Irish charge in the third and fourth quarters. Behind fierce blocking he ripped the Wildcat line to pieces, twice blasting across for touchdowns and a 13–10 victory.

"Great game, great game!" Rock bubbled later in the dressing room, clapping Enright on the back. "It was nice for a good Presbyterian like you, Rex, to save the new Catholic's ball game from those Methodists."

Because of the unremitting interest in his conversion, however, Rockne felt that sooner or later he was going to have to make some sort of public statement about his decision. He was speaking at a businessman's convention when he steered his talk around to the subject almost without his audience being aware he was getting into it. He described it this way:

"I was always impressed by the thought of my players receiving Communion every morning, but I'd begun to realize how incongruous it must have appeared when we arrived in another city for a game and the public saw my boys rushing off to church the moment they got off the train while the coach rode to the hotel and took his ease.

"One night in the East before a big game I was nervous and worrying about the game the next day and was unable to sleep. I tossed about in bed and finally decided to get up, get dressed and sit downstairs. About five-thirty in the morning, while pacing the lobby, I unexpectedly ran into two of my players hurrying out.

"I asked where they were going at that hour—although I had a good idea. Within the next few minutes a dozen more hurried out and I suddenly decided to go with them. They didn't realize it but these youngsters were making a powerful impression on me with their devotion, and when I saw all of them walking up to the Communion rail, and realized the hours of sleep they'd sacrificed, I understood for the first time what a powerful ally their religion was to them in their work on the football field . . ."

Rockne's conversion, in a country still largely suspicious of Catholicism, created much comment—and respect. Within a matter of weeks, however, Rock would have another kind of "conversion," this one destined to bring him intense embarrassment.

14

Building the Program

> *Notre Dame was often accused of excessive zeal in recruiting players, and the charge irritated Rockne tremendously, especially when it was suggested that parish priests in communities across the land were putting pressure on parents to send their athlete sons to Notre Dame. "If I ever heard of any evidence," Rock once growled, "I'd be the first to phone that priest and tell him to get busy with the sinners in his flock and leave the innocents alone."*

Knute Rockne was well aware that the job he faced at Notre Dame was not going to be easily accomplished. Tradition, earlier national acclaim, and financial muscle were not his to harness in his drive toward the top. He wanted to win games—but he also wanted to win the right games. Building a schedule and a continuing, successful program was more easily desired than done.

Very early in his career Rock had found it tough to get games with Big Ten teams. He'd attend all the Conference meetings but they didn't think Notre Dame was well enough known to fit him into their schedules. The Irish were too tough to be an early-season breather but not good enough to supply any prestige in beating them.

Soon, Big Ten sentiments changed markedly. The Irish were succeeding so dramatically that not more than a couple Big Ten teams would be willing to play them each season. But money talked. And as the Irish drawing power increased, they became a more attractive opponent. To get spots on Big Ten schedules Rock agreed to abide by their eligibility and procedural rules, and more than one Conference athletic director admitted that Rock was more scrupulous in observing them than many of the brothers in the lodge.

He'd always wanted to schedule games with Michigan but never could land them. Yost, at Michigan, who for years had considered himself the paragon of all Midwestern coaches, plainly jealous of Rock's success, always thought that Notre Dame was a sort of outlaw football factory—so patently untrue—and refused to meet the Irish. And there was at least one Big Ten athletic director who was anti-Catholic and simply wouldn't consider a series.

Other Big Ten teams didn't mind playing him but always went through a tizzy of juggling games so they could schedule the Irish late in the season because they didn't want a discouraging early-season loss.

"And another thing," Tug Wilson said wryly. "Once scheduled, we had a dread of playing Rock right after one of his rare defeats. A situation like that was just short of murder. You know, only once in his entire career did Rock ever lose two in a row."

There was another situation where Rockne was apparently as reluctant to schedule a game as the opponent. His opposite number was Bob Zuppke, of Illinois, and the only time their teams had played was in both coaches' absence at Taylorville.

Once Walter Eckersall, the sportswriter and football official, bumped into Zup at the Auditorium Hotel during a Big Ten schedule meeting.

"Look," said Eckie, "Illinois and Notre Dame have never met in football. Why don't you get on Rock's schedule for next fall?"

"Why don't you ask Rock about it," Zuppke suggested.

So Eckie collared Rockne and said Zup wanted a game. A minute later Rock and Eckersall bumped squarely into the little Illinois coach.

"Oh, hello, Zup," Rock began. "I, uh, I hear you want a game. I have a date or two open."

Zuppke raised a finger and, straight-faced, said, "Yeah, Rock. Wait right here. I'll check it out with George Huff."

Huff was the Illinois athletic director.

As Zup hastily shoved off, Rock turned to Eckersall. "Be back in a minute," he said. "I have to make a phone call."

As Eckersall told of it later, with a broad grin: "Nothing, of course, came of it. Neither one ever came back."

Rock did have his scheduling successes, however.

He always had a special relationship with Army. He once confided that Notre Dame's rise to national recognition could be traced, in great part, to the series with the Cadets—beginning with the seminal game on the Plains in 1913. Then he took a truly giant step in the early 1920's when he convinced West Point officials that the Notre Dame–Army game had outgrown the remote facilities up the Hudson.

"Let's play in New York City," said the astute Rockne, knowing how much razzmatazz the press would make of it.

It made sense to Army, too, with all that extra loot in the offing. They set it up at the Polo Grounds, home field of the New York baseball Giants. (Once it was shifted to Ebbets Field in Brooklyn because of a World Series conflict.) Then it became a fixture in Yankee Stadium. The game became the biggest annual sporting event in New York. Rock was right about the razzmatazz. In 1923 the performance of the Four Horsemen there made both Notre Dame and Knute Rockne national celebrities.

A year later Rockne scored the biggest coup in his gaudy national schedule policy but it took some roguish manipulation by an outsider to swing it. Harry Grayson, the colorful Scripps-Howard writer, working on the Coast at the time, took the credit.

"Rock had known Howard Jones, the new USC coach, from Jones's Iowa days," said Grayson. Jones's Iowa team had whipped Rock in that great upset in 1921. And ironically, Jones had been hired at USC on Rock's recommendation.

"Well, USC was small-time in the early 1920's. Until they hired Jones they were going nowhere. The minute Jones reported in January 1925 I went to him and said: 'You're not going to be considered big-time until you play someone who means something. The best way you can make a quick impact is to schedule Notre Dame, even if you're not ready for them. You can build it into a great intersectional series.

" 'I don't think Rock would give me a game,' Jones said.

" 'You know what I think?' I said to Jones. 'I think you're afraid to play him!'

" 'I've never been afraid of anyone in my life,' Jones snarled.

"I just smiled and let it go at that. Then I phoned Rockne, whom I'd met a few times. 'Rock,' I said, 'why don't you really widen your schedule and play somebody here on the Coast? How about USC? Give you a helluva intersectional trip, too.

" 'Nah,' said Rock. 'They don't mean anything yet.'

" 'Neither did Iowa when Howard Jones beat you then,' I shot back. 'What's the matter, Rock? You afraid of him?'

" 'Who, me?' Rock roared. 'I've never been afraid of anyone in my life!'

" 'Good,' I said. 'I've gotten very close to Jones, and I'll arrange it.'

"And that's how it happened. Turned out to be the greatest intersectional game in football."

Most of Rockne's big annual games were away from home, however, and with good reason. Rock was always embarrassed at coaches' conventions when he faced the gentle barbs of colleagues who kept asking when he'd be getting out of the antediluvian Cartier Field. True, its rickety stands had been enlarged to hold 20,000, but that was minor league stuff compared to the monuments built at Illinois, Ohio State, California, Stanford, Michigan and elsewhere. He'd been pleading for action with Father Walsh. He'd even been promised an eventual stadium during the heyday of the Four Horsemen. But the administration kept telling him of priorities for classrooms, laboratories, dormitories and other facilities—all of which were able to tap football receipts which went into the general college fund.

Sometimes it was all Rock could do to keep his bitterness from surfacing.

"How do you think I feel," he complained in a rage to his Bonnie, "presenting a first-rate production in a third-rate setting?"

She put his metaphor into proper, if only temporary perspective:

"As long as the critics keep telling you it's the best production in the country," she said, "that's the important thing. Besides, remember where you are. This is Notre Dame, and I'm afraid they'll always have a way of putting first things first. But it'll come, I'm sure . . ."

From the time Rockne arrived, athletics at Notre Dame had been a penny-pinching operation. Without the help of larger income from a bigger stadium, Rock was left to his own devices. He was always hustling the buck. Immediately following World War I he made a personal appeal to businessmen of South Bend:

Mr. Frank Bilinski,
227 Laurel,
South Bend, Indiana.

Dear Friend:
A selected list of representative citizens of South Bend has been prepared, a list of live men who will promote any plan to boost South Bend. Your name is on the list.

The Notre Dame football team travels from coast to coast and they advertise the city of South Bend in a very effective manner. Notre Dame plays the best teams in the country— away from home. I know that the people of South Bend want to see these teams. The only difficulty in bringing them here is the payment of a reasonable guarantee. Our gate receipts have been too small to warrant bringing the best teams here to play. . . .

. . . If I receive a return which shows that South Bend is willing to back us I will guarantee to bring Purdue and Nebraska here for the fall of nineteen twenty. I will bring Indiana and some other strong team here for the fall of nineteen twenty-one. . . .

To secure this needed support I am enclosing a season ticket. Please return in the enclosed envelope your check for five dollars or the season ticket. This ticket is good for all athletic contests at Notre Dame and includes four football games, about eight basketball games, four track meets and ten baseball games. We believe that this co-operation will be of mutual benefit and will secure more firmly the pleasant ties which already bind our city and our university. We welcome any suggestions or any constructive criticism which enable us to further this project.

Very sincerely,
K. K. Rockne.

We aren't told whether the sale of season tickets was successful.

In the meantime, Rock was also soliciting funds inside the university, and in this task he used a shrewd sense of bureaucratic infighting. In *We Remember Rockne,* a series of reminiscences collected by John McCallum and Paul Castner, Paul Manion, former dean of the Notre Dame Law School and a member of the Athletic Board in Rock's time, tells how Rock could slide around a negative ruling.

Rock had longed for a tarpaulin to cover the field. At a meeting of the Athletic Board, Father Michael A. Mulcaire, the chairman, asked him how much it would cost.

"Ten thousand dollars," Rockne said.

Father Mulcaire rejected the purchase out of hand as too costly. The money simply wasn't available. When discussion indicated that Mulcaire's position probably would be supported unanimously by the board, Rockne quickly changed the subject.

A few weeks later Mulcaire and Manion wandered over to watch practice. A truck rumbled up and several student managers began unloading huge heavy rolls.

"What's that?" Mulcaire asked curiously.

"A tarpaulin for the field," a manager said.

Mulcaire was almost apoplectic as he turned to Manion. "You were there when we voted down the project!" he shouted. "He has deliberately defied us!"

"Not quite, Father," Manion said calmly. "No official motion ever was made to purchase or not, and no vote was ever taken. And since the Board took no official action, I suppose Rock just added the tarpaulin to his next order of soap and towels."

One of the first and smartest things Rockne did, as he began to cope with the 1920's, was to realize that his fledgling football program was going to need some good publicity. The weekly game coverage by two South Bend newspapers and the nearby Chicago papers was effective enough, and the wire services put out satisfactory stories on each game. But Rock sensed the depth of coverage wasn't there, and it was too local.

The best way to augment that coverage, Rock figured, was to scout around for a bright young Notre Dame student who knew something about the game and could write. Under his plan, he wouldn't have to pay him anything. He would let it be known that the student was his official campus correspondent, entitled to cover practice sessions and provide feature stories for any papers that cared to print them. The papers would pay the kid space rates, so much per inch. Naturally, an eager young student would produce as much material as possible; the more inches, the more loot.

The correspondent would come up with a daily practice angle if he could, for one of the two South Bend papers which Rock would select on an exclusive basis (depending on which he was feuding or not feuding with in a given year). If the correspondent could peddle practice stuff to the Chicago or Indianapolis papers, fine. But Rock particularly wanted material to be fed to Indianapolis, Detroit, Cleveland, St. Louis, Minneapolis and especially New York. "New York is the heart of the whole matter," he told his first student reporter. "That's the big time. When they start noticing us there, everybody else will fall in line."

With his sure reportorial and publicist's instincts Rock trained the kids himself. Rule one: Concentrate on the school and players; never mind trying to build up Knute Rockne. Rule two: Clear the substance of the story with him so that no secrets are divulged. Rule three: Write with a great respect for the English language. Pure Rockne.

Several of the students he picked during the 1920's clearly proved Rock knew how to judge other than football talent. His first correspondent was Arch Ward (who had actually graduated a year or so earlier), later to become the renowned sports editor of the Chicago *Tribune,* and the man who conceived the idea of the annual baseball and football all-star games. Following Ward was Francis Wallace, later to become a brilliant sportswriter in New York, a novelist, movie scenarist and magazine writer of note.

Wallace came closest to being Knute Rockne's Boswell. Next came George Strickler, whose own football career had been cut short by injury. It was he who claims credit for the famous nickname and photograph of the Four Horsemen. He also went on to become a sports columnist for the Chicago *Tribune.* Subsequent correspondents were Paul Butler, later Chairman of the Democratic National Committee, and Walter Kennedy, Commissioner of the National Basketball Association.

"We sure piled stuff into print," Strickler recalled years later, "and I know Rock really appreciated us. And in order to let us have some fun as well as make some spending money, he let us travel with the team on road trips. 'Let us' is just one way of putting it. What he did was look the other way when we slipped aboard the train with the team—knowing, of course, that we had no railroad tickets and would have to depend on our own ingenuity as far as conductors were concerned."

Frank Wallace later wrote: "We were known as 'Road Scholars.' " It was a pretty neat turn of phrase, and that's just what they were. They were students, and they had to be scholarly sharp to figure out ways to beat the conductors.

"Fortunately," said Wallace, "we traveled in Pullman sleepers, always leaving at night, and we stayed out of sight while the conductor collected tickets. Then we'd pile into a berth with one of the players—usually picking one of the smaller guys—to spend the night with the curtains drawn.

"Once I got caught. The conductor decided to check some of the berths. I was in a lower. He looked at me suspiciously and demanded my ticket. I mumbled something that wasn't very satisfactory to him and he told me exactly how much money I had to cough up on the spot—or else. Rockne heard about it in the morning and took me aside. I figured he'd really rake me over. He just fixed me with that steely look of his and said: 'Next time—upstairs, where he might miss you!' And he pointed to an *upper* berth. Naturally, I took his advice—and never got caught again."

As the team went through winning season after winning season, Notre Dame was often accused of excessive zeal in recruiting football players. The charge irritated Rockne tremendously, especially when it was suggested that parish priests in communities across the land were putting pressure on parents to send their athlete sons to Notre Dame. "If I ever heard any evidence," Rock once growled, "I'd be the first to phone that priest and tell him to get busy with the sinners in his flock and leave the innocents alone."

He also raged against allegations that Notre Dame players were being paid. "Not only is it a filthy lie," he said, "but I wish those critics who say so would have to work as hard as some of our players do to earn their keep."

It was true that Rock never visited a recruit in his home or telephoned a potential star. But if a boy wrote to him, Rock would reply with an enthusiastic letter. And if one of his former players called about a prospect, Rock would encourage the alumnus to recruit the boy for Notre Dame.

"But *someone* was doing a job for him," Tug Wilson recalls wryly. "I was on a train one Saturday morning in late November, going to South Bend for a game. I noticed one of the cars almost full of strapping seventeen- or eighteen-year-olds, and something about them aroused my interest. A companion quickly put me straight. 'They're a gang of football prospects rounded up in the Chicago area, going to see the game.' "

It was highly unlikely that they'd even get to meet Rock. He would be much too busy, and besides, he preferred to remain aloof from recruiting. By the mid-1920's, the program sold itself anyway. A weekend close to this place and this man was enough to set a high school player panting for further association. It worked more often than not.

"Actually," Rock once confided, "I dislike applying any kind of sales pressure to a high school boy. I have the fear that if I recruit him personally there'll be an obligation on my part to play him. And what if he isn't as good as we thought he'd be? So I want a boy to come to Notre Dame because that's his own solid choice. You'll never see me in this crazy scramble to convince a kid he'd be better off here and a better football player at Notre Dame. I can't make promises like that—and I won't."

Once the players arrived at Notre Dame, Rockne saw that they were treated well in the football program. For one thing, he was a nut on equipment. He designed his own and put it on the market for anyone who wanted it. His shoulder pads were tight-fitting and remained in place. He was the first to install locked-in, skintight thigh pads, and the first to recommend detachable hip guards, although they didn't appear until after his death. He introduced sleek gold satin silk pants which he claimed not only streamlined the figure and presented a smaller target for a tackler, but also cut down on wind resistance.

Rock also had a thing about his players' appearance on the field. He found uniforms with a tapered fit, with jerseys so snug they wouldn't wrinkle, and pants fitting tightly at knee and thigh. Ribbed stockings had to be pulled up tight, and the short white sweat sox, after protruding from the shoes, had to be folded over just so. "I want you to *look* like football players, even if you're not," he told his boys.

He simply hated slovenly men and slovenly football players (although his own appearance was usually nothing to boast about). He insisted that a man who didn't care for his uniform or how it looked on him was likely to be a failure at anything he tried later in life. There was only one thing he hated more, even though he admitted it was irrational. He detested boys who walked slowly, believing this showed a lack of spirit and willingness to use their bodies to best advantage.

Rockne's relationship with his players was an amalgam of coach–surrogate father–Dutch uncle–confessor–taskmaster, and in the close-knit Notre Dame community he was forever demonstrating the need for all. "In the first place," said halfback Johnny Niemiec, "everyone called him 'Rock,' from freshman to varsity star. We had to because . . . well, he was so 'intimate.' Anything else would have been unnatural. Once in a while an assistant coach or an old friend would call him 'Swede' but with the players it was just 'Rock.' "

"He always ate dinner with us at the training table," said Norman Barry, a halfback. "Promptly at six-fifteen. We'd be waiting, he'd walk in, and we'd dig in. We always had meat for dinner but it wasn't in superabundance and every once in a while Rock would have to get up for a phone call, or a reporter would wander in, and when Rock returned all the meat would be gone before he'd had his. He'd glare around at us, put his hands on his hips and roar: 'You can't trust *anybody* around here!'

"We knew he wasn't angry, of course, because he'd gladly give up his share for a kid who was hungry."

But a serious breach of conduct, personal or on the field, could turn his intimate paternalism into steely disapproval and in a flash the intimacy would vanish—but only for a while. Rock never carried a grudge around in his hip pocket, and a day later nobody would ever have guessed a boy had been chewed out.

"But waiting for that familiar, warm rapport to return," said Niemiec, "was a form of purgatory."

As a result, Rock seldom had a disciplinary problem. His wrath was enough of a deterrent. In one area, however, he was unbending. A boy who broke training rules rarely if ever got a second chance. There was a right way, a wrong way and Rock's way. One night he decided to visit one of his fullbacks in his dorm at 9:45 P.M. The boy was out.

Rock waited until 10:20, twenty minutes past football curfew. No show. Next morning Rock sent word for the boy to report to his office.

The player admitted he'd gone downtown and hadn't returned until 11:00 P.M. "I regret this," Rock said evenly, "but I'll have to ask you to turn in your suit." There was no appeal and no discussion. It was a loss to the team but the loss was not the priority in Rock's scheme of things. Yet on the two or three occasions, over thirteen years, when he had to bounce a boy off the club, he never let it be known why the boy was fired. He always made up some plausible excuse why the boy had given up the sport.

There was no mistaking Rock's rules. Nine hours of sleep every night. All lights out by 10:00 P.M. Coffee allowed at breakfast only. No smoking or drinking in any form.

Although his players frequently saw him with that big black cigar jutting from his face, he had a snappy answer to any hint that they might like to light up, too: "Don't do as I do; do as I say. It all depends on who you are and what you're trying to do. You're football players trying to prove you're the best. A doctor advising a diabetic to avoid sugar doesn't have to follow his own advice."

Despite his rigid training rules, Rock sometimes gave a strange order to Scrap-Iron Young, his trainer. "Jimmy so-and-so is overtrained and needs to relax. Take him out and buy him a couple of beers—but don't tell him it was my idea."

Rock's prescription for his own drinking was: "Drink the first. Sip the second slowly. Skip the third."

There was no end to the range of Rockne's interest in his kids. When Chet Grant, the brilliant quarterback of 1921, showed him his academic schedule, Rock noted that he had an advanced English course and asked who the teacher was. Grant told him it was Father Crumley. "Rock's eyes lit up," Grant recalled. " 'Tom Crumley, eh?' he said. 'Good! He knows *words!*' Rock had a remarkable sensitivity to language and phrasing and he was always delighted when he saw any of his players taking advanced English courses."

Whenever a player came out of a game, Rock always patted him on the back. Once, following a game, a kid, naked, on his way to the shower, skidded to a stop and rushed back to Rockne.

"Hey, Rock," he said, "I didn't get my pat."

Rock, talking to a sportswriter, turned on a mock glower. "Get outta here, or I'll pat you on your head. Hard!"

The boy grinned. He'd made his point.

Fred Miller, captain of Rockne's 1928 team the heir to a brewing fortune, was rather affluent as a student. But he wanted to earn his own spending money, so one of Rock's assistants arranged a campus job for him—a tough, back-breaking physical labor detail. When Rock heard that Miller had been given a campus job, he suggested to his aide that the boy be put on the payroll under a different name. "If the priests find out," he grumbled, "they'll accuse me of depriving some poorer kid of a job." Then he snickered. "But I doubt if many kids on this campus would be interested in the kind of work Freddie is doing."

Miller remembered. "I was only a freshman then. Rock knew every freshman but didn't let on that he did. He preferred to stay aloof from them until they were eligibile for varsity. But every time the frosh went on the road for a game we always found a warm telegram awaiting us from him, wishing us good luck.

"He was always sensitive to bruised feelings," Miller added. "Always fearful that a boy might be emotionally scarred for life.

Once, against a Big Ten team, Rock sent in a second-string back to punt on our own 5-yard line. The guy was so nervous he dropped the snap, and the other team recovered and scored. It didn't cost us the game but Rock knew how miserable the guy was.

"Next week he put the kid into the game again and the guy blew a signal. Rock didn't take him out. He knew how critical it was for the boy. I remember Rock, himself, telling about it later in a speech. He said he simply had to show the kid he hadn't lost confidence in him. He could have ruined him for good by letting him ride the bench the rest of the year."

The girl friend of one of his substitute backs came to town for a weekend and accidentally bumped into Rockne on the campus. Naturally, she recognized him. Out of sheer innocence or unwarranted boldness—take your choice—she asked Rockne if her boyfriend was going to get in the game that day. Rock drew back, then asked who the player was. She told him. Rock smiled gently. "Why, of course!" Actually, he had no plans to use the boy that day, but he saw to it that he got into the game and carried the ball at least once.

Even after they'd graduated, Rockne couldn't resist staying involved with his players. He carried on a ceaseless, tireless campaign to place his boys in high school or college coaching posts. But he was not blindly loyal. He'd always take a long look at their qualifications and would recommend them only if they met standards he applied to the coaching profession.

A boy might have been an excellent player but Rock had some firm ideas on what coaching should be all about: patience, teaching ability and psychological insights to a player's character and personality. If he didn't think a boy had the makings of these qualities, he wouldn't recommend him. Then he'd give him some clear ideas on why he'd be better off in business or a profession.

One player didn't take Rockne's advice and got a coaching job on his own. Two years later he phoned his old coach. "Rock," he said, "you were right. This racket isn't for me. I'm going into business." Within three years he was a huge success.

In Rockne's constant travels he'd often drop in, unannounced, at high schools where some of his ex-players were coaching, but rarely did he leave before talking to the players or diagramming a play.

Once he went to Philadelphia for an alumni meeting. "But he happened to arrive a day early," recalled Harry Stuhldreher, who was a young coach at Villanova then. "We were having our football banquet and Rock just popped in to say hello. Not that he needed an invitation, because who wouldn't have been delirious to have an added attraction like that?

"But the most dramatic thing about his few days there was his discovery that some former Notre Dame football players in the area—including myself—had been preparing for a game with the Pottsville Pro's. He tried to talk us out of it, arguing that we were over the hill, out of shape and would probably get hurt.

"As usual, Rock made sense, but all our guys were already in town, posters had been put up all over, the game was only a few days off and a lot of tickets had been sold. We couldn't call it off.

"Later we found out that Rock had sneaked down to our practice field the day before the game and hid behind a big tree while watching us work out. One of the guys, arriving late, spotted him. Rock was embarrassed but recovered enough to tell him very sternly that we looked awful. No snap or rhythm. As our old coach, he just couldn't bear to leave town without taking a look at us."

15

The Embarrassments

Columbia was furious. Unofficially, they insisted Rockne had signed a bonafide contract. But they didn't want to expose him as a contract jumper, and felt it wouldn't be a happy marriage if both partners entered the union with any embarrassment. After a day of conflicting reports Knute Rockne told reporters, "I'm going back to South Bend," adding, with feeble humor: "Of course, I don't know if there'll be a job there for me."

Just three weeks after news of Rockne's baptism as a Catholic, fans, coaching colleagues and the press were rocked by the big, black headlines:

ROCKNE TO LEAVE
NOTRE DAME TO
COACH COLUMBIA

Rock had gone east on business the second week of December in 1925, and for a day or two none of his friends nor anyone at Notre Dame was quite sure where he was. Last reports were that he'd been in Philadelphia. The story carried by all the wire services, however, stated that he'd signed a three-year contract with Columbia at the then staggering salary of $25,000 a year, which would make him the highest paid football coach in the land. News of the signing set off shock waves of seismic proportions—and, for

Rockne, produced the most embarrassing moments of his career.

Within hours the city of South Bend, the Notre Dame campus and a few hundred sports editors throughout the country were coming unstuck as their frantic efforts failed to locate Rockne for confirmation. Finally, at midnight, Knute Rockne slipped into his hotel room in Philadelphia and made a phone call.

Next morning, Father Matthew Walsh, president of Notre Dame, gave a statement to the press: "Mr. Rockne phoned me from Philadelphia after midnight last night," he said, "and asked if I'd heard a report that he had accepted the job as football coach at Columbia.

"When I told him I had indeed, he said I should pay no attention to the reports. He had signed no contract and had no intention of doing so. Mr. Rockne told me that he would be at Notre Dame next season, and not Columbia. That ends the matter."

Well, not quite. Columbia authorities insisted Rockne had signed. But when reporters hurried up there to find someone who would stand on that statement or display the contract, nobody was around, from the president's office on down. A man named Joe Byrne, prominent in Notre Dame alumni circles in New York and one of Rockne's close friends, stepped forward and said he knew Columbia had been after Rock for several months but never did Rock give them real encouragement. Sign a contract? Ridiculous!

Tracking down Rockne in the East became the big game for the next forty-eight hours. He had slipped out of Philadelphia. On his way to Boston? New York? Washington? The man who was always the easiest man to find in all sports (just look for a room full of sportswriters) had disappeared without trace. Actually, he was in New York sweating it out with well-hidden Columbia people. In all likelihood, there *was* a contract between Columbia and Knute Rockne. He had probably signed it. But Rockne would confide to friends later that he'd sent up a verbal rider that "it all depended on getting a friendly release from Notre Dame."

Truth of the matter was that Columbia wanted a big-name coach and figured Rockne was ready for a new challenge. They were probably right. They caught Rock at the perfect, psychologically vulnerable moment. His nerves had apparently been rubbed raw from the 1924 and 1925 seasons. He had approached the Notre Dame administration about a new stadium to replace old Cartier Field and had been rebuffed. He loved New York City and the theater. And he was a sucker for flattery—which the Columbia people laid on with a trowel.

There had been all sorts of mild feelers for his services in the last five years. Northwestern, Princeton, Michigan State, Wisconsin and others. But he was enamored of Notre Dame and still building —still rising to a challenge unfulfilled. He never seriously considered any of them. But *Columbia?* Prestige. The East. New York City. A small fortune . . . Maybe this was the time and place.

Columbia allowed the statement by Walsh to become the official word. But actually Columbia was furious. Unofficially, they insisted Rockne had signed a bonafide contract. At the same time, however, they didn't want to expose him as a contract jumper, and felt it would not be a happy marriage if both partners entered into the union with any embarrassment.

After another day of conflicting press reports, Knute Rockne hurried aboard a train at Grand Central station, bound for South Bend, trailed by a dozen reporters. "I'm going back to South Bend," he told them, adding, with feeble humor: "Of course, I don't know if there'll be a job there for me."

There was, but only after Father Walsh rather coolly told Rock it was entirely up to him. Notre Dame would not stand in his way if he wanted to leave. If he wanted to stay, he could, but nobody wanted to pressure him into it. It was the first and only time that his bosses under the Golden Dome had dealt with him with anything but deference or the kind of attitude reserved for a favorite son. For the first time, Knute Rockne almost seemed humble.

Those close to him, even those who loved and understood him the most, agreed that Rock possessed one flaw—if it could be interpreted as such. Perhaps he was only human, after all. There was in Rockne a craving to be wooed by other schools. It was his only vanity, and if he flirted with other offers, other climes, he possibly never meant it to be serious no matter how it looked. He had simply let the Columbia affair get a little out of hand.

Shortly after he'd returned to South Bend and the thing had started to simmer down, the Notre Dame Alumni Association put the cap on it. Within two days they'd raised funds to buy Rock a new car as "a small token of their appreciation and affection."

A somewhat emotional Knute Rockne had already proclaimed: "Notre Dame has been wonderful to me. It took me in as a poor boy and educated me and gave me my life's opportunity. I am truly indebted. When I stop coaching at Notre Dame, I will be through with football."

Until the next time, that is. It would take only a few years before the temptation became another tempest . . .

Much was made of Rock's suicide schedules, which lured fans to the gates, and Rock began to draw criticism. It wasn't fair, the critics began to sniff, to subject his players to such pressures. Rock bristled. "Let people condemn me," he snapped, "but my boys thrive on them. So why should critics complain if my kids don't? Besides, we're not losing too many games with those schedules, are we?"

No, they weren't. But Rock's next loss would prove particularly memorable and even less happy than usual.

On Monday, November 21, 1926, Rockne, walking to the practice field with assistant Hunk Anderson, said: "Hunk, I'd like you to handle the team when we play Carnegie Tech next Saturday."

Anderson shot a questioning look at his boss. "But, Rock, that game's away, you know. In Pittsburgh."

"I know, Hunk, but I'm going to take the day off."

He then explained it to his aide. The Tech game was the last one before the big finale with new foe Southern California, at Chicago's Soldier Field. If they whipped the Trojans, they'd be nailing down another undefeated season and, undoubtedly, the national championship. So, thinking ahead to the Trojans, Rock didn't regard Carnegie Tech—loser of two games that year—as much of an obstacle. He knew exactly how to handle Tech and had mapped fail-safe plans. Anderson could carry them out while Rockne went to Chicago that weekend to see the Army-Navy game at Soldier Field. Navy was going to be new on the Irish schedule next year and it would give Rockne a chance to scout both service teams at once.

Anderson was flattered. "Thanks, Rock, and don't worry. We'll take care of Carnegie Tech."

They practiced all that week for the Carnegie Tech game, but with Southern Cal more prominently in their mind's eye. On Thursday night Anderson took the team to Pittsburgh. On Friday morning Rock went up to Chicago to hobnob with some Big Ten athletic directors. Saturday he went to the Army-Navy game with his trainer, Scrap-Iron Young. Rock cherished Young as a gabbing partner and sounding board for ideas.

They witnessed a spectacular 21–21 tie between Army and Navy, and Rock was satisfied that he'd learned plenty about the two teams. Then, as Young recalled it, "We were leaving the stadium at the end of the game and newsboys outside were shouting their football extras. We stopped dead in our tracks as one kid hurried by, screaming: 'Carnegie Tech upsets Notre Dame!' I rushed after him, grabbed a paper and came back to Rock. 'It can't be true,' he said quietly, but his eyes gave him away. And there it was in the headline. CARNEGIE TECH 19, NOTRE DAME 0.

"We went back to our hotel and Rock sat there stunned and speechless for twenty minutes. Then he put through a call to Hunk Anderson in Pittsburgh and talked long and quietly. The press was storming our door, seeking a comment from Rock.

"He no sooner had hung up when the phone in our room began to ring. And for the next half-hour Rock was besieged by calls from friends in South Bend, and alumni in Chicago and New York who knew where he was and demanded to know how this monstrous thing could have happened. And all Rock kept saying, softly, was: 'It isn't Hunk's fault. I'll take all the blame.' "

Rock had inadvertently put Hunk Anderson in a box. He had given Anderson an ironclad game plan to take advantage of known, serious Tech weaknesses and ordered him not to change the plan under any circumstances. Two things happened. It was a bitterly cold, wet day in Pittsburgh, and the field soon became chopped up. And for some strange reason, the Tech apparent weaknesses turned out to be their strengths. Perhaps more important, the Irish had been led to believe by Rock himself that Tech was a bunch of humpty-dumpties and there was nothing to worry about. They went into the game with no emotion or fire—and fire was what they needed that day.

The shock troops opened the game. They didn't score, and the regulars couldn't mount a decent drive when they came in. It may have been the only time in Irish history when a Notre Dame football team panicked. Anderson stuck to Rockne's imposed plan. He used a close box defense against what was supposed to be a miserable Tech kicking game, even when Tech punts—often on second or third down—kept booming way past Irish safety men, bottling up the Irish offense time and again.

Then the Tech offense, realizing that they were holding their own against the invincibles from South Bend, began to move the ball. Behind the brilliant leadership of quarterback Howard Harpster, later to become an All-America, they smashed for three touchdowns and won, 19–0.

Critics later said it was the only tactical mistake Knute Rockne had ever made in his career. It probably was, and he continued to maintain it was his fault. Later he said, "It would have been easy for Hunk to disregard my orders, considering how the game was going in the first half. But considering the beating he was taking it took courage on his part to display his loyalty and confidence in me."

Rock shocked the squad by holding a Sunday practice the next day, but he spoke just two sentences about the fiasco in Pittsburgh. "It was my fault, so don't blame Hunk. Let's just be glad we have a chance to redeem ourselves against Southern Cal."

On Monday morning the team left for Los Angeles. On the train each man found in his bag something Rockne had smuggled in: It a program of the Notre Dame–Carnegie Tech game.

The gamblers made Southern Cal a 7-point favorite. With one minute to play, the Trojans were leading, 12–7. It looked to be all over. Rock put his arm around the shoulders of a third-string quarterback named Art Parisienne, a 160-pounder who, for some strange reason, always passed beautifully in enemy territory but had difficulty putting an entire game together. "This is our spot, Art," Rock said calmly. On his first play, Parisienne completed a twenty-yard toss down to the Trojan 28. On the next play he fired a perfect pitch to Johnny Niemiec in the end zone, and the Irish won it, 13–12, in the last fifteen seconds.

In 1927 there was another loss to Army and a tie with Minnesota, but there was a rare distinction coming out of the Navy game. Played at Soldier Field, Chicago, it drew the largest crowd ever to see a sporting event in America—slightly more than 120,000 people. No one was surprised. Fans were being turned away wherever the Irish played, and it got to be a standard ploy to announce how many fans failed to gain admittance.

One day, late in 1927, Rock was told there was a go-ahead on a new stadium. "I'm sure you'll have some ideas for it," Father Walsh said, smiling, "so be certain to confer with our architects."

As if any architect could design Notre Dame's stadium *without* talking to Knute Rockne.

One man who recalls Rock's interest in the project was Harry Smith, a cameraman-director for the old Pathe Newsreel company. Smith, now in his eighties, recalled how he first became acquainted with Rockne:

"I had shot a couple of his games for the newsreels," he explained, "but I'd never met him. Now my company had signed a contract to make twelve two-reel films on Rockne and his football techniques. They were to be made in the spring and just before the season opened. I came out to South Bend with a camera crew and found the most dynamic and positive man I'd ever met in all my film travels around the world.

"Without insulting me or putting me down in any way, Rock seemed to take over. He was a born director. He could sense when I wasn't doing the right thing or, when filming, catching what he thought it should be. We restaged a lot of famous Notre Dame touchdown plays in stop-and-go motion and slow motion. Rock was fascinated with the process, and he learned more film technique in three weeks than many cameramen or directors learn in a year.

"But he wasn't very tolerant with his players during the filming. He demanded absolute perfection. He wanted nothing to look phony and his players were terrified that they might not deliver.

"Once he restaged a play with his star halfback. The halfback really ran hard but there was no gain, so Rock took him out and raked him the way he would have in a real game.

"Our crew lived in a dorm, and Rock would come over every night to talk about film. Then one night he got me aside and said he was building a new stadium and wanted to know my ideas, as a cameraman, that might help. The stadium was still in the drawing stage, he explained, and he thought I could tell him something about press box facilities and filming stations. He knew how important newsreels were to promotion of football, and he didn't want a camera crew stuck just anywhere. I gave him my ideas and he was grateful as hell."

But while one dream was coming true, there came a sudden blow —a dissonant counterpoint to the lovely tune of trip hammers and riveters he soon expected to hear at old Cartier Field. He knew it would be only a matter of time before he'd have his team on top again, but there came a day when it looked as though his whole world lay shattered, his glittering hopes for continued supremacy just so many shards of disappointment.

Now he sat in Father Walsh's office while the Notre Dame president told him that the administration was troubled. As gently as possible he explained that there was a growing fear among critics of the football program—that Notre Dame would become known as nothing but a football factory, an institution obsessed with football and unconcerned with a university's true function. Even friends and supporters of the university might begin to think that way. The administration felt that the tail should stop wagging the dog. No one was saying that football *was* too dominant at Notre Dame, but perhaps a nine-game season was long enough, and post-season football was not in the best interests of the student athlete and the university.

The philosophy and the niceties aside, there was only one thing Rockne was hearing. No more Rose Bowl—no more opportunities for his football teams to clearly demonstrate they were the best in the land.

Rock knew there was no use arguing. Much earlier he'd been quoted as recognizing that the faculty must run the school and a coach must accept the fact that football is an extracurricular activity just like the Glee Club, the campus newspaper, the drama society or whatever. Even though the faculty or administration might interfere, or lack sensitivity or understanding, Rockne conceded that they must have the dominant responsibility for the university's overall excellence.

So Rockne suffered still another embarrassment—that of telling his coaching colleagues that the Bowl game was out. The administration was true to its word. Although Bowl games proliferated in later years, no Notre Dame team ever appeared in one until forty years after Rockne's death.

16

The Pied Piper

When introduced by the toastmaster, Rock would stand there a dozen seconds or so, silently looking out at his audience. It would always seem longer than he actually held the look, and, as one observer put it: "It was as though he knew he had the power to attract and hold them, and they, in turn, were willing and waiting to be held . . ."

Rockne's love affair with the press, his enjoyment of writing, his ease as a communicator with people on all levels, did not come too easily. They were, in fact, an outgrowth of his great talent as a public speaker. Quite possibly, it was from the dais of a banquet hall that he made his biggest impression on the largest number of people.

Strangely enough, when he was first appointed head coach, he was unable to make a speech of any kind without floundering and faltering. Listeners seemed to feel sorry for him.

He never could understand why he had such trouble. In Notre Dame theatricals he had been a natural. In getting across to his players and coaching colleagues he was loose, fluid and marvelously vibrant. With such superb communicative rapport with the drama club, with students and football players, why, then, his inability to get on his feet a dinner before "civilians," as he put it, without blushing, stammering and fumbling?

Soon aware of his failures in those earlier days, he walked into President Cavanaugh's office and bluntly blurted out his problem. Could Father Cavanaugh help?

Cavanaugh nodded, smiling softly. "I think I understand your difficulty, Rock," he said. "You think you have to operate in two different worlds. The classroom and football field is one, and the outside world is the other. But you should regard it then as the same thing.

"I've heard you in the classroom, Rock, and on the field. You are superb. So, it's just a matter of confidence when you're on your feet in other circumstances. You're underestimating the "civilians." You're overanxious to make everyone in your audience understand what you have to say. So, maybe you're too loosely knit, too repetitious or too long."

Rockne, the teacher, proved he could also be taught. He became one of the most exciting speakers in America. Within a couple of years he was so much in demand that he was booked three or four nights a week. He developed a technique in his preparations which, for him, was foolproof. He wrote his speech in advance—never more than a fifteen-minute address—and rehearsed it two or three times, making changes as he went along. Players or professors passing his office often could hear him, in that unmistakable, flat but dramatic voice, rehearsing a speech for that evening.

He got great benefit from his wide and voracious reading. No matter what the audience, or the message he had in mind, his speeches were that of a cultured and educated man. He laced them through with topical references or lines and anecdotes from favorite authors. He could take something from the England of Charles Dickens and adapt it to modern America. He improved upon old jokes and by applying them to a variety of new situations always got a fresh laugh.

He took his prepared speeches with him on trips but never brought the manuscript to the dais. He merely used it for one last look before he left his room. The only time he deviated from this routine was at a dinner in a Midwestern city, where, for some unaccountable reason which he later wasn't able to explain, he took the manuscript to the dais and referred to it a few times as he went along. Within three minutes he sensed—and so did his audience—that his speech was flat and mechanical. Missing was the Rockne magic, the full flavor of the man used to holding an audience in his spell. Suddenly he stopped in mid-sentence, snatched up his manuscript and in full view of his startled audience hurled it away from him. Then, with a small, almost apologetic smile, he began to talk again. Within a minute he was the real Rockne and was a smash hit.

When introduced by the toastmaster, Rockne would stand there for a dozen seconds or so, silently looking out at his audience. It would always seem longer than he actually held the look, and, as one observer put it: "It was as though he knew he had the power to attract and hold them, and they, in turn, were willing and waiting to be held. It was always a breathless moment of dramatic anticipation. Actors and professional speakers often said they could rarely if ever manufacture that kind of moment."

As Rock's reputation spread, his talents became commercially marketable. One day in the mid-1920's he received a phone call from the director of the Chicago Automobile Show. Would Rock be willing to make a fifteen-minute speech at the show? For a fee? the man added. Would $500 be suitable? Rock quickly accepted, and when he hung up he mentally asked himself: how long has *this* been going on! He was a hit, of course, and the Studebaker Corporation back in South Bend, latched on to a good thing when they saw it. Over the years he signed at least three contracts to talk to Studebaker sales meetings all over the country. In early 1931 he was offered a position as Studebaker's sales promotion director. It was an offer he would accept but never implement . . .

Knute Rockne may well have been the best after-dinner speaker in the nation. One night magazine columnist, Hugh O'Donnell, bumped into a friend, clad in a tuxedo, coming out of a New York hotel. O'Donnell asked where he'd been.

"At a miserably boring dinner," was the answer. "Probably a thousand people there for some big corporation conference. I got dragged to it by a businessman who insisted I come along. Terrible dinner and terribly boring statistics served up afterwards."

"Sounds like a total disaster," said O'Donnell.

"Not completely," the man said. "There was one guy with a foreign-sounding name. An athletic coach or something from some college or other. I missed his introduction but I swear he almost brought those people to their feet cheering.

"He was supposed to talk about business and he did, but he put so much humor, drama and punch in it that it was the best speech I ever heard."

The next day O'Donnell had lunch with Rockne and reported what the man had said.

Rock looked up from his soup. "You aren't kidding me, are you? The guy really said that?"

O'Donnell never saw him look so pleased. Because of his love affair with words, some friends thought he'd rather be regarded as a good after-dinner speaker than a great football coach.

Smaller schools or organizations often were embarrassed or afraid to approach him—and often were stunned by his immediate acceptance when they did. And no audience could be certain what he would say. The Izaak Walton League of fisherman asked if he'd say a few words on how he developed character in his players, perhaps thinking it would be a comfortable topic for him.

"I don't know what you mean by that tired phrase 'character building,'" he said. "But if you mean it was stopping boys from smoking, swearing or keeping late hours, I'm not your man. I know that general idea. But it's the place of the home and Sunday School to take care of those things. If I ask a boy to quit smoking, it's only to test his will power and make a better athlete out of him.

"There's too much of a mistaken idea about this character stuff," he went on. "It's like culture. I love good music and I like to play the flute, myself. I also enjoy literature. But too many of our boys regard culture as lipstick, rouge, tea-dancing and a corsage of narcissus flowers."

But it is Chet Grant, the octogenarian ex-quarterback, who puts Rockne in proper perspective as a speaker. "I was coaching Christian Brothers Military School in St. Paul: "I asked Rock to come up and talk at our banquet, before a mixed group of men, women and students.

"Let me put it this way," he said with charming hyperbole. "Had he ordered us at the close of his speech to play follow the leader, all hands would have swarmed after him in any direction. As a student of American Indian history he could have piped these enchanted adults down the Mississippi to Lover's Leap rock where the Indian maid, Red Wing, and her sweetheart had jumped in their legendary suicide tryst. At that point, had Rockne enjoined us to leap likewise there would have been no alternative but to plunge en masse into the waters of the Mississippi. Finally, had he then charged us to SWIM, SWIM, SWIM, obviously not a single death by drowning would have ensued."

Knute Rockne could never get used to the fact that by the late 1920's he was virtually public property, as well-known as movie stars and celebrated politicians, and that anything he said or did was going to be quoted and chronicled from coast to coast. He had a reasonable tolerance for interviews and never did he turn down a request from a legitimate newspaperman. But he could work himself into a rage over the liberties often taken with him.

Once he was on an unannounced business trip to an Eastern city. Coming out of an office building, he bumped into a sportswriter who recognized him. Rockne had known the man slightly. The man asked him how he was and what brought him to town. Rock simply said he was there on some brief business and that he was feeling fine. Politely, he asked the writer how *he* was and wished him and his newspaper good luck. The writer said he'd never felt better and the paper was doing fine. The two men parted.

When Rockne left town the next morning, he picked up a copy of the man's paper. The guy had written an "interview" two columns long. Or, as Rock put it sourly, "two columns wrong." "I wish," he said, "I could give my football teams so little and get so much in return."

Another time a Midwest sportswriter asked what he thought was the reason for an apparent decline in the quality of Eastern football. Rock ducked the question for the most part, but couldn't resist a brief touch of light banter and said maybe the Eastern kids were wealthier than boys in other parts of the country, and, because they were used to so much luxury, some of them might be unused to football's hard-nosed demands.

The reporter, seizing his opportunity, whipped the single line into a *cause célèbre*. The wire services picked it up, and next day, all over the country, there were headlines such as: ROCKNE SAYS EASTERN BOYS CAN NO LONGER TAKE IT.

Rock's coaching colleagues in the East, as well as personal friends, were upset and bombarded him with mail and phone calls. He tried to tell them he had uttered the merest of fripperies, with no denigration intended, and that he had been grossly misquoted and certainly mishandled. Knowing Rock, most of them believed him.

Back in South Bend, friends worried that the remark would cost him a few Eastern players. With his eye unerringly on the mark, he said: "Any Eastern boy who decides not to come to Notre Dame because of what I've been purported to say will be staying away for only one reason: because he knows down deep that he *isn't* tough enough to play for us. For the good prospect it'll be a challenge to prove he *is* tough enough. So, we lose nothing."

Most writers generally knew Rock's habits and tried not to take up too much of his time. They also knew when and where he liked to do his talking. They would leave him alone just before a game, and very early they found out there was no point in asking what happened after a defeat. "I won't know," he said acidly, "until my barber tells me on Monday." Then he went on to invent one of football's most colorful and penetrating phrases: "Everybody," he said, "likes to be a Monday morning quarterback. It's so easy to call the plays a day or two later."

Clearly, however, Rockne was the all-time pet of the sporting press. The late Harry Grayson, the colorful Scripps-Howard columnist, who had been one of the earliest to realize that Knute Rockne was en route to a super-image on the sports scene, had covered Rockne from coast to coast.

"Nobody," he once said, "nobody—not Dempsey, not Tunney, not Ruth, not Jones—nobody was as adroit at handling the press as Rock was. He knew whenever he came to town for a game the sportswriters were going to pitch camp in his hotel room and there was no escape for him. He was operating without a high-powered publicity man—except for his kid student correspondents—so anything the writers wanted to know they just zeroed in on him.

"But he was the slickest operator I ever met, in avoiding something he didn't want to talk about. His storytelling was always the dominant part of any gab session with Rock and everybody ate it up. But he was so clever that he could veer off onto an anecdote or a story about somebody and grab your attention so neatly that you'd never know until later that he'd taken you off the track. And even if you caught on right away you didn't dare interrupt a Rockne roll because everyone else would be teed off on you. Damnedest broken field interview subject I ever encountered."

For the most part, Rockne was very open with reporters— mostly because he admired their profession and life style—but on occasion his openness came back to haunt him when they violated his confidence. Such as the time en route to a Southern Cal game. Working out in Tucson, Arizona, he invited all the writers accompanying the team, plus several others from Tucson and Phoenix, to attend a secret practice session at the University of Arizona.

Arriving in Los Angeles two days later, Rock picked up the local papers and exploded out of his chair. There, on the sports pages, was a pretty accurate description of some special offensive and defensive tactics he was intending to use against the Trojans. He was stunned at what he considered a breach of ethics. "Serves me right for trying to be nice to certain sportswriters," he said bitterly in his first interview on the Coast. "From now on I'll have to be careful who I treat as friends."

But the only writer who ever really brought a sense of hurt to Rock's heart was Westbrook Pegler, the Chicago *Tribune* syndicated columnist. Rock had shrugged off the time that Pegler had once described him as having the face of a battered oilcan, but after Rockne got himself heavily involved with writing, radio shows and speaking tours on behalf of the Studebaker Corporation, Pegler wrote: "I now perceive Mr. Rockne as a modest man who doesn't think much of himself, who is constantly amazed to find himself a great national celebrity, but who now wants to make all the money he can, lest the public gets next to him."

Rock always thought it was a low blow. He enjoyed money not because it was money but for what it could do for his family. At

Rock's death, Pegler—and many of Rockne's intimates—were surprised that his estate would be valued at slightly less than $45,000.

Rockne's own direct association with the press was one of the love affairs of his life. He loved to write and leapt at the chance to join Christy Walsh's sports syndicate, for which he wrote a daily column in the fall. He served up his views of Midwestern football, wrote special features on any phase of sports, including coaching, and even did a Friday column in which he picked winners of the next day's big games. Other coaches frowned on this and some bitterly rapped him as unethical and, at least, meddlesome. They didn't think it proper for someone of Rock's stature to publicly call the turn on their efforts.

He regretted their reaction—it was the only awkward thing in his relations with his coaching colleagues—but he never considered giving up his football commentary just to please them. Truth of the matter was that Knute Rockne at no time ever earned more than $12,000 a year coaching the Notre Dame football team, and with a family of four kids he always felt the need to earn more money.

His first writing venture, in 1925, had been a juvenile novel called *Four Winners,* in which the hero was a physically handicapped high school boy who made the varsity through hard work and determination. As literature it was feebly Victorian and convoluted writing, and no critic hailed Rockne as a threat to Theodore Dreiser or Sinclair Lewis, but it made him a few thousand dollars and whetted his appetite for more.

Next he turned out a couple of technical books on coaching, but, clearly, his greatest enjoyment came from his newspaper work. He found deadlines tyrannical, though, and once said to Bill Cunningham, a famed Boston columnist: "How do you guys do it? How do you come up every day, week after week, month after month, with something people want to read—and yet write it in a way that entertains them?"

Cunningham grinned. "It's like facing Army or Southern Cal every day, hey, Rock?"

"I'll take Army and Southern Cal," Rock conceded.

He constantly sought tips on the trade from his columnist friends and admitted that the most important trick he had to master was not to bury his most interesting or important stuff in the middle of his piece or at the end. "Up front—at the top" was what they hammered at him, and soon his material began to improve.

Yet Rockne, in the nether reaches of his mind, thought he'd be retiring from coaching in a few years and become a full-time sportswriter. In fact, a few weeks before his death it was reported that he'd been offered $25,000 a year to work for a Chicago paper which would syndicate him. When the Hearst newspaper chain heard about it, they asked him not to sign anything until they polled all the editors in the chain to see how high they'd go for an exclusive Rockne—with $50,000 as a jumping-off figure. In all probability, the Chicago offer was from the *Tribune,* where he would have been successor to Walter Eckersall, his boyhood idol as Stagg's quarterback at Chicago.

Shortly after Rockne became heavily involved with syndicate writing for Walsh, he heard Bob Zuppke, of Illinois, doing a radio broadcast of a football game in Chicago.

Zuppke, who was one of Rockne's chief rivals for national acclaim, and who had come up with Red Grange at the same time Rock was working with the Four Horsemen, had long been a friendly and respected irritant in Rockne's psyche. Zup had also started to make a reputation as a fine oil painter, and when he took a plunge into the new medium, radio, with rather good notices from the critics, Rockne felt a sting of jealousy—as well as a sense of challenge. He sidled up to a newsman pal. "Y'know, I'd kind of like to try that broadcasting thing sometime. D'you think you could help arrange it? I've got a week off after the Army game before going out to the Coast to play Southern Cal. There must be a good game I can broadcast on that open date."

There was—and Rock's friend set it up for him. On November 24, 1928, Knute Rockne broadcast the Northwestern-Dartmouth game over KYW, Chicago, from Dyche Stadium in Evanston. He called the play-by-play, and also did the color stuff. He was not only superb on his play-by-play, as the newspapers commented the next day, but he did something no broadcaster had ever done before.

He called many of the plays in advance, telling his audience just what was coming, and why. For Rockne, it wasn't a hot-dogging gamble. He was familiar with both teams' tactics and personnel, and rarely was he wrong. Once, when he seemed to hesitate, he pointed out that Northwestern could do one of two things—one of which was daring and the other which was good football.

The Wildcats chose to go, in that instance, with "good football," and Rock dryly commented, when things broke right for Northwestern: "They were lucky I wasn't their quarterback on that one."

Though he did no more play-by-play broadcasting, he was so excited by the medium that he urged Christy Walsh to get him other spots on the air and that winter he frequently appeared not only on sports commentary programs of his own but as an exciting guest on variety shows. He got a note from his good friend, Will Rogers: "Okay," said Rogers, "so you're coming over to my racket. Well, just don't start learning any rope-twirling tricks and start thinking about the Ziegfeld Follies or I'll take up coaching."

Knute Rockne's relationships with coaches—his own assistants and opponents—as well as the press were constantly marked by his humor. The funniest incident is probably one that happened near the Naval Academy at Annapolis.

Rockne was in a car with assistant Hunk Anderson, writer Frank Wallace and a Navy athletic official. The Navy man was driving and got into a right-of-way dispute with a big truck. Rock exchanged words with the burly truckdriver. Finally Rock let go with a beaut, and when both vehicles screeched to a halt near an intersection the trucker bellowed a challenge to Rock, got out and advanced ominously toward them. Rock smirked and turned to Anderson, his hard-bitten line coach. "Go get 'im, Hunk!" he said, chuckling. But before Anderson could do his chief's bidding, the Navy official quickly executed a quartering maneuver, slammed his foot on the gas pedal and sped away.

Next to Army, Rock's fiercest rivalry was with Nebraska. One year when the Cornhuskers came up to South Bend, Dana Bible, their coach, whom Rock loved to needle, was standing with Rock during pre-game workouts. Bible gestured toward five Irish teams going through signal drills.

"Which one is your first team, Rock?" he asked.

"To tell the truth," said Rock, airily, "it doesn't make much difference."

"Three hours later," recalled Bible, "I found out he was right."

Rockne always had special relationships with Army coaches. He once confided that Notre Dame's rise to national recognition could be traced, in great part, to the series with the Cadets.

Army always dispatched scouts to the Irish games before their annual date, and after one Notre Dame game at South Bend two Cadet scouts came up to Rock and complimented him on his victory but admitted there'd been one play the Irish had unfolded which they didn't understand. To their amazement he hustled them to a blackboard in the dressing room, grabbed a piece of chalk and went into a furious X and O routine.

"This is the one," he said, "a spinner off our shift, ending in a wide sweep or a pass." Rapidly he explained the maneuver and then said: "Any questions?"

They stared at each other, with slack jaws. They couldn't believe it. They asked him about several points and he filled them in completely.

"Rock," said one, "you're sure you aren't giving us a variation of your play? After all . . . we ARE Army . . ."

Rockne clapped him on the shoulder. "I've given it to you straight, mister. That's the real Notre Dame play I've just given you. I'll just add this: it's not the play itself which is so successful. It's the execution."

The Army scouts went back and reported to Cadet head coach Biff Jones.

"He's *got* to be tricking us, Biff," said one of the scouts.

Jones shook his head. "No, that's just the way it works, and we'll prepare for it just that way."

It didn't help much. Notre Dame 12, Army 6.

It wasn't the first time Rock gave away his plays. Once, with one of his better teams shaping up, Rock sensed that overconfidence was setting in almost from the first day of practice. He was opening with two breathers, to be followed by a couple of toughies. The coach at the small school the Irish played first was a good friend of Rock's. Rockne sent him a complete set of plays and formations he'd been using—and included some ideas on how to stop them. The Notre Dame varsity was stymied when they found their blocking assignments all fouled up and had to struggle all day. From then on there was no hint of overconfidence among the Irish.

No coach in football history enjoyed such a meteoric rise to success, and a collateral effect was the power he had in recommending other coaches for jobs. Time and again he'd get phone calls from athletic directors asking his opinion of so-and-so. But he was at his peak of effectiveness when he grabbed the phone himself and called a college to tip them off to someone he felt was just right. Never, however, would he knock other candidates for the job.

In the winter of 1925, shortly after his team had demolished Stanford in the Rose Bowl, he got a call from Southern California. The Trojans were in the market for a new coach. Would Rockne be interested? No, he wouldn't; he was flattered and all that, but no thanks. Could he recommend someone, then?

Rockne didn't hesitate. "There's a guy at Duke, who's only been there one year, but I bet he'd be willing to come out there. Name's Howard Jones."

"Jones? Oh yes, he was at Iowa for a while." The voice at the other end wasn't heavily stocked with interest.

"Yes, and he beat one of the greatest teams I ever hope to have," Rock snapped, "and that convinces me he knows what he's doing."

So the Trojans, on Rockne's word, hired Howard Jones, who became one of the nation's all-time great coaches.

When the University of California was looking around for a coach a few years later, Rock called the Coast and told the California athletic director that the Bears could never do better than hiring Navy's Bill Ingram. Ingram immediately became a top candidate—but a few days later Rock heard through the grapevine that one of the California selection committee didn't like Ingram's personal appearance. Rockne got on the phone again and with the most cutting verbal acid he could muster told the top California official: "If that's your prime consideration, don't worry about it. I'll buy Bill Ingram a hundred-dollar suit myself." Ingram got the job.

"I've never known a big-time coach who was as unselfishly helpful as Rock," Tug Wilson recalled. "I was walking with him once when a high school coach came over and asked him something about a play. In a flash, Rock was down on one knee, in the dirt, scratching out a formation the guy was interested in."

Rock wasn't as helpful to officials. Although he didn't bait them, they always knew he was around. In a game with Southern Methodist he was visibly aggravated when referee John Schommer called an infraction on a Notre Dame lineman just as the Irish were on a long drive to break a scoreless tie.

Rock flung his arms in the air and screamed: "John, you can't do that!"

Schommer glared over at him. "The hell I can't, Rock! I've already done it!"

Rockne let his arms fall limply to his sides and with a lopsided grin said: "Well, okay, John . . . as long as you've done it."

An official named Joe Lipp worked a lot of Notre Dame games and was not often, Rock thought, sympathetic to the Irish cause. Once Lipp called more penalties against Notre Dame than Rock could tolerate. At the end of the game Rock bumped into Lipp coming out of the officials' dressing room.

"Oh, hello Cyclops," he greeted him stonily.

"What's this Cyclops thing?" Lipp asked suspiciously.

"Well, obviously you only had one eye out there today," Rock snapped. "Look it up."

Officials were often the butt end of his sharpest barbas at banquets. His favorite was about an official working an Irish game on the road. "A real homer," Rock said. "There was a fumble, followed by a frantic pile-up from both sides, to recover the loose ball. The ref blows his whistle, dives into the pile and burrows his way to the bottom. Finally he comes up clutching the football, shouting, 'Our ball!' and turns it over to the opposition."

With his great personal ease and his ability to reach his listeners, he became one of the first coaches to establish coaching schools. Rock's schools mushroomed all over the land and he held seven or eight each summer, from Massachusetts to Texas, from Pennsylvania to California. He'd lecture from 8 A.M. to noon and follow with a practical session on the field in the afternoon. Still doing much of the tough demonstrating himself. It went on like this most of the summer while most of his rival coaches were fishing, resting or planning their fall strategy. He once conducted a coaching course in Hawaii, luring at least a hundred mainland mentors to make the trip with him.

His style was informal, never arrogant; he never appeared to assume the role of master with pupils. Once, at Bucknell, he was unavoidably a day late. Coaches, anxiously awaiting his appearance, were told that he was arriving that night and would start lecturing promptly at 8 A.M. the next day. Every coach got up extra early to be sure to get a good seat, and all were on their way toward the lecture hall by 7:30. As they neared the lecture building at 7:35, they saw a blocky man sitting on the top steps, his hat tilted on his head, legs dangling before him, dipping into a sack of peanuts, munching quietly and tossing some to the pigeons. It was Rock, of course, disdaining a dramatic entrance and just being himself.

Although completely natural in his delivery, he also took delight in occasionally using a highly literate word or phrase "just to keep the franchise," as he put it. "Somebody might think I'm a smart guy—you never know," he explained.

One of his favorite stories was about fancy words. At a coaching school in Texas, one of the coaches seemed a bit fuzzy on Rock's discussion of signals. Rock was explaining one system in which the first two digits added up to the signal, the call "three, eight" adding up to the operative signal of eleven.

"The guy looked perplexed," Rock recalled, "and said 'digit—how do you spell that?'

"I told him, and went on to explain how the juxtaposition of the digits was the key to the system.

"The coach yelled: 'Juxta-what?'

"So I repeated it, spelling the word carefully.

"Say no more, Rock,' the coach called out. 'Digit and juxtaposition, hey? Them two words are all I'll ever need. I'm a success right now.' "

But none of his coaching school ventures could match the imaginative but quixotic plans he made for the summer of 1928. The announcement came in the spring from, of all places, the Cunard Line in New York. Coach Knute Rockne, the news release said, was chartering a Cunard liner to the 1928 Olympic Games in Amsterdam for football coaches and their families. En route, and on the return, Rockne would be conducting his famous coaching school aboard ship.

"My God!" rumbled old adversary Pop Warner. "Only Rock could come up with a stunt like that! I can see the news report now: 'Joe Smithers, football coach at Old Siwash, spends too much time at ship's bar and falls overboard during Knute Rockne's football drill.' "

If it was a stunt, it was a remarkably successful one, as a couple hundred coaches plus several hundred plain football nuts rushed forward to book passage for these pigskin rites as sea. Rock, of course, was very serious about the clinic and it was an artistic and professional success.

Meanwhile, he had contracted with the Scripps-Howard papers to cover the Olympics for them once he got to Amsterdam. It was a labor of love for the old track coach. And with the instinct of a feature writer he went behind the scenes and wrote about things missed by writers concerned with the daily winning and losing. He particularly aimed at athletes from small nations like Finland, Haiti and Belgium, and when he got back to New York he went to Joe Williams, sports editor of the *World-Telegram,* to find out whether his material was well-received. He had instructed Williams, when he left, that he didn't want any rewriting of his material. "Print it just as I write it," he told Williams. "Don't try to pretty it up or make it slick. If I misspell a word, fix it, but otherwise leave my stuff alone." Williams later assured him that his stuff had been among the widest-read of all the Olympic coverage.

In one of his first interviews on returning to America, the talk inevitably got around to football, which would be under way in a week or so. What would his team be like?

"First of all," Rock said, "I'm predicting we'll lose four games. We're just not up to our usual standards this year. Secondly," he told his astonished listeners, "you can describe us as 'Minute Men' this year, because that's all it'll take before the opposition scores on us."

Everybody laughed. Rock laughed in return, but his mirth was somewhat metallic and on the macabre side.

17

The Ghost of Gipp

Now Rockne stood there, his double-breasted over-coat unbuttoned, his brown fedora hat nudged back from his high forehead, his hands clasped behind his back. And when he started to talk, some of the natural rasp was missing from his voice. "You've all heard of George Gipp, of course," he began . . .

As long as Notre Dame plays football—as long as any shred of romance remains of the Rockne legend—there will never be a moment more lasting than one which Knute Rockne himself came close to regarding as sacred. It occurred at Yankee Stadium, in New York, on November 12, 1928.

Already that season, events had begun to support Rock's wry prediction after returning from the Olympics—that this was the season his team could be called the "Minute Men." If the Irish could do no better than beat Loyola of New Orleans, 12–0, in their opener, then trouble was double-parked right around the corner. Just a week later, Rock almost got blasted out of Camp Randall Stadium in Madison as Wisconsin won, 22–6. Two weeks later, in Atlanta, Georgia Tech shut out the Irish, 13–0. It was turning into the kind of season that would produce, for the only time in Rock's career at Notre Dame, the transient but heretical belief that maybe Knute Rockne wasn't as smart as some folks said. There was even a rumor that his tenure at Notre Dame might be a tad shaky. Nobody except the few rumor-mongers ever bought a flimsy of it. The Irish won their next two games, but for Rockne, a sensitive man, a combative man, it was all wormwood and gall as he prepared his team for the big one—the annual showdown with Army. Nobody more than twenty miles north, south, east and west of South Bend gave him much of a chance. On Wednesday night his next-door neighbor, Tom Hickey, dropped in to say goodbye and wish him good luck.

Rock was just at that moment lighting a fresh cigar. He puffed vigorously once or twice, peered over a cloud of smoke and said: "We'll whip Army on Saturday, Tom."

"Damn right you will, Rock," said Hickey. It was the conventional if not the sensible thing to say, and Hickey tried to put some enthusiasm in it. Army was probably the best in the business that year, led by Chris Cagle, the best running back in Army history until Glenn Davis came along almost two decades later. John Murrell wasn't far behind him as a fullback. Bud Sprague was an All-America tackle. Biff Jones was a brilliant coach, and the Cadets were on a six-game winning streak, headed for an unblemished season.

Rockne had . . . well, Rockne's team was a year away. John Law was an All-America guard; captain Fred Miller a respectable tackle; his substitute was a raw-boned sophomore named Frank Leahy. Two hard-nosed, marvelously spirited halfbacks named Butch Niemiec and Jack Chevigny carried the offensive load. Oh, yes—there was a sophomore quarterback named Frank Carideo, and another sophomore, fullback Joe Savoldi, both showing great potential. Rock could hardly wait for 1929, but the priority right now was to prevent 1928 from turning into a complete disaster.

Biff Jones brought his troops down to New York from West Point on Friday morning. The papers indicated that Rockne had all but conceded the game, which didn't fit Rock's character but nobody at Army was thinking of that. Jones took his team to a workout on Travers Island. Even the rain couldn't dampen the Cadets' spirit; they were riding a physical and emotional high. After the workout they checked into the Astor Hotel on Times Square.

Rock and his kids stayed, as usual, in the subdued atmosphere of the Westchester Country Club, and sportswriters who came up there noted that the Irish were almost depressed. At 11:30 Saturday morning Rock led his team into Yankee Stadium, where they began the silent, gladiatorial ceremony of suiting up and getting taped. Witnesses thought it was the most subdued Notre Dame team ever to climb into uniform.

Outside, photographers from all the New York papers were scrambling for shots of the famous, the powerful and the notorious who always decorated this event: senators, congressmen, generals, movie celebrities, gangland lords and their gussied-up ladies—straight out of Damon Runyon. Plus, of course, the legitimate football fans and wave upon wave of Notre Dame's curbstone alumni. There were only 75,000 legitimate seats in Yankee Stadium. But this was Carnival Time. Festival Week. Rio. The Roman Colosseum. The last year for uninhibited binges. Exactly a year from now, Wall Street would send up the signal that the Roaring Twenties were over. Now, however, people wanted into Yankee Stadium to see if a fading Knute Rockne had any magic left. So another 15,000 seats were sold *somewhere* in the place, putting the crowd at 90,000—the largest for any sporting event ever held in New York.

At about 12:45 the Irish took the field for their pre-game workout, resplendent in their gold satin pants and bright green jerseys, a much more colorful aggregation than the somber, black-shirted Army players at the other end of the field. But expert eyes in the press box were peering down at the confident, more powerful Cadet squad. There, the lithe, fluid Chris Cagle . . . there, the bull-shouldered John Murrell . . . there the tough Bud Sprague, the spunky Spike Nave, the rangy Ed Messenger. This was the pride of the East, the team that, clearly, was going to claim the national championship.

A half-hour later Rockne summoned his men back to the dressing room for a final word. There hadn't been much fire and fury, or biting sarcasm that year. It had been a somewhat subdued Rockne in dressing rooms throughout the country, as though Rock knew this was a year which called for realism on his part, the year of lowest ebb in talent, and there was no use to call for more than could be reasonably delivered week after week. Yet this was Army, and perhaps there *should* be something different.

Now Rockne stood there, his double-breasted overcoat unbuttoned, his brown fedora hat nudged back from his high forehead, his hands clasped behind his back. And when he started to talk, some of the natural rasp was missing from his voice. "You've all heard of George Gipp, of course," he began . . .

Of course. These players had all been in grammar school in Gipp's day and the years have a way of muting the paeans to minor heroes. But every player in that cold, concrete and steel-girdered dressing room knew who and what George Gipp had been at Notre Dame, and accepted him as the one legend that was destined for immortality.

"You all know that I was at his bedside the day he died," Rock went on. "And you may or may not have heard that just before he died he said to me: 'Rock, someday when things look real tough for Notre Dame, ask the boys to go out there and win one for me.'

"Well, I've never used Gipp's request until now. This is the time. It's up to you . . ."

Years later Jack Chevigny said: "There wasn't any big show of emotion—no pounding or storming out of there the way other teams had responded to a particular Rockne pep talk. But this time we all seemed to feel something terrible deep that brought us individually to a great pitch. We were simply ready to play the game of our lives."

At midfield for the coin toss, captain Bud Sprague, commander of A Company, 1st Battalion, shook hands with Fred Miller, and the game was under way.

On the first play from scrimmage, Chris Cagle swept wide, and was chased back and dropped for a fifteen-yard loss. From then on, the first quarter was a punting duel. As time slipped by, press box observers expected that the awesome Army attack would gear up any minute. The desperate Irish defense would have to fold sooner or later.

It came as a shock, then, when Fred Collins, Rock's fullback, got loose for twenty-five yards. Jack Chevigny got five and then Collins again got six, and the Irish had a first down on the Army 5. A moment later Collins cracked over guard and was blind-sided. The ball popped out of his arms and into the end zone, where Army's Murrell smothered it for a touchback. On the sideline Rockne's eyes glowed. "We're still in this," he muttered hoarsely to assistant Tom Lieb.

It was a scoreless tie at the half. Cagle got untracked early in the third quarter. He ran for ten and eight. Then, faking a sweep, he stopped, dug in, and pitched a perfect forty-yard pass to Messenger on the Irish 14. Four more running plays and then Murrell battered over from the 1. It didn't seem to matter to Cadet fans that the extra point was missed.

Jimmy Brady, in at quarterback, put a few things together on a subsequent Notre Dame drive. Coolly, he stayed on the ground, picked his spots, and got great blocking from Freddie Miller, John Law and the others up front. Butch Niemiec, Jack Chevigny and Fred Collins began ripping off five- and six-yard chunks. On a fourth and one, Chevigny on a second effort, sliced for a first down by inches on the Army 2.

On the next play, the Irish choreographed into their shift (now a shadow of its old-time dazzle because of rules changes). The ball came back to Chevigny again and, when the hole he was to hit didn't open, he hurtled over the defenders instead, into the end zone for the touchdown. He bounced to his feet and in the same motion flung the ball upward exultantly. And he said it . . . he *did* say it . . . "That one was for the Gipper!"

But Notre Dame missed the conversion, too, and it was 6–6 as the game entered the final quarter. Rockne slapped Frank Carideo on the rump and sent him into the game at quarterback. On both sides the blocking was intense, the hammering of the backs was ferocious. But neither team could break the big play, and neither would permit the other a long drive.

Chevigny missed a long field goal attempt, but moments later the Irish got the ball back and pierced to the Cadet 16 on shots by Niemiec, Chevigny and Carideo. Then there was a busted play and the snap from center sailed back to the Irish 32. There was a mad scramble for the ball and Chevigny recovered—but was knocked silly as he did so. Rock took him out. He sent in a halfback replacement, then turned and yelled: "O'Brien!"

With the single word, another legend was in the making as Johnny O'Brien replaced Ed Collins at end.

Referee Walter Eckersall told Carideo there was less than two minutes remaining. Neither O'Brien nor the substitute halfback could talk until one play had been run off. But Frank Carideo needed no message. Johnny O'Brien had a nickname: "One-Play O'Brien." At least three times that season, events had determined how appropriate the name was. It was incredible that Army had not learned its history homework. Carideo knew exactly what the play should be.

It was third and twenty-six on the Army 32. O'Brien was 6'2" and the Cadet safety man was 5'9". Rock was well aware of that. Carideo knew it, too, and so did Butch Niemiec. Carideo barked his signals. The snap came back to Niemiec as Carideo, Collins and the entire line blocked desperately. Manny Vezie, the other Irish end, cut toward the sideline, drawing off one defender. O'Brien raced diagonally toward the corner of the field, his long legs pumping.

Holding until the last split second before the rush got to him, Niemiec fired the ball in a high, looping arc. Cagle, the Army halfback, had gone with O'Brien, but O'Brien gave him an inside fake and came back to the right, toward the corner. Only the short, squat Cadet safety man, Nave, was with him now. At the 2-yard line O'Brien and Nave went up for the ball. O'Brien snagged it, came down with it and tumbled over the goal line for the winning score.

The pandemonium in Yankee Stadium continued on through the missed Irish conversion attempt.

The uproar also continued right through the Notre Dame kickoff when Cagle took the ball on his own 10 and raced fifty-five yards, being stopped only by Eddie Collins, the last man between Cagle and the goal line. Two plays later Cagle ripped his way to the Irish 10-yard line and seconds later had to be taken from the game, completely exhausted.

His substitute, Dick Hutchinson, tossed a quick pass, good to the 4, then on the next play hurled himself to the Notre Dame 1. He had failed to score and the Irish took over on downs just as the gun went off.

On the sideline, Rockne was curiously calm. "I figured it would be something like this," he said as his players mobbed him. Then he put his arm around Jack Chevigny's shoulder. "Well, we got it for him, didn't we, Chev . . ."

The Gipper had been there, and Frank Wallace, then reporting for the New York *Daily News,* chronicled it just that way in a story the following Monday, as an afterpiece to his actual game coverage.

It was headlined:

GIPP'S GHOST BEAT ARMY
Irish Hero's Deathbed
Request Inspired
Notre Dame

Strangely enough, Rock was upset over Wallace's piece. He thought Wallace had violated a confidence, that his locker room speech never should have been made public. Wallace, mindful of his own sense of integrity and his feeling for the public interest, told Rock—and often repeated the story—that he'd never considered it a breach of confidence, that the story rightfully was entitled to become part of football tradition. Rock looked at his one-time student correspondent and nodded gently, and did not contest it further. He knew a simple truth when he heard it.

The Irish lost their last two games; to Carnegie Tech, their first loss at home since 1905, and to Southern California. It was the only time in Knute Rockne's career he ever dropped two in a row. Somehow it didn't seem to matter that much. The emotionally charged victory over mighty Army had in large measure salvaged his worst season ever. He had predicted he'd lose four that year and he did.

But he was in no way depressed. Ground was to be broken the following spring for his long-sought stadium. And even though it meant the Irish would have to play all their games away in 1929, he had reason to believe his road club would be an instrument trumpeting the Irish return to the heights.

*   *   *

Could it be that Knute Rockne would never learn? Rockne, the omnivorous reader, might have paid heed to Oscar Wilde, who said: "In all the world there are only two tragedies. One is getting what you want. The other is not getting it."

Early in December, 1928, at an NCAA business meeting, L. W. St. John, athletic director at Ohio State, got a phone call from Maj. John L. Griffith, Commissioner of the Big Ten. The Buckeyes were in the market for a new coach to succeed Dr. John W. Wilce, who was fed up with the developing recruiting rat race and longed to return to the full-time practice of medicine.

"Saint," said Griffith, "I know a guy who'd just love to be a candidate for the job you have open."

"Who?" said St. John eagerly. He knew Griffith's contacts and his record for integrity.

"He's sitting right here in my room with me," said Griffith. "His name is Knute Rockne."

St. John pulled back from the phone. "You're crazy, John," he said flatly, "and I can give you forty reasons why."

"I know all the reasons you do, Saint," Griffith replied tartly, "but you'd better talk to him if the idea appeals to you."

How could it not? Knute Rockne at Ohio State? What a parlay. He got hold of Rock and they went to St. John's room, St. John all the while thinking it was incredible. Yet Griffith must know something, because it was just a couple years ago that Rockne had gone through the Columbia flap.

In the next hour, St. John divined, among other things, that Knute Rockne just might feel he'd accomplished all he possibly could at Notre Dame—and that he'd always had a secret hankering to be part of the Big Ten, the nation's premiere conference. He'd never fully forgiven the league for not granting membership to the Irish, but this might be another way of joining up. And how exciting it would be to dominate this powerhouse lodge.

St. John was right on target. From Rock's viewpoint there was undoubtedly more. It would give him a yearly crack at Michigan. Fielding Yost, who had earlier broken off relations with Notre Dame and never had had a kind word to say about Rockne, was now retired, but Rock was still nursing a residual grudge against the Wolverines. And now L. W. St. John, who had steadfastly refused to schedule Notre Dame, was offering him a job. Sweet were the uses of adversity.

Suddenly, wonder of wonders, Knute Rockne was telling St. John that he'd like to take the job, but . . . well, only if no word got out until he returned to Notre Dame and got his people to release him from his contract.

No one ever knew how it leaked. But a Columbus newspaper sniffed out the story, and by the time Rockne got back to South Bend Father Walsh was waiting for him.

"Nothing to it, Father," Rock said with a nervous wave of his hand. "Yes, I was approached by Ohio State," he added, "but I have no intention of leaving Notre Dame."

Father Walsh nodded and was silent for a moment. Then he said: "Good. After all the plans you made for our new stadium . . ."

No doubt there were other things he left unsaid.

There is no record of anyone having observed Rock mopping his brow as he came out of Walsh's office. But, spiritually, he might have. He *should* have.

He had wriggled out of it once more, but he knew it must not happen again. There were limits . . .

With spring practice coming up, Rock was soon nursing rosy hopes for Notre Dame's return to supremacy. The 1928 season may have been disastrous but several classy sophomores had looked good while losing.

With Rockne, any guilt feeling was a transient thing. Why, of course he was staying at Notre Dame . . .

18

The Cripple

They rolled him to the sideline in a wheelchair, wrapped in blankets, his feet in heavy black galoshes. He sat there strangely immobile, no resemblance to the crackling, staccato-voiced Viking chieftain who normally was on top of every play, every situation. But he was furnishing a force that was unmistakable Rockne—his presence.

It was going to be a strange season for Notre Dame in 1929. The grandstands on venerable Cartier Field had been torn down; the steelwork for Knute Rockne's dream stadium was in place and everything was proceeding on course for a glorious dedication in the fall of 1930.

Meanwhile, the Irish football team, dispossessed from its home grounds, was going to be the travelingest team in the history of big-time college football. Every Irish game—nine of them—was going to be on the road, and their new nickname—"the Ramblers" —would be appropriate. Rockne and the administration, however, detested the name despite the need for a complete road schedule. It smacked too much of a carefree academically negligent program at a time when the excesses of big-time football were much in the news. The Carnegie Corporation had just issued a 327-page report that condemned overemphasis on football in colleges, and Rock was worried that the sensation the report caused would damage the sport.

No matter. Nothing could be done about it. The Irish were away every weekend. On October 5, 1929, they opened at Indiana. Midway into the first period came the fateful moment that would change Knute Rockne's entire life. A Hoosier play swept wide toward the Irish sideline, and when the ball carrier was hit by two Notre Dame tacklers the momentum carried all three into a pileup near the Irish bench—but not before they had smashed into Rockne, who was unable to get clear in time. Rock went down, and then came up rubbing his left leg. "It's nothing," he said to a concerned assistant. "Just a bump. It'll go away."

The Irish whipped the Hoosiers, 14–0, but the pain in Rockne's leg didn't go away. By Sunday it had gotten worse. He was sure he knew what the trouble was. In the spring of that year he'd had three infected teeth pulled, and he suspected that the infection had left him with some form of sciatic rheumatism. The bump on his leg no doubt had brought it back again. "Obviously," he grumbled, "I've let too many of those clumsy ends and tackles get into my legs during live blocking drills."

By Wednesday he was in intense pain. Dr. R. L. Sensenich, his physician, suspected something more critical than the bump, or a return of the rheumatism. Tests indicated that he might well have a blood clot in a vein in his left leg which could lead to something serious. He ordered Rockne to bed for a week.

Rock stared at Sensenich incredulously. "A *week!*" he exploded. "I've got a meeting with a very tough Navy team in Baltimore, Saturday, and I intend to be there!"

He had no idea how wrong he was going to be . . .

Complete rest and immobility of his leg was the only cure Rock's doctors could suggest. Otherwise, the pain was almost unbearable. As soon as he moved his leg from its propped-up position, the pressure on his weakened veins increased and the pain shot through his entire leg.

Navy wasn't the only team on Rockne's mind. It was the toughest schedule in Notre Dame history—and every foe would be met on the road. Navy, Carnegie Tech, Georgia Tech, Southern Cal and Army were the big games ahead. Even Wisconsin, Drake and Northwestern had good teams that year and would be upset-minded.

After the 5-4 season of 1928, his worst ever, Rock felt he was ready for an upward bounce. Many of his players were young and unproven, but he had a great guard in Jack Cannon, a fine tackle in Ted Twomey, and a promising end in Tom Conley. But his spirits really rose when he considered the men behind the line.

He had a junior quarterback who had played just sparingly as a sophomore. He was a crack punter and a good passer, and—best of all—Rock sensed that with a couple of games under his belt he'd show some brains. His name was Frank Carideo, a stocky 5'8", 175-pounder.

There was a transfer from University of Pennsylvania named Marty Brill whose father was a transit tycoon. Brill's father thought Marty hadn't been getting a fair shake at Penn and convinced his son to transfer his supposedly mishandled talents to South Bend. Brill was a blocking fool whose life seemed dedicated to knocking people down.

The real glint in Rock's eye, however, was a reflection of what he saw in a 5'10", 192-pound Italian who had come to the United States at age thirteen. If the boy was occasionally betrayed by the language, Joe Savoldi was never a disappointment with a football under his arm, thundering toward a hole in the line that didn't seem to be there. Joe Savoldi would make it happen.

Savoldi, not a quick study, had spent his sophomore year making sense of the signals and the Rockne system. Another coach might have given up on him, but Rock saw his raw power and told Tom Lieb, one of his two assistants, to spend some extra time with Savoldi in spring practice.

Lieb, after a month, wasn't optimistic: "I don't know, Rock," he said. "He has the strength of a bull but about the same amount of finesse and agility. I don't think he'll make it."

"To hell with the finesse," Rock growled, "if he can learn the numbers he'll do it on strength."

When fall came, it seemed that Lieb was right. Savoldi, discouraged, quit the team. But Rock tracked him down. "Okay, Joe," he said, "if you're as good as you think you are, no more shock troops. I'll give you a shot at the first team."

Savoldi returned, and Rock kept pumping him up with compliments, even when they weren't merited. It was the Rockne psychology at work and Savoldi began to respond. Rock figured that along about the third game Savoldi would be ready. But all that was before Rock got upended on the sidelines in the opener, and now here was his doctor telling him he'd have to go to bed for a week—with Navy coming up.

Rockne listened crossly as the doctor explained what might be happening in his leg. He knew something about medicine and was too reasonable a man to reject the doctor's opinions as merely speculative. "It's thrombophlebitis," the doctor told him. "The pain is not the important thing; more serious is the fact that a clot can cut off circulation in that leg . . . And if a clot breaks loose and lodges in your lung or heart or brain, it will kill you. What I'm saying, Rock, is that you are courting disaster if you don't do what I say."

Two days before the team was supposed to leave for the Navy game, Knute Rockne went to bed. He put Tom Lieb in charge of the team. On Thursday night Lieb came to Rock's house, along with his quarterback, Carideo. Rockne covered every eventuality and quizzed Lieb and Carideo on every possible game situation, outlining everything he wanted them to do. It was the first of the almost nightly sessions Rock would have in his home that fall. Ends, tackles and guards would meet with him twice weekly. The halfbacks and fullbacks, three times. The quarterbacks, four nights a week. Lieb was there every night. Bonnie Rockne was torn between reporting Rock to the doctors and making sure his players had enough sandwiches and hot chocolate before they left the house.

On Saturday noon before the Navy game Rock was in bed in South Bend. But his mind was in Baltimore. Three or four good friends from downtown were at his bedside. Finally, against doctor's orders, he put through a phone call to the Notre Dame dressing room in Baltimore.

"When that phone rang and I heard Rock's voice," said Lieb, "it was a godsend, even though I knew he should not have done it. But I sensed our kids were flat. It was the first time they'd ever gone into a game without their coach—and being away from home sure didn't help. They needed something, and I wasn't sure I could provide it."

One by one Rock got every starter on the line. He went over the boy's duties, then gave each a little pep talk. He concluded the session with Lieb. "When the game starts," Rock instructed him, "I want you to have someone on the long-distance phone from the press box, giving me a play-by-play description."

Lying in bed, mostly with his eyes closed, his fists clenching and unclenching episodically, Rock said hardly a word to his cronies as the Irish won, 14–7. Then, finally, a succinct comment when the gun ended the game: "We've got a great quarterback." He meant the junior, Carideo.

With Rock still in bed all the next week, the Irish handled Wisconsin, 19–0. But Rock suspected there was something missing from the Notre Dame attack.

Coming up was the first big hurdle, Carnegie Tech, always a problem for the Irish. "I'm going to have this one even if it kills me," he told Lieb. And, against a violent protest from his doctor, he got out of bed and went to the practice field, where workmen had hastily erected a twenty-foot-high platform from which he could overlook the field. With an assistant helping from below, he slowly climbed to the platform, dragging a megaphone with him.

But there were continuing and mounting frustrations. Rock was used to demonstrating what he wanted his players to do. He was not content with telling an end how to box a tackle; he wanted to get in there and do the hitting himself. Now he couldn't.

Lieb tried to reassure him, but Rock brooded darkly. "It isn't your fault, Tom," he said, "but those kids are still making mistakes they should have corrected two weeks ago. And I'm not getting across to them like this. They're feeling sorry for me and trying to make things easier for me, and nobody's fooling anybody."

Meanwhile, he had decided that something special was needed for the Tech game. He figured Joe Savoldi would be that something and spent most of his transient energy bellowing orders to Lieb, Carideo and Savoldi. Then, drained, he would go back to his house and, after dinner, hold a meeting with all three.

Everyone in South Bend knew Rockne had been ordered to bed

for two weeks. On Thursday night people at the South Bend railroad station seeing the team off were shocked to see him rolled into the depot in a wheelchair and put aboard the train, a grim-faced doctor alongside him. Friday morning he was whisked to his suite in the Pittsburgh Athletic Club to rest. Some rest. Immediately he was surrounded by sportswriters and pals from South Bend. As usual, he told jokes and stories nonstop, took phone calls, handed out game tickets to a favored few—and drove his doctor crazy.

It was raining, so the Irish squad was taken to a local gym. Rockne insisted on being trundled into his wheelchair, down the elevator, into a limousine and over to the gym where he supervised a signal drill.

Later that afternoon he collapsed into bed, exhausted, with terrible pains shooting through his leg. Dinner was brought to his room. Nobody saw him that night or the next morning. The team went to the stadium without him. The dressing room was silent, haunted by the absence of a man who said he'd be there. Lieb, in charge, was nowhere in sight. Suddenly the door to the dressing room opened. Lieb stood there, behind Rock in the wheelchair. He rolled the chair into the room, silently, then grasped Rockne under his arms and lifted him onto a rubbing table. Rockne's face was white and seemed to twitch slightly. He closed his eyes for a few seconds, and when he opened them they seemed to burn with a high, blue intensity. His doctor stood off to one side, shaking his head imperceptibly, helplessly. Silence enveloped the room. Then Rock raised his head a bit, the round, brown fedora hat tipping up slightly.

Finally he spoke and the tension was broken. "A couple of years ago," he began, his voice strangely thin, "I did a dumb thing and went off scouting when we were playing this team here. I should have been here with my team. We lost, and I've never forgotten."

His voice grew stronger. "The doctors said I'm taking a big chance coming over here, but I don't care. I don't care what happens after today but . . . I didn't come here to see you lose."

It was possible, according to Frank Wallace, who was there, that Rockne at that moment wanted to win more than he wanted to live.

Pause. They were hanging on every word. "Never have I wanted to win a game as badly as I want this one. AND YOU CAN DELIVER IT TO ME!" he shouted, his face working. "But only if you go out there and hit 'em, hit 'em, hit 'em like they've never been hit before, like you've never hit *anyone* before! DO YOU UNDERSTAND? DO YOU KNOW WHAT YOU HAVE TO DO?"

Now he was pumping his arms and screaming, and there were many who thought he was sobbing. On each player there may have been a slightly different effect, but the sum total added up to one common reaction. They didn't even wait for his command to go out there. They poured toward the door, their animal roar expressing full acknowledgment that Rockne's pain and desire was now coursing through them, too. When they were all past him, Knute Rockne sagged forward toward the edge of the table. His doctor caught him just in time. He mopped the sweating face and reached for Rock's pulse.

Rock insisted that he be wheeled out to the sidelines, where they wrapped him in blankets and buckled on his heavy black galoshes.

He sat there strangely immobile, no resemblance to the crackling, staccato-voiced Viking chieftain who normally was on top of every play, every situation, every possibility that might arise. But he was furnishing a force that was unmistakable Rockne—his presence.

It may have been the most physical game a Rockne team ever played. The hitting could be heard in the stands. The blocking was savage on both sides, but the defense was just as potent and neither team could mount a consistent drive.

They wheeled Rockne back inside during the half. He said little, but what he said was comforting: "Don't worry. We'll get our break. And when we do, we'll make it work for us. Count on it."

The break came, just as he predicted, just as they knew it would. Jack Elder, the 166-pound sprint star, gathered in a Tech punt at midfield and raced it back to the Tech 7-yard line.

Tom Lieb sent in a sub and after the first play, when he could legally transmit a message, the sub told Carideo that Rock wanted Joe Savoldi to carry it in.

It was the psychological spot for the big Italian kid and Rockne knew it. Savoldi pounded to the 5. He smashed at the merest suggestion of a hole for two more yards. Straight ahead again, without looking to see if daylight existed between center and guard. No hole, but he got a yard. Fourth and a yard away. On the sideline Rock was silent, his eyes boring straight at the stocky Savoldi hopping into the shift. He took a direct snap and blasted in, up and over.

Both teams were too exhausted to muster a threat in the final quarter. Rock had met the first big test of 1929. His doctor said to Lieb, grimly: "Even if you go through undefeated, I hope you realize Rock might not live to see it."

The drugs that could keep phlebitis under control were still decades away. When Knute Rockne returned to South Bend, bed rest was the only prescription. But there was no one strong enough or dictatorial enough to keep him there. Bonnie Rockne tried, but she was hopelessly subservient to her husband's single-minded desire for victory. Once she made a feeble plea "on behalf of the children" but felt too ashamed to press the point any further. His doctors were completely helpless. All they had going for them was the knowledge of their science and the concern that kept them from walking away from their patient.

Some of his colleagues suggested that Notre Dame's president issue an order for Rock to stay in bed, or at least stay away from the football team. But they knew Rock would never forgive them if such an order were given.

Everyone sensed it was expecting too much for this human dynamo, this man of perpetual motion, this man in constant conflict with imperfection, to completely immobilize himself. At least twice a week he hauled himself to the top of the platform at the practice field, muffled in two sweaters and a hood against the wind, and bawled out comments through his loudspeaker. And even in his pain and discomfort he couldn't refrain from dishing out the barbs and humor so much a part of his coaching philosophy.

Jack Cannon, his All-America guard, was noted for his ranging, unorthodox tactics on defense. Playing without a helmet, he attracted the fans' eyes as he roamed the field, making spectacular tackles, often out of position. What the fans didn't realize was that while he was stunting, somebody was protecting his vacated territory. The somebody was tackle Ted Twomey. Nobody knew better than Rockne that Twomey often made Cannon look good. Rock's problem was to make Cannon aware of it.

One day, from his platform, Rock quietly told Lieb to leave Twomey out of the varsity line-up during a scrimmage. Although Cannon played his normal, roaming game, the offensive scrimmage team, made up of reserves, knew his style and knew, too, that a substitute tackle was playing alongside him and not very good at covering for Cannon. They slammed big gains through Cannon's position. After five or six such gains Rock painfully straightened up in his chair atop the platform and put the loudspeaker to his lips.

"Hold it a minute," he barked. "We've got to bring in Cannon's pal, Twomey, because it looks as though he can't get along without him."

The Irish won their next two games, one against Georgia Tech, with Rock staying home. Rock hardly lost touch, however. He was upset that Joe Savoldi played poorly against Georgia Tech and Tom Lieb had to take him out of the game. Rock worried that Savoldi's failure might destroy his self-confidence and set him to brooding.

Now the team faced Southern Cal at Soldier Field in Chicago. The Trojans were tough and Savoldi would have to have one of his better days to ensure a victory. A few days before the game, Rock summoned Joe to his bedside. He told him that several prestigious Italian lodges in Chicago wanted Rock's okay to make next Saturday Savoldi Day in Chicago. Rock told Joe he'd held up his permission until he could talk to him.

"It's a great honor for you, Joe," Rock said, "but no honor at all to you or Notre Dame if you play the way you did down in Atlanta." He paused. "Should we tell them to cancel that celebration Saturday in Chicago? Maybe we shouldn't take the chance."

Savoldi's black eyes glittered. "Hell no, Rock! Don't you cancel *nothin'!* Tell 'em to go right ahead for a Savoldi Day!" On the Tuesday before the Southern Cal game, Rock got out of bed with a new gimmick. He went to the field but spent only part of the time up on the platform. The rest he spent in his car, which was fitted out with a loudspeaker. He could bellow instructions across the field and confer at the same time with Lieb and Carideo.

By now Rock had discovered that even in a Pullman bedroom a railroad car's vibration was bad for his leg. When the Studebaker Corporation heard about this problem, they adapted their largest model car into a plush, flat-bed job so that Rockne could be driven to Chicago in relative comfort. He had ruled out an ambulance as too theatrical.

Once again a drawn, pain-racked Rockne was wheeled into the dressing room to muster, for just thirty seconds, whatever vitality he could feel in his affliction. It is likely that he needn't have said anything at all. His players knew that if Knute Rockne unloaded one of his famous pep talks he would be a candidate for an autopsy report. His sacrifice and risk in just coming to the game was painfully evident. It would not go unanswered by Rock's kids.

Again the wheelchair was rolled out to the sidelines, and again Rock tried the impossible: remaining impassive during a Notre Dame football game. At his nighttime bedside conferences at home, and in two appearances at the practice field tower, he had designed something special for the Trojans. The Irish were a running team which passed infrequently, and Southern Cal knew it. So Rock set up an aerial surprise that was a shocker. He told Lieb to fashion a pass play with Jack Elder, the sprinter, doing the throwing. Elder had never thrown a pass in his life. Rock knew he was a fine athlete who could rise to the occasion. With the Irish trailing, 6–0, Elder faked a run against the Trojans, stopped short and tossed a perfect TD strike to end Tom Conley. It brought a wide smile to Rock's face. Something else almost brought him to his feet, choking, a few moments later. Russ Saunders, the Trojans' own speedster, returned the second-half kickoff ninety-five yards for a touchdown, the first time anyone had ever done that against a Rockne-coached team. It gave Southern Cal the lead but then it was Savoldi's turn. Tearing huge gaps in the Trojan line, he led a Notre Dame scoring drive that pulled out a 13–12 victory.

They took Rockne back to the Auditorium Hotel in downtown Chicago. He was in agony, and there was no thought of trying to get him back to South Bend that night.

Lieb tried to be a buffer for him as players and sportswriters poured into the suite, everyone wanting a piece of the congratulatory action. When the players came in, Rock wouldn't let the pain show in his face and voice. Instead of accepting congratulations from them, he made a big show of bestowing kudos on the kids who had done the winning on the field.

He got through the ordeal with about thirty seconds to spare. After the last player had left, after Lieb had hustled the last newsman out the door, Rockne sagged completely.

"I can't take this much longer, Tom," he said through clenched teeth. "This thing is closer to beating me than anything I've ever known in my life." He covered his eyes with his hands. "I think I'm at the end of the line, and I've given up any idea of going to New York for the Army game. You and the kids have done it mostly without me this year, anyway. I'll count on you winding it all up the same way."

Lieb nodded. "Don't worry, Rock. Just two Saturdays to go."

Rock wasn't particularly worried about the next game with Northwestern, and the Irish breezed, 26–6. Army would be something else. The annual Army-Navy series had been terminated (temporarily) the year before because Army refused to accept the three-year eligibility rule and was still using players who came to West Point after previously starring for two or three years in college. And there was no doubt that the Cadets now considered Notre Dame the high spot of their schedule.

There was color and anticipation enough in this head-on clash at Yankee Stadium between two great teams. Even though the stock market had its frightful and historic crash just a couple of weeks earlier, tickets were being scalped for as much as $75 each. A couple dozen Army planes flew into Mitchell Field on Long Island the morning of the game, carrying a hundred or more top Army brass from posts all over the nation. Several hundred red-hot fans from South Bend had come on two chartered trains. An early winter sent the thermometer plunging to 10° by game time, but more than 80,000 fans were there, wrapped and cosseted against the numbing cold.

Early that morning Lieb had talked to Rock on the phone.

"That field will be frozen hard," Rock said. "Round up a few dozen pair of rubber-soled basketball shoes or we'll never have any traction."

Shortly before the Irish were to take the field for practice, the shoes hadn't arrived.

On the telephone from his bed, Rock gave a quick order. "Get hold of some files from the stadium maintenance people and tell the kids to file their cleats as sharp as they can, so they'll penetrate that icy turf."

Rock knew that any edge at all might provide the difference against this great Army team that had lost two games on incredible bad breaks to Yale and Illinois. Chris Cagle was an All-America halfback; John Murrell, the best fullback Notre Dame had faced all year. And the Cadet line outweighed the Irish by twelve pounds per man.

Then Rock told Lieb he wanted to talk to every one of the starters. Lieb hesitated, but followed instructions. "This time Rock was very calm," Lieb recalled. "No fireworks. It was as though he was telling every kid that there was nothing to worry about. He had confidence in them and simply expected them to go out and do their jobs. It was the perfect approach for this spot. With Rock's supreme confidence, they no longer had to be worried about the ten-degree temperature or the heavier and more experienced Army team."

The filed cleats were the only thing that kept Notre Dame in the game. That and heroic line play as the Irish forwards blunted three Cadet drives deep in Notre Dame territory. Then, midway in the second period, the Cadets blocked an Irish punt and had a first down on the Notre Dame 13. Two line plays failed on the icy turf, and on third down, from the 8-yard line, Chris Cagle raced wide, came to a miraculous halt on the treacherous footing and flipped a pass to end Ed Messenger on a crossover pattern. Messenger reached greedily for the sure TD. But Irish halfback Jack Elder, the 9.5 sprinter, cut in, stole the ball virtually out of Messenger's hands on the 4-yard line and stumbled toward the sideline, tippy-toeing the first five strides to stay in bounds. He recovered his balance, barely escaped two diving Army tacklers, and was gone, streaking down the sideline. One lone Army defender had a last, desperate diving shot at him on the Cadet 5, but Elder took the glancing blow and swept on past, for a ninety-six-yard TD.

It was no accident that Elder had picked off that pass. All that previous week Rockne had warned Lieb that Cagle liked to fake a sweep and then toss a flat pass. "He goes to his right," Rock said, sitting up in bed and gesturing with his arm, "so whenever they get into passing territory I want Elder to take the defensive position on that side of the field. He just might nip one off."

In bed back home, Rockne was listening to the broadcast by Graham McNamee, radio's first famed sportscaster. As McNamee's rapid, metallic voice began describing Elder's flight up the boundary line, Rock raised two clenched fists and howled hoarsely: "That's it! He'll go all the way!" And when McNamee breathlessly reported that Elder had crossed the Army goal, Rock's eyes blazed as he grinned at thre pals in his bedroom.

In the second half Army continued to thwart Notre Dame and made several deep penetrations into Irish territory. But each time the Notre Dame line stopped them on downs. And each time Frank Carideo added to the Cadet frustration by punting the Irish out of danger, often out of bounds in the coffin corner, preventing an Army return. Carideo kicked eleven times that day, in a brilliant display of defensive punting.

It ended 7–0, with the desperate Cadets, who had played the entire, bitter game with their original eleven starters, backing the Irish up to their own 10-yard line as the gun sounded.

That was it—the perfect season Rockne wanted so much, sweeter than any other because of the pain and frustration he had overcome to achieve it.

In South Bend an exhausted Rockne turned off the radio. He had cheated by tuning in. A month earlier his doctors had flatly forbade him to listen to Irish games on the radio because they excited him too much and sent his blood pressure skyrocketing. He was ordered to confine his game-day activity to a phone call from Lieb at the end of the game. But Rock couldn't bear the thought of enduring the Army finale without knowing what was going on. So he tuned it in.

He had already been stripped of all his outside activities: speaking engagements, radio talks, writing his syndicated column and even answering his mail. A columnist had claimed that normally he was a busier man than the President of the United States, which, at the time, may have been only a short punt from the truth.

One thing he insisted on following through with was the annual selection of the All-America team by the All-America Board of Coaches. The Board, organized by Christy Walsh, included Pop Warner of Stanford and Bill Alexander of Georgia Tech. They met at Rock's beside, with a half-dozen roistering reporters lining the room on bridge chairs set up by Bonnie so they could kibitz the proceedings. Rockne, bright-eyed and chipper despite the ten weeks of pain, was, as usual, the dominant figure. The reporters were startled at his intimate awareness of leading players in all sections of the country and impressed by his insistence that players from smaller schools be given consideration. They were even more impressed when he hesitated voting for Pest Welch, Purdue's great triple-threat back.

"I tried not to vote for Welch," Rock later wrote in his autobiography, "because his coach, Jimmy Phalen, had been one of my boys at Notre Dame. I wanted to be sure I wasn't allowing my regard for Jimmy to interfere with my true evaluation of other contending backs. Every report I had from Big Ten coaches said Welch was the best in his league but I wanted to be sure that representatives from other sections had a chance to come up with their candidates."

Only when Rock had the full facts about Welch, and others, did he finally cast a ballot for the Purdue star.

"It seemed like an awful waste of time," Pop Warner rumbled amiably to one of the sportswriters later. "Rock knew Welch belonged."

The sportswriter shook his head negatively. "Pop," he said, "I don't think Rock ever in his life, consciously or otherwise, has wasted a moment of his time."

The compliment may have gone over Warner's head.

A week later Rock's doctors gave him an order. He was to go to Florida for two months of complete rest and relaxation, allowing his leg to soak up the sun on the beach. But the sun made him feel better than he was. Within two weeks he accepted an invitation to make a short banquet speech in Miami. At the end of the dinner he collapsed and had to be carried to a hotel room.

That was it. His doctors in South Bend brusquely made all the arrangements and then told him he was to be on a Pullman the next morning, bound for the Mayo Clinic in Rochester, Minnesota. Two weeks at the Mayo confirmed the fact that he was indeed suffering from serious thrombophlebitis. The venous swellings in both legs would have to be kept bound in tight, rubber bandages except when he slept at night.

"A couple of weeks?" Rock asked suspiciously.

"Until we say so," was the flat answer. "It may be a year or more." Pause. "Or until you get out of coaching."

Rockne's face grew white.

He never knew that the doctors, privately, had told intimate colleagues that Knute Rockne might not live more than three years unless he *did* give up coaching.

There was one other thing that disturbed Rockne. He had heard —and had seen muted references in the papers—that many people around the country didn't quite believe the seriousness of his illness. Rock was just being his colorful dramatic self, they scoffed. After all, the day after alarming medical reports, they would read that Rockne was on a long train trip with his team. Obviously, thought the cynics, the condition and prognosis couldn't be all that grave.

They just didn't know Rock's flaming spirit and his sense of self-sacrifice. There was no way he could tell them, so he brooded over it, and it didn't do his health any good.

19

Return to the Top

The first touchdown in the new stadium came on just four SMU plays, the last play being a forty-eight-yard scoring pass. On the sidelines, Rock growled: "We've got to come back quick, or those guys will get delusions of grandeur and pass us to death." The Irish comeback took exactly twelve seconds. Joe Savoldi gathered in the SMU kickoff and raced it back ninety-eight yards for a touchdown.

All week long Rockne's right halfback had been showing more drive and spirit than his coach could recall. On Saturday the undefeated Irish would be at Franklin Field, Philadelphia, taking on Pennsylvania. Rockne nudged Hunk Anderson, his assistant, and nodded toward their right halfback, who was looking awfully crisp and businesslike in signal drill. "Marty's been really sharp this week, hey, Hunk?"

Knute Rockne, the supreme psychologist, had subtly changed some offensive plans that week, so casually that reporters and even most of his players weren't aware of it. Frank Carideo, his quarterback, knew, of course. Marty Brill, the right halfback, was primed for the game of his life . . .

On November 8, a record crowd of 80,000 had jammed Franklin Field far beyond capacity—a crowd content to forget for about three hours that the papers the last few weeks had been full of ominous signs of what was being referred to as "a deep and worsening depression." It was exactly a year since Wall Street had done its dizzying flip-flop and the ripple effect was lapping at everyone's consciousness.

No matter. Knute Rockne and one of his greatest teams—possibly his greatest—were in the East, and that was a signal for instant and rampant excitement, and an event as social as it was sporting. To add to the excitement, Lud Wray's tough Pennsylvanians had some legitimate expectations of derailing Rockne's runaway express.

Marty Brill, Notre Dame's senior halfback who had transferred, disgruntled, from Penn, didn't have to remind anyone of the short-sighted view the Quaker coaches had taken of him as a freshman and sophomore. The press had been reminding people all week.

For two seasons Brill had been the primary blocker for his backfield mates, although he was a slashing runner in his own right. Now, against Penn, Rock turned him loose. Carideo at quarter, Marchie Schwartz at left half, Joe Savoldi at full, and Brill at right half were awesome in their display of speed, power and precision.

The Irish rolled for 43 points in the first half on their way to a 60–20 victory, the greatest number of points Rock had ever tallied against a topnotch foe. Brill, running for almost two hundred yards, scored on touchdowns of sixty-six, thirty-six and twenty-five yards.

After the game the rumor circulated that Brill's wealthy industrialist father had offered him $1,000 for every touchdown he scored against Penn but Rockne hotly denied it. Brill, he said, didn't need the money and didn't need additional motivation.

It was a season of high drama from beginning to end—even more dramatic than the previous year, when Rockne had been desperately ill.

In September Rock was moderately healthy, recovered from the acute stage of his phlebitis, but he set a somewhat less strenuous pace as he faced the toughest schedule in Notre Dame history.

The schedule hadn't worried him. Much of his undefeated team of 1929 was returning, most notably the backfield, with Carideo, Brill and two devastating fullbacks in Moon Mullins and Joe

Savoldi. The other halfback, replacing Jack Elder, was the new sensation, Marchmont Schwartz of New Orleans. Bert Metzger, fourth in a line of watch-charm guards (Noble Kizer, 164, Clipper Smith, 163, John Law, 164), weighed only 149. Every ounce of it tough-gristled hostility.

The beautiful new stadium was ready—an excitement unto itself —and was to have its official dedication on October 12, when the Irish met Navy in the second game of the season. But getting past the opening foe, Southern Methodist, might have killed the Rockne of the previous year. Yet, as he explained after the season was over: "I was able to survive it because I'd spent two weeks at the Mayo Clinic that spring. The docs had told me I was a 90 percent new man—and I say to hell with the other 10 percent. My bad set of tonsils had been removed, my nerves were in good shape, and my friends and assistants said I'd never been in better mental spirits."

At least he'd hoped so. He'd spent five weeks at Miami Beach during the winter, in the final stages of his inactive recuperation, and had been absolutely miserable as he followed the doctors' orders. By spring practice he was permitted to attend every day, although half the time was spent, as a precaution, in his canvas camp chair on the sidelines.

For the first time in his career, he had ample help—by 1930 standards. Now he had four full-time assistants: Hunk Anderson, Jack Chevigny, Ike Voedisch and Tim Moynihan. He also had a full-time equipment manager, business manager, trainer and ticket director—all the trappings of a big-time operation which his rivals had enjoyed for years. For the first time, too, he had a team doctor who traveled with the club. At long last, despite his own knowledge of medicine and the human body, he felt his players had the full protection of professionals.

Rockne needed all the comfort of his improved conditions against Southern Methodist on opening day, October 4. "We'd heard stories about something called 'the Aerial Circus' which Matty Bell had developed at SMU," quarterback Frank Carideo recalled. "But what hit us was more cyclone that circus. I think Rock and we learned more about pass defense in that game than two dozen of his lectures could have done for us."

The first touchdown in the new stadium came on just four SMU plays, the last being a forty-eight-yard scoring pass. On the sidelines, Rock growled: "We've got to come back quick, or those guys will get delusions of grandeur and pass us to death."

The Irish comeback took exactly twelve seconds. Joe Savoldi gathered in the SMU kickoff and raced it back ninety-eight yards for a touchdown.

Early in the second period Carideo returned a punt forty yards to set up another score, but just before the half ended SMU completed four straight passes to tie it up, 14–14. Rockne's nerves were getting a workout. In the third quarter Carideo passed to Ed Kosky for the go-ahead touchdown but the Irish missed the extra point.

"We'll win it on defense," Rock said tight-lipped to Hunk Anderson. He was right. Carideo punted the hide off the ball, several times bottling up the Mustangs deep in their own territory. And three times Tommy Yarr, the half-Irish, half-Indian center, blunted SMU drives with pass interceptions.

Although there had been an opening game in the new stadium, the formal dedication was saved for the Navy game the following week, highlighted by a monstrous demonstration the night before. It seemed the entire city of South Bend had joined with the student body in a blazing torchlight parade, punctuated by fireworks and the Notre Dame band blaring the Victory March at its loudest.

Rock came close to choking up when he spoke at the dedication ceremonies. Notre Dame's stadium—the fulfillment of his dream —was an actuality and he didn't need the pompous words of a Navy admiral, also on the speakers' list, to tell him so. Gilbert K. Chesterton, the famed British writer, was then lecturing at Notre Dame, and he'd been astounded by the festivities the night before. Observing the frenzy as it poured out before him, he murmured in monumental misunderstanding: "Good gracious, but they're angry!"

There wasn't a game in the 1930 season that didn't provide Rock with a soaring high spot or element of drama. Navy was sunk, 26–2. The gamblers then, strangely, picked a tough Carnegie Tech team as the favorite but Rockne used the slight to make a scathing pre-game pep talk and the Irish blew Tech out of the stadium.

Another week, another dramatic highlight. Pitt, just a few years earlier, had hired as its coach a dour but brilliant young Scots dentist who had been pursuing two careers simultaneously, and this year his club was picked to go through undefeated. The headlines blazed: SUTHERLAND SET TO HALT IRISH WIN STREAK.

Could be, said many experts, investing the game with national championship flavor. "It can't happen!" Rock snapped to a couple of close sportswriter friends the night before.

Rock now had a new star to fit in with Carideo, Brill, Savoldi and Mullins. Marchy Schwartz could do almost anything, superlatively, with a football: he was a brilliant runner, fine passer and great punter. He was deadly on defense and probably the best all-around back Rock had coached since the immortal Gipp. Schwartz led the Irish to four touchdowns in the first half as they trampled the Panthers, 35–19, with all the Pitt points coming against the reserves. Later, Jock Sutherland admitted it was the only time in his career that a team could have scored 100 points on him if they'd had a mind to.

This was a game, incidentally, when Carideo and Savoldi put their Italian heritage to good use, but then got caught at it. Both had learned to speak Italian in their homes. Savoldi, often to Rock's displeasure, would forget a signal and look over appealingly at Carideo. Carideo would repeat it in Italian. But then a Pitt tackle began crashing through and dumping Savoldi before he could hit the hole. Nearly always, it seemed, when Savoldi was getting the repeat signal in Italian. Finally the astute Carideo straightened up and walked over to the Panther side of the line of scrimmage before the ball was put in play. Casually, he called out in Italian: "Any good Italianos here?" The Pitt tackle obligingly held up his hand. "Thanks," Carideo said in English. No more signals were called in Italian.

Of all the Rockne-Savoldi stories, none was more typical than one in which Rock was about to send him in to a game. When putting in a sub, Rock always made sure the player knew the entire situation: score, down and yardage, defensive alignments, anything to help the kid do his job. The Irish were in a time-out as Rock put his arm around Savoldi's shoulder.

"Joe, it's third and five. We have the ball on their 25, okay?"

"Uh, yeah, Rock, yeah," said Savoldi.

"What defense are they using, Joe?"

"Oh, uh, defense . . . that's uh . . ."

"They're using a 6-2-2-1, Joe. Got it?"

"A 6–2–2 . . . uh, sure, Rock. It's . . ."

"Have you been watching Mullins? Do you know what he's been doing?"

"Well, uh, sure . . . Moon's been . . ."

"Particularly on that short-side play, Joe. Notice how he's been handling it?"

"Yeah . . . I mean . . ."

"Okay, give it all back to me. I want to see if you have the full picture. Now, what down is it, Joe . . . ?"

At that point Savoldi straightened up and shrugged Rock's hand off his shoulder. "Dammit, Rock, I dunno! You just send me in there and I'll win the goddam ball game for you!"

Rock did. And Savoldi did.

By all rights, the Savoldi story should have ended with big Joe making unanimous All-America. But this was the season for drama at Notre Dame. Joe Savoldi put in a memorable performance against Penn—the game in which Marty Brill had provided the high note. Savoldi had been a devastating blocker for Brill and Marchie Schwartz and had ripped off big yardage himself.

But the next day headlines screamed:

JOE SAVOLDI SUES FOR DIVORCE

No one even knew he'd been married. Joe had kept it secret for almost a year, but then the marriage had failed.

Divorce? A student at Notre Dame? Where students were not even supposed to be married, let alone involved with an action that was anathema to the church?

The story hit the Notre Dame community with poignant but immutable impact. Savoldi was a favorite of everyone, including Rock. But the administration had no choice. Savoldi would have to leave school. Rockne, with a heavy heart, summoned him to his office. It was the worst news he'd ever had to break to an athlete. And as much as Rock hated to lose Savoldi as a football player, he was even more heartsick that Savoldi would have to leave Notre Dame with graduation just seven months away.

"Don't worry, Rock," Joe said gently, more concerned with his coach's feeling than his own. "I understand how it is, Rock."

Rockne nodded vacantly, then cleared his throat. "Uh, Joe, I don't know what you'll do now . . . Get a job, go into business . . . I don't know what you might have in mind. But times are getting tough . . ."He paused, then his hand dipped into his pocket for a piece of paper. "You'll need a cushion until you get started. I want you to have this, and I won't listen to anything you say against it."

Savoldi looked at it. It was a check for $1,000, and it had come out of Rockne's personal funds. Joe knew Rock would be hurt if he refused it. He put it in his pocket, then stuck out his hand. Neither said much. Nothing needed to be said.

Joe Savoldi went right out and became a professional wrestler, and in his first year on the circuit he earned $80,000.

It was not the first time Rockne had dipped into his own pocket to help his former players. At one of his coaching clinics held in a Midwestern city, two of his former stars, Joe Boland and Jack Chevigny, were assisting him. On the last night they were there, a thief broke into their room and ripped off all their money and jewelry.

It left Boland, particularly, absolutely destitute, and Rock knew that Boland was leaving the following week for a new assistant coaching job in Minnesota.

Rock came into Boland's room while Joe was packing, a cloud of gloom on the young man's face. "Cheer up, Joe," Rock said, and tossed a folded pad of bills on the bed. "This should hold you until you collect your first pay check."

Naturally, he reimbursed Chevigny the same way.

The story is also told of Rockne's largesse to a rather more remote recipient. As his fame grew, he was asked to become a director of a South Bend bank. Within a couple of years the bank folded. Many depositors lost much of their money. One such was a charwoman who worked at Notre Dame. A friend of the woman happened to mention to Rock that the woman had lost her savings of $150. Without a word, Rock wrote a check for $150, gave it to the woman who'd reported it to him and told her to take it to her friend.

Rock's willingness to help a friend, a player, or anything connected with the university was seemingly limitless. One day, he hopped in his car and, leaving no word as to where he was going, drove down to Indianapolis, the state capital.

Plans for a new state highway had been revealed showing that it would pass through the outskirts of South Bend and through an old cemetery. Several graves, including those of several former Notre Dame faculty, would have to be disturbed and moved to another cemetery. Rock took a dim view of these plans. Without consulting anyone at the university, he laid his displeasure on the legislators. Within a half-hour, he was promised that the highway would be rerouted around the cemetery.

About a month before the 1930 season ended, the B. F. Keith-Orpheum vaudeville circuit came to Rockne and offered him a glittering deal for a one-month, five- or six-city tour in January. All he had to do was get on the stage for a half-hour, twice a day, tell some jokes or stories and talk about football. His salary for the stint would exceed that of four years of football coaching. Something told him to reject it. Not that it didn't appeal to him artistically —the stage was a life-long magnet for him—but he still had fears for his health.

But in other ways he still overcommitted himself, especially if he could help advance a worthwhile cause. His real trouble was he couldn't say no to friends.

The Depression was now deepening all over the land. Millions were already out of work, and in the big cities long lines were beginning to form outside of soup kitchens that were providing a bit of daily sustenance for the unemployed.

In New York City, Mayor Jimmy Walker had an idea for a big charity event that would surely raise a bundle for the unemployed:

a football game between the pro New York Giants and—who else?
—the darlings of those thousands of New York curbstone alumni:
the Fighting Irish of Notre Dame. No, not Rock's current Irish,
but a bunch of old-timers, including many of the Four Horsemen
crowd. Walker got on the phone to Rock. Would Rock get in touch
with his former players and bring them to New York?

For Jimmy Walker, Rockne didn't hesitate. The date was set for
Sunday, December 14, in the Polo Grounds, and Rockne immediately went into motion. A few letters here, a few phone calls there,
and he had about eighteen commitments. "I assume you're all in
shape," he told them. "After all, you've only been out of football
a half-dozen years." He was thinking of the pro games he'd played
when he was even older than they were.

It apparently was all set. But a couple of days before the Army
game in Chicago Rock went to his doctors for a physical and they
blew the whistle. No charity game in New York. Not only did they
ban him from taking part in something like that in the cold weather
of mid-December in New York but they wanted him to go straight
to Florida immediately after the season for a month on the beach.

Rock sent a telegram to Jimmy Walker, telling him he couldn't
make it. The USC game on the Coast, December 6, would put too
much travel strain on him. It would mean another long trip back
to New York.

Walker was terribly upset. He phoned Rock and said that more
than $50,000 worth of tickets had already been peddled and the
whole city had been excited by the impending event. Without
Rock's presence the game would be a fizzle and he'd have to
consider calling it off. Rock said he'd let him know in two or three
days.

He hadn't even bothered to tell his pal Jimmy that he'd already
committed still another bunch of his former players to a similar
charity game in Chicago against a team of former Northwestern
stars, to be played on Thanksgiving, two days before the Army
game.

His old Notre Damers had already checked into South Bend and
during that week (the mind boggles slightly at this) he was not only
coaching them but was, at the same time, readying his varsity for

a crucial game with Northwestern in Dyche stadium. What he didn't need right then was a blizzard, but he got it. The old-timers and his varsity worked indoors on the dirt floor of the old gym. So did the indoor track squad. The word for that week was chaotic.

Rockne's final season was now rolling into its climactic final weeks. First, there would be Big Ten champion Northwestern with probably its greatest team ever. Followed by vengeful and tough Army. Winding up with a brilliant Southern Cal club that had lost to the Irish by a single point the previous year. It was already decided by the press and fans that if both teams were undefeated when they met, the winner would be national champion. Nobody had ever won the national crown two straight years. Rockne wanted to be the first.

Northwestern would be the first real test since he'd lost Savoldi to the divorce courts. And Moon Mullins, now the top fullback, was sub-par with a bad knee. In his pre-game speech, Rock flung all his passion at his players. Blow this one, and it won't matter what they do against Army and USC. The season would be in ashes. "It'll probably take more fight then you possess," he told them, "and the fact is, you've never completely demonstrated just how much you have this season. But today you can't duck it, because if these guys beat you, THEY can be national champions." There was more, crackling in the damp, cold air, and they got the message. Actually, he spoke for less than one minute.

It was a scoreless first half. In the dressing room Rock didn't rave or rant. This time he was calm, cajoling, sympathetic. He had a word for every regular. Give us two or three superb plays, he pleaded.

With five minutes to go in the game they gave him a big one as Marchy Schwartz zipped off tackle. Seven potential tacklers were flat on the ground as Schwartz raced fifty yards for the TD. Three minutes later the Irish got another score from in close and it was all over.

In the entire second half the Wildcats never crossed the Irish 40-yard line. And although Northwestern had one of the best aerial attacks in the country, they completed only three passes all afternoon. Later, Rock said it was the finest pass defense he'd ever seen any football team put up.

The pressure on Notre Dame—and Rock—seemed unusually heavy. The prospects of back-to-back national crowns, and rumors that Rock's health was degenerating again, lay heavily over the campus. Added to Rockne's personal load was his uncertainty over the big charity game in New York. To make things worse, the charity game in Chicago on Thanksgiving was a bust. The temperature had plunged to zero, and fewer than 5,000 fans showed up. When ticket sales failed to meet expenses, Rockne wrote a personal check for $2,500 to cover the loss.

This year the Irish weren't going through the razzmatazz of the junket to New York to play Army. The Cadets were coming to Soldier Field in Chicago, instead, because the Notre Dame team was leaving Monday morning for the Coast, and their final game against USC. It would have been impossible for them to go to New York and then head right for Los Angeles.

Just a few weeks earlier, incidentally, Rockne had been dismayed by a report that Army wanted to terminate the annual series because it was no longer just a football game but a circus event not consistent with West Point's idea of athletic propriety. It took a hasty, private meeting with Major Ralph Sasse, the new Cadet coach, and Rock at his most charmingly persuasive, to keep the series going.

Now, on November 29, at Soldier Field, the Irish faced the Cadets. More than 110,000 fans sent up a rolling murmur of shock as workmen pulled back the huge tarpaulin and a covering of straw to reveal a field coated with ice. The temperature was 14°.

In the dressing room before they took the field for the kickoff, the Irish sat waiting for Rockne's spiel. He sat there with them, staring down at his hands folded in his lap. For an eternity, it seemed, he sat like that, as though there were nothing he could say that would mean anything at that point. Finally, he stood up, looked out at their set, young faces and made the briefest pre-game talk of his life.

"Let's go get 'em," he said quietly.

For three quarters, and for eight minutes into the final period, it was a punting duel, both teams kicking on second or third down, as the backs on both sides slithered and careened helplessly on the slick surface, toward holes which linemen failed to open because nobody's cleats could get enough purchase for an effective block. On the sideline, Rockne ceased his usual running comment and was strangely silent.

Then, following a punt by Army, which Carideo returned to the Irish 47, Carideo called a play which hadn't worked all day. When he came back with it now it seemed to have a new look. Not really, of course—but no one ever completely shut off one of Rock's pet plays.

It was his classic cutback over tackle. Out of the shift came a box to the right. Little Bert Metzger, all 149 pounds of him, pulled out at the snap, raced through a hole created by tackle Joe Kurth and end Tom Conley, and took out an Army defensive halfback. Conley, after a brush block on the Cadet tackle, raced downfield to pinch off the other Army halfback. Marchy Schwartz, with the ball, was into vacant territory by then, and on his way to a fifty-four-yard touchdown dash that had developed so quickly that nobody in the stands was fully aware it was happening.

Frank Carideo place-kicked the extra point for the Irish 7–0 lead, and with only four minutes to play it looked as though Rock was only one game away from another perfect season.

But with less than a minute to go, Carideo had to punt from his own 10-yard line. Something went awry in the blocking assignments, and an Army end, Dick King, sliced through to deflect the kick. The ball bounced back into the end zone, and Harley Trice, an Army guard, smothered it joyously for the touchdown.

Pandemonium in Soldier Field. The Irish were about to be tied in the last fifty seconds of play. Knute Rockne was just another victim of fate's fickle finger.

Rockne had often worked on an emergency situation such as this. His tactic called for a nine-man rush, with at least two feints to open up an alley. He watched grimly from the sideline as the Army center prepared to snap the ball.

Chuck Broshus, a substitute Army quarterback, was standing on the 12-yard line with arms and hands outstretched, waiting for the ball. He was that far back because he was a drop-kicker—one of the last of the breed. The Cadet center had already wiped the ball on his jersey to remove all traces of mud and slime. Broshus would have to handle it cleanly in dropping it to the turf for his rebound.

The snap swept back to Broshus perfectly, belt-high. He bent slightly at the waist as he prepared to drop the ball and then kick it on its rebound. The kick never got more than two feet off the ground as at least three Irish linemen burst through and smothered it.

Two plays after the succeeding kickoff, the gun went off, signaling the 7–6 Notre Dame victory.

Rock took his cigar out of his mouth and looked at it. It had long since gone out. He flung it away, satisfied.

Monday morning in Chicago, he shepherded his squad onto the Notre Dame special train bound for Los Angeles. A trip to a Southern Cal game had become a skylarking peregrination for Notre Dame. A dozen or more sportswriters piled aboard the special to chronicle every phase of the trip, which would take at least five days. The team stopped in New Orleans and Tucson, Arizona, for a day each so Rock could put his kids through a widely advertised and much photographed drill. At Phoenix, the junket would be joined by a half-dozen Los Angeles sportswriters who made the last leg of the journey milking Rock for any number of pre-game columns. The whole nation knew it when Knute Rockne and his road-happy Irish went west to meet the Trojans.

The night before he left South Bend, Rockne sent a telegram to Mayor Jimmy Walker of New York. The annual Notre Dame–Army game played there had helped, in great measure, to give the Irish their national constituency. And Manhattan was Rock's second home, with the theater, and marvelous all-night sessions with great orchestra leaders such as Isham Jones, Paul Whiteman, Carmen Lombardo, Ben Birnie and others, who always had the latchkey out for him whenever he came to town. It was a huge emotional debt which Rock felt he owed New York. In his telegram he told Jimmy Walker he'd show up for the charity game, December 14 . . .

But on the way to the West Coast, Rockne knew he had a problem at fullback. Joe Savoldi was a victim of the divorce courts. Moon Mullins was out with a bad knee. His third-string fullback, Dan Hanley, was hard-working but slow, and had played very little. Rock knew he had to get more speed into his attack. Suddenly he had an idea.

Let the Trojans think Hanley was going to play. They'd fear nothing from him and probably would react accordingly.

Meanwhile, there was Bucky O'Connor . . .

O'Connor was a fine senior reserve halfback with great speed and breakaway moves. Yet not powerful enough for fullback in the system Rock was now using. But if Rock could somehow . . . *somehow* . . . get O'Connor in at fullback . . . *posing as Hanley* . . .

By the time the expedition arrived at Tucson for a workout, it was all set up. In Tucson, Bucky O'Connor, wearing Dan Hanley's number, went through signal drills and a dummy scrimmage. On Rock's instructions, O'Connor, the impostor for Hanley, deliberately messed up a couple of plays.

On the sidelines, Rock gloomily turned to several writers, including those from Los Angeles. "I'm afraid Dan Hanley just isn't up to it," he said. "He hasn't played enough to really know our system and mesh with it."

"Kind of slow, too, isn't he Rock?" said one L.A. writer.

"He sure is," replied Rockne. "I wish we had Moon Mullins in there, but he's out for good with that knee."

Just then some photographers started coming across the field. Reporters might be fooled but pictures getting back to Los Angeles might blow the whole thing. Rock sent both Hanley and O'Connor to the dressing room, with orders for Hanley to get his own jersey back from O'Connor and to return to the field for photos while O'Connor stayed out of sight.

When the photographers took a shot of the starting team it was Hanley who appeared at fullback. At that point Rock put an end to practice.

Two days later during the final workout in Los Angeles, Bill Henry, football columnist for the L. A. *Times,* wanted to meet the new fullback, Dan Hanley. He went to Francis Wallace, who had made the trip out from New York, and asked Wallace to introduce him. Wallace, as he later wrote, had to do some fancy footwork. He took Henry over to Bucky O'Connor (Hanley) and said, very clearly and carefully: *"Dan Hanley,* I'd like you to meet Bill Henry . . ."

O'Connor, catching on immediately, pulled it off beautifully, chatted for a few seconds and then excused himself before Henry could ask any personal questions.

Rockne was playing it skillfully, appearing glum and discouraged. Alerted by his instructions, his players went through their drill with a marked absence of spirit and snap. Los Angeles writers noted the team's sluggishness in their stories. The gamblers made the Trojans a solid favorite. It was obviously a battered, tired Notre Dame team going with a slow, inexperienced Dan Hanley at fullback. Rock had the Trojans all set up.

It wasn't even close. USC kept defending against an Irish attack that was supposed to bog down because of a plodding fullback. Obviously, the Trojans merely had to key on Marchy Schwartz. They did, and kept Schwartz in check.

No one could understand why they kept letting the slow-footed "Dan Hanley" rip off so much yardage.

Bucky O'Connor ran for three long touchdowns, each for fifty yards or more, as the Irish plastered the Trojans, 27–0. Knute Rockne had his two back-to-back undefeated seasons and national championships.

He barely took time to accept congratulations. While his team returned to South Bend by train, Rock flew there to spend two days in his office, then took another plane to New York, getting there just three days before the charity game. He took one look at the smiling crowd of former Notre Damers who met him for a couple days of practice at the Polo Grounds, noted the flab around the middle of Jimmy Crowley, Rip Miller and a few others, and knew it was going to be a long, cold Sunday afternoon.

"I guess we were a sorry lot," recalled Crowley. "None of us exactly an ad for physical fitness. Rock just sort of shook his head but there wasn't much he could do with us at that point. Benny Friedman, the ex-Michigan All-America quarterback, had a pretty good bunch behind him on the Giants and they'd been playing together for a couple of years. But we did have some good laughs out of it to go along with the bruises."

It didn't take long for the Old Notre Damers to realize what they were up against. "Hey, how much time is left?" Elmer Layden asked after he'd carried the ball on the first play from scrimmage. He asked the question while flat on his back, two Giant tacklers astride him.

A couple of minutes later, Crowley, somewhat in the same situation, said to the ref: "How many people are here today—and why are they all wearing Giant uniforms?"

Hunk Anderson and Noble Kizer, playing guard, were having a dreadful time of it. Anderson wiped some blood from his lip and said to Kizer, a future head coach at Purdue: "I think their next play is going to the outside. Instead of going on through, I'll pull out so I can be in better position to stop it. You cover my hole."

"You're nuts if you think I'm gonna stay here and let all those gorillas tromp over me!" Kizer snapped back. "I'm pulling out with you." The play, of course, came through the big gap they left and went for twenty yards.

Rip Miller was playing alongside Anderson. He noticed that Hunk was doing a real needling job on Miller's man. As a result, the Giant was really belting Miller around. Miller finally turned to Hunk and said wearily: "Hunk, I wish you'd confine your sassy talk to the guy directly opposite you. This guy has been murdering me all day and I've had it."

"They beat the stuffings out of us," said Crowley dryly, "by several touchdowns, as I recall. We caught Rock smiling on the sidelines a couple of times, as though he enjoyed seeing some of his old stars get their lumps."

Not likely. If Rock had reason to smile it wasn't because he was losing.

At a banquet that night, Jimmy Walker called on Rockne to say a few words. The game had cleared almost $200,000 for the unemployment fund and Rock beamed, despite a growing pain in his leg. He kidded his former stars and told them they were the real heroes. He'd only had to sit on the bench and watch them collect their bruises. They had risked their hides to play and he knew they were doing it because they felt it was for a good cause.

Jimmy Crowley, of course, had the proper perspective. "Sure, we were concerned for the poor, but we were there getting cracked around for only one reason—because Rock asked us to."

The Mayor's Committee handed Rock a wad of money for his personal expenses in coming to New York. He tried to refuse it but they insisted. He pocketed the cash, but when he got back to South Bend he mailed back his personal check for the amount.

Right after the first of the year, at his doctor's orders, Rockne was scheduled to return to the Mayo Clinic for another checkup. Although he had long since given up his chemistry teaching and other administrative details, he was as busy as when he'd worn seven hats. Earlier on he'd been a somewhat limited, *local* personality, as it were; now he was a national figure with all sorts of physical and emotional demands and requests being pressed upon him.

He was lucky if he found time to jump into his car and hit the streets of South Bend on a personal errand. And luckier still if he could get anything done there. He was instantly recognized, bigger-than-life to the locals, and could not say no to anyone who wanted to pass a word with him when he stopped in at Rocco's barbershop, popped into the newsstand at the Oliver Hotel for out-of-town papers, dropped into a delicatessen for German potato salad which he loved, or pulled into a filling station for gas.

Shortly after the New York charity game he was scheduled for an interview with Bill Cunningham of the Boston *Post*. Rock arrived on the sleeper from New York at 7:30 A.M. He was on a brief tour for Studebaker, and Cunningham noted how snazzy Rock looked in a pressed gray suit with handkerchief in the breast pocket, and a Ziegfeld blue shirt. "He'd just had time for a bath and breakfast," wrote Cunningham, "and by nine o'clock he had seven writers in his hotel suite. I wanted to talk football but Rock wanted to talk literature.

"The telephone kept ringing but he didn't have to answer it. Studebaker had supplied him with a traveling secretary who kept putting off the callers unless it was something vital. Rock never thought anything was vital except football or what he was discussing at the moment."

Rockne had a luncheon engagement at the Harvard Club and it was only after lunch that Cunningham was able to get him alone. "Rock shucked off his jacket and vest," said Cunningham, "and hitched up his pants legs. Then he began unrolling a set of rubber putties he always wore to keep his bad legs firm. He hoisted his freed legs to the table, and then sighed."

Cunningham wanted to know how he flexed his ends. "Never mind about flexing ends," Rockne told him. "Tell me how you writer guys go about grabbing your readers by the neck and holding them through stuff you know might be dull, but what you want them to be sure not to miss."

"And *that's* what we talked about—not football," said Cunningham.

Soon afterward, Rock spent a week at the Mayo Clinic. He was told that his phlebitis, though apparently vastly improved, was merely in an arrested state and could worsen at any time. He was to cut down on his activities. He could continue with his Studebaker dates (a lucrative contract) but the quid pro quo was the elimination of all other speaking appearances and at least half of his writing. And he was to go to Florida for at least six weeks before starting spring practice.

Returning from Rochester, Rock stepped off the train in Chicago, his lined face wreathed in a broad smile. The usual dozen reporters and photographers were on hand to record his return.

One of them said: "Hey, Rock, I hear you're pretty poor at math. Is that story true about a couple of your checks bouncing?"

Rock grinned. He'd mentioned to a reporter friend before he'd left for Minnesota that he'd been neglectful and had overdrawn his account. "Yeah," he said. "A couple of them came back marked 'no funds.' That was okay, but when one came back stamped 'no bank' I knew I was in trouble."

Good old Rock. Gimpy legs or not, a helluva guy, right? And those strangely recurring rumors that if he didn't get out of football soon, he wouldn't be long for this world—well, hell, who could believe *that?* Rockne out of football? Then it wouldn't be football . . .

*　　　　*　　　　*

In January 1931 Rockne went to Florida, as his doctors had ordered. There, on the beach, a friend from New York found him playing joyfully in the sand with his youngest son, Jackie.

"You look great, Rock," the visitor said.

"Good enough," Rock countered. "They're letting me go swimming now. A year ago they only let me sit at the water's edge and wet my toes.

"My legs are a lot stronger and I can play miniature golf." He smiled crookedly. "No marathon dancing or steeplechase races. But maybe by next summer."

His face brightened. "Best news the docs gave me was that I won't have to conduct spring practice from a chair." Then he wagged his head in mock sadness. "But I won't be able to use my sympathy-for-my-illness gag with the players any more. I'll have to think of something else." A pause. "Good Lord—I may have to rely on straight football!"

Early in March he left Bonnie, Jackie and Mary Jean in Coral Gables and flew back to South Bend to organize spring football— which he was to interrupt for Easter Week while he went to Hollywood to sign a film contract. On March 29 he went to Chicago to spend a day with his mother, to celebrate her birthday. On the night of the thirtieth he left Chicago by Pullman for Kansas City.

There, Knute Kenneth Rockne, age forty-three, had a rendezvous with Transcontinental Western Flight No. 599, departing 9:30 A.M., March 31, for Los Angeles.

20

Aftermath

More than 100,000 people stood along the route, lined all the way by police, firemen and Boy Scouts, all standing at attention. South Bend's population was only 100,000. Thousands had come from nearby towns and farms to be part of an historic moment they regarded as deeply personal. Trains on the New York Central and all buses leaving or approaching South Bend came to a full stop for one minute . . .

Bonnie Rockne had been in Florida for Easter vacation with the two younger children, Mary Jean, eleven, and Jackie, five. It was the last day of their stay and they were to leave for South Bend next morning. She had taken the kids to the beach at Coral Gables with the Rocknes' good friends Mr. and Mrs. Tom O'Neil of Akron, Ohio. On the way back to the O'Neils' home they stopped at a filling station. A mechanic took O'Neil aside.

Then, his face ashen, but maintaining control, Tom O'Neil came back to the car. "Bonnie," he began, "I have some very serious news . . ."

He told her that Flight 599 had crashed in Kansas and that Knute had been killed.

Bonnie gathered her two children to her on the drive back to the Rockne quarters, and then broke the word to them. Mary Jean was visibly affected. The lone girl in the family, she was very close to her father. Little Jackie was not quite comprehending.

The first thing the maid handed to Bonnie as she entered the house was a telegram. It was from Knute, sent from Kansas City that morning—typical of the cheerful, warm, loving messages he always sent her before starting on a trip.

The O'Neils helped her pack their personal belongings. Little Jackie played with his marbles and a popgun, then got out a football and kicked it around the living room, something he would not normally be permitted. The football was the last object Bonnie Rockne noticed before leaving the house. She asked Tom O'Neil to be sure to pack it with the rest of her things to be sent north. Knute and Jackie had played with it on the beach a couple of weeks earlier. He had blown up the ball himself.

Bonnie had already made certain decisions about her husband's funeral. Shortly after returning from the beach she'd received a phone call from Dr. D. M. Nigro, president of the Notre Dame Alumni Club of Kansas City, and one of Knute's closest friends. She asked Nigro to take charge of her husband's body as soon as possible and bring it back to South Bend.

Nigro had rushed out to Pembroke School in Kansas City to break the news to Knute Jr. and Billy, before they heard it from other sources. They sobbed until he said to them: "Take it like real sportsmen, the sons of a great man."

In Chicago every radio station was blaring word of the crash. One of Rockne's sisters, Mrs. Martha Stiles, heard it on WGN. Numbly she phoned the station and was told that while Knute Rockne apparently had been listed as a passenger, his body had not yet been positively identified.

Mrs. Stiles phoned her sisters, Louise and Florence, who lived with their mother, and a third sister, Mrs. Anna Leggett. They all gathered at their mother's home. The sisters told their mother only that Knute had been hurt. The strong, resolute Viking lady who was Knute Rockne's mother went calmly to the telephone and, without identifying herself, called WGN and asked if it were true that Knute Rockne was dead. She got an affirmative answer and turned to give the corroboration to her daughters. Louise fell to the floor in a faint.

Just the night before, Mrs. Rockne and Louise had gone to a

movie and had seen a newsreel showing Knute conducting spring practice.

On Wednesday morning, April 1, the investigation into the fatal crash of NC-999 opened in Cottonwood Falls, Kansas, thirty-four miles southwest of Emporia. (Anthony Fokker, the Dutch designer of the craft, was in Los Angeles and said he would fly to Cottonwood Falls to testify. "But," he said, "it is out of the question to consider the airplane itself was defective. I inspected it personally two days ago and found it in perfect condition.")

The inquest was headed by Coroner Hinden and Leonard Jurdon, Department of Commerce inspector. They listened to airline officials and three of the farmers who had witnessed the catastrophe, and put together what was known and what was surmised. There were no sophisticated methods in that era to determine causes of plane crashes. It was believed that ice had formed on the plane, especially on the wing. Its weight had snapped off one side of the wing to send the plane spiraling into the snow-covered pastureland.

Another theory was that pilot Fry had come down blindly through the clouds when he'd lost his bearings—had thought he was too close to the ground and nosed up sharply again. The terrific jerk, amplified by the power of the three motors, had put too much stress on the wing and ripped the right section away. With ice causing more than 50 percent of lift to be lost, the plane had no chance to zoom up again. Air mail pilot Paul E. Johnson testified that he had been in the vicinity. He, too, had been fighting ice and had seen Rockne's plane maneuvering to escape clouds. Since the two planes were so close, Johnson assumed ice had been a problem for NC-999, too.

When R. S. Bridges, the airline traffic agent from Kansas City, stood up to read off the names on the passenger list, the crowded courtroom was alive with spectator buzzing. The first name was: "Knute K. Rockne . . ." The buzzing stopped as though cut off with an invisible knife.

Officialdom rendered a brief, pragmatic final report: there had been no explosion and nobody was burned. All eight men had been killed instantly on impact. The plane was not overloaded, with only six passengers and sixty-five pounds of mail. It was only a year old and had been inspected every twenty-four hours. Cause of the crash must have been structural failure due to the stress of ice. Case closed.

From that moment on, the focus of the nation would be on Knute Rockne's funeral.

Three assistant coaches from Notre Dame, Hunk Anderson, Jack Chevigny and John Voedisch, were waiting in silent anguish in the Kansas City railroad station as midnight, April 1 neared. Suddenly a railroad official came toward them and nodded. Rockne's body had arrived from Cottonwood Falls.

Anderson, Chevigny and Voedisch, like outriders from Valhalla, had come to Kansas City to guard their chieftain's body on his final trip home, although officially Bonnie Rockne had asked Dr. Nigro to take charge of all arrangements and shepherd her sons, Billy and Knute Jr., from Kansas City.

The three coaches allowed no one else to touch the gray box in the transfer to the Santa Fe train that would pull out at 4:34 A.M. for Chicago. The three husky young men hoisted the box into a special funeral coach and stayed with it all night long, sleeping not a wink.

At 7:45 P.M., April 2, the train arrived in Dearborn Station, Chicago, and was immediately transferred to a special New York Central train for South Bend. Boarding it at Chicago was a committee of prominent Notre Dame alumni from Chicago to accompany the body. If Dr. Nigro and the three assistant football coaches felt any infringement on their own function, they kept it to themselves.

The train pulled into Union Station at South Bend at 11:20 P.M. Anderson, getting off first, stared in disbelief. The station was jammed with thousands upon thousands of people, all hoping to catch a glimpse of the temporary casket. It was a great shifting sea of faces, with hundreds of handkerchiefs pressed to eyes like white-caps rippling the silent surface.

Once again Anderson, Chevigny and Voedisch lifted the box and bore it to a waiting hearse to be taken to the Louis McGann funeral parlor on North Michigan Avenue, where the body would await the return from Florida on Thursday of Bonnie Rockne and her two younger children. They were taking a train called, ironically, *The Dixie Flyer.*

Until Franklin D. Roosevelt's death in April 1945, fourteen years later, there simply wasn't a funeral in American history that produced as much emotional impact as the funeral of Knute Rockne in April 1931.

Now started the messages of sympathy from the nation's famous —the expressions of regret from every quarter. The Maryland legislature was the first such body to pass a resolution acknowledging the loss of a great leader. Within days every legislature in the country had done likewise.

President Herbert Hoover referred to a "national loss" even more than football's. His telegram to Bonnie Rockne read: I KNOW THAT EVERY AMERICAN GRIEVES WITH YOU. MR. ROCKNE SO CONTRIBUTED TO A CLEANLINESS AND HIGH PURPOSE AND SPORTSMANSHIP IN ATHLETICS THAT HIS PASSING IS A NATIONAL LOSS.

Variations on the theme came from General Douglas MacArthur, former superintendent of West Point; from Charles Lindbergh and Will Rogers; from King Haakon of Norway, the land of Rockne's birth (Haakon also sent a special delegation of Norwegians from his embassy in Washington to attend the funeral); from every governor, senator and congressman and every famous football coach in the land.

Sermons were prepared for delivery not only in Catholic churches but in hundreds of Protestant churches and Jewish synagogues. Purdue University, in nearby Lafayette, Indiana, set its campus flag at half-staff and was followed quickly by every school in the Big Ten.

The Columbia Broadcasting System sent representatives to South Bend to arrange for a coast-to-coast radio broadcast of the funeral services scheduled for Saturday, April 4. It would be the most extensive such broadcast ever attempted, also going by short-wave to Europe, South America and Asia.

Friday night before the funeral there would be a one-hour CBS network memorial tribute headed by Ted Husing, then the nation's preeminent radio sportscaster.

At first there were urgent suggestions that the funeral services be held in Notre Dame's new stadium, which had been dedicated the previous autumn—a stadium Rockne had virtually designed himself. It would be only fitting, said many people, for the symbolic structure to be used to commemorate Rockne's brilliant career.

Bonnie Rockne would have none of it. Services, she said firmly, would be held on the Notre Dame campus at Sacred Heart Church, a replica of a thirteenth-century French Gothic cathedral.

The seating capacity would be limited to 1,400, of course. Although it was Easter Week, many students had decided to remain in South Bend for the funeral. And, to begin with, more than 250 honorary pallbearers had been invited (with hundreds more hoping to have been summoned). On the favored list were such as Will Rogers, Mayor Jimmy Walker of New York, Olympic chieftain Avery Brundage, as well as a clutch of big-time football coaches headed by Pop Warner of Stanford, Jock Sutherland of Pitt, Tad Jones of Yale, Bill Alexander of Georgia Tech, Dana Bible of Nebraska, and others.

The actual pallbearers, selected by Bonnie Rockne, were obviously emotional choices. Six Notre Dame football players were chosen: Tom Conley, captain of Rockne's last team in 1930, Tommy Yarr, captain-elect for 1931, and the famous 1930 backfield—Frank Carideo, Marchmont Schwartz, Marty Brill and Moon Mullins.

Virtually every starting player Rockne had coached at Notre Dame was on his way to South Bend, including more than 200 of whom were now coaching either in college or in high school. Every member of the famed Four Horsemen team of 1923–24 would be there, including, of course, the Horsemen themselves—Harry Stuhldreher, Don Miller, Jimmy Crowley and Elmer Layden.

Bonnie Rockne had arrived home from Florida on Thursday morning. Knute's body now reposed in a bronzed casket at the modest Rockne home at 1417 East Wayne Street in the Sunnymede section of middle-class houses. The famous and near-famous made a shrine of it as the funeral services drew near.

Mayor Jimmy Walker stood at the doorway of Rockne's den and murmured: "Just what I expected it to be like." It was a simple room, where Rockne had done most of his planning and writing —a desk, a large chair, an upright floor lamp, a room chockablock with newspapers, books, file folders and football memorabilia, yet nothing really in disarray, everything seemingly ordered and available.

The room was dominated by a large oil painting of Rockne in a sweat shirt, with a football under his arm, his rough-featured face gazing out quizzically. Painted by Gerrit A. Beneker, it hung directly across from the doorway, the first thing to be seen upon entering.

Only two photos were on his desk: one of Bonnie and the other of Rockne in cap and gown when he graduated from Notre Dame in June 1914. His framed diploma marking his degree in chemistry from the department of pharmacy—and his proudest personal possession—hung on the wall.

On Saturday, April 4, the city of South Bend was closed down of all activity by mayoral proclamation. Wayne Street and the blocks on either side of it were closed to traffic.

Inside the house, Bonnie Rockne stroked the smooth side of the bronze casket that had lain there for two days, and kissed the crucifix fastened to the top—her farewell to the man who was leaving their home for the last time. At 3 P.M., on schedule, the six Notre Dame football players picked up the flower-draped casket, decked with a blue and gold Notre Dame monogram blanket, and carried it outside, where 250 honorary pallbearers lined the sidewalk six-deep from the house to the hearse at the curb. Hundreds of people were beyond the honorary pallbearers, but, as one observer put it, "they were so quiet you could actually hear the sighing of the birches on the Rockne lawn as the wind rustled them."

Then Knute Rockne's final journey began. Slowly, west on Wayne Street to Eddy. North on Eddy to Jefferson and to Notre Dame Avenue. North on Notre Dame Avenue to the university. Past the new stadium, its entrance entirely draped in black and white. Past the stadium to Sacred Heart church, already crammed with 1,400 students, close friends, university people, the press and the nationally famous. In front were Bonnie Rockne, her four children and Knute's mother and four sisters.

More than 100,000 people had taken up positions along the route, lined all the way by police, firemen and hundreds of Boy Scouts, all standing at attention. South Bend's entire population was only 100,000. Thousands had come from neighboring cities, towns and farms to be part of an historic moment they regarded as deeply personal.

Trains on the New York Central railroad and all buses leaving or approaching South Bend came to a full stop for one minute. The night before, the radio audience which was tuned in to the weekly Friday night fights in Los Angeles listened to an eerie effect. The ring announcer asked everyone to rise for ten seconds of silence. A gigantic rustle was heard as the crowd stood, and then, at one-second intervals, came the clanging of ten strokes on the timer's bell. Rock was "out" but never kayoed.

Grief and splendor vied for emotional impact at Sacred Heart church, and flowed together fittingly in a common bond of reverent beauty. From the belfry the church bell boomed out a full-throated, solitary note. Solemnly it reverberated on the still April air—over the campus, over the new stadium, and seemingly to the nearby Mishawaka hills, echoing back again. A public address system had been set up so that about 10,000 people outside the church could hear the services.

Inside, four huge but graceful streamers of black and white dropped in magnificently rich folds from the ceiling in front of the altar where the casket rested. Red lights flickered in silver lamps hanging over the sanctuary.

The full panoply of the church was assembled for the rites. Bishop John F. Noll of Fort Wayne was the celebrant; Reverend Michael W. Mulcaire, the deacon; Reverend John F. O'Hara, the subdeacon. Father Mulcaire, head of the faculty athletic board, was to read the service.

Bishop Noll appeared, capped with white miter, a cape of rich black draping in lustrous folds from his shoulders. There was a whispering of robes from his retinue, priests in cassocks of black with white surplices. A choir of young seminarians opened the services with the chant of *Miserere*.

Never did the high ritual of the Catholic Church seem more impressive than for the Norseman, born a Lutheran, lying at the altar.

Reverend Charles L. O'Donnell, often called "the poet president of Notre Dame," was to deliver the eulogy. Later, he was said to have exceeded even his great gifts of spiritual and literary power.

Father O'Donnell stared for a moment at the assemblage before him, forgetting for the time being that his words would be carried across the nation, and to foreign countries as well. His voice trembled and almost broke as he began, but he quickly steadied himself. It is worth recording here, in part, what he had to say:

". . . In this holy Week of Christ's passion and death, there has occurred a tragic event which accounts for our presence here today. Knute Rockne is dead.

"And who was he . . . ?

"Ask the president of the United States, who dispatched a personal message of tribute and comfort to a bereaved family . . . Ask the King of Norway, who sends a special delegation to these solemn services . . . Ask the state legislatures who have passed resolutions of sympathy and condolence . . .

"Ask the various university senates, the civic societies and bodies without number . . . Ask the bishops, the clergy, the various religious orders who have sent assurances of their prayers . . .

"Ask the thousands of working newspapermen whose labor of love in his name has stirred a reading public of one hundred twenty-five million Americans . . .

"Ask men and women in all walks of life . . . Ask the boys of America . . . Ask any and all of these: Who was this man whose death has struck the nation with dismay and has everywhere turned heads in grief . . . ?

"Was he, perhaps, a martyr who died for some great cause? A patriot who laid down his life for his country? A statesman, a soldier, an Admiral of the Fleet? Some heaven-born artist, an inventor, a captain of industry or finance . . . ?

"No . . . he was the director of athletics and football coach at Notre Dame, and a great American . . ."

Father O'Donnell went on: "In an age that has stamped itself as the era of the 'go-getter,' a horrible word for a ruthless thing, Knute Rockne was a 'go-giver,' a not much better word for such a divine thing . . .

"He made use of all the proper machinery and the legitimate methods of modern activity to be essentially not modern at all: to be quite elementarily human and Christian, giving himself . . ."

Father O'Donnell's voice was barely audible when he finished. Nearly all the 1,400 people inside the church were weeping.

When the rites were concluded, the hearse left the church at 4 P.M., the scheduled time—the kind of precision and planning that Rockne, the master co-ordinator and planner, would have admired.

South, now, on Notre Dame Avenue to Jefferson Boulevard; west on Jefferson to Michigan. North on Michigan to LaSalle, and then Lincoln Way West, the packed thousands once more lining the route. Out Lincoln to Blaine . . . to Portage . . . and then north to Highland Cemetery where the graveside rites were held.

Two days earlier Bonnie Rockne had gone out to the cemetery and selected the spot herself. Old Council Oak, its leaves preparing to burst forth with new spring life, had been a symbol of peace for more than 150 years, a meeting place of Indian chiefs and white men. There, under its spreading branches, Knute Rockne's grave had been prepared.

It was done now. And when the count was taken it was judged that more than 1,600 of the nation's 1,700-odd daily newspapers had carried editorials on Knute Rockne's death. Not just the giants in New York, Chicago, Detroit, Philadelphia. There were also tributes in the Casa Grande, Arizona, *Dispatch,* the Eufaula, Alabama, *Tribune,* the Smackover, Arkansas, *Journal,* the Henderson, Kentucky, *Gleaner.*

The heads over the editorials told it all:

ET TU, ROCKNE—Terra Bella, California, *News*
ROCKNE IS NOT DEAD—Boulder, Colorado, *Camera*

ROCKNE GOES TO VALHALLA—Springfield, Illinois, *Courier*
SKOL! KNUTE ROCKNE! SKOL!—Boston *American*

The editorial cartoons were predictably of a piece, but poignant nevertheless. A huge black-crepe-wrapped football. Black-draped goal posts with a wreath lying on the goal line beneath them. A prone Knute Rockne, with sweat shirt and whistle, lying on the field, surrounded by an army of football players, heads bowed. A wreath-wrapped goal post merging into a black background labeled THE GREAT BEYOND.

And then there was the poetry. Hundreds upon hundreds of spontaneously composed verses, by professional poets as well as just plain fans, which poured into newspaper offices, much of it beautiful and bittersweet, and published on the editorial pages.

In sum, the South Bend *News-Times* perhaps said it best:

> Knute Rockne of Notre Dame, who lived so that the world might be better for his having lived, and who died with his faith and his fame like a mantle about him, was left to his eternal rest today . . .

It was over. A man whose full measure as a personality, as a force for good, was gone from the American scene. Symbolically, Knute Rockne's death brought down the final curtain on that crazy, frenetic, kaleidoscopic, nonpareil era known as the Golden Age of Sport. Done. Its warp and woof assigned to a tapestry of history that was more legend than plain fact and footnote.

A week after Rock's death, a tearful Will Rogers, the famous forelock dangling over his right eye, got to his feet at the prestigious Los Angeles Luncheon Club. He smiled a lopsided smile and his first words were not really for the audience, though it was meant to hear them:

"It takes a mighty big calamity to shake this country all at once, Knute, but you did it . . . You did it, Knute . . ."

Rock was supposed to have been inducted into the club the previous week. The chair he would have occupied on the dais was vacant, under a large portrait of him.

At his death, Knute Rockne was forty-three years old.

Forty-five years later, on the Notre Dame campus, there are people who will look you straight in the eye, and without trying to romanticize, without meaning to be maudlin, tell you that Knute Rockne never died, and never left this place.

When you consider who he was, and what he did, you almost have to believe them.

ABOUT THE AUTHOR

JERRY BRONDFIELD *is the author of* Woody Hayes and the 100-Yard War. *A former newspaperman, he has been a frequent contributor to national magazines, has written for television and is currently a staff editor for Scholastic Magazines, Inc. He is a graduate of Ohio State and his favorite hobby is serving as chief alumni recruiter in the New York area for the Buckeye football team. He lives in Roslyn Heights, New York, and grows strawberries in his spare time—some, he claims, big enough to feed a family of four.*